The Man Who Made
Babe Ruth

ALSO BY BRIAN MARTIN
AND FROM MCFARLAND

*The Detroit Wolverines: The Rise and Wreck of a National
League Champion, 1881–1888* (2018)

Pud Galvin: Baseball's First 300-Game Winner (2016)

*The Tecumsehs of the International Association: Canada's
First Major League Baseball Champions* (2015)

*Baseball's Creation Myth: Adam Ford,
Abner Graves and the Cooperstown Story* (2013)

The Man Who Made Babe Ruth

Brother Matthias of St. Mary's School

BRIAN MARTIN

McFarland & Company, Inc., Publishers
Jefferson, North Carolina

This book has undergone peer review.

LIBRARY OF CONGRESS CATALOGUING-IN-PUBLICATION DATA

Names: Martin, Brian, 1950– author.
Title: The man who made Babe Ruth : Brother Matthias of St. Mary's School / Brian Martin.
Description: Jefferson, North Carolina : McFarland & Company, Inc., Publishers, 2020. | Includes bibliographical references and index.
Identifiers: LCCN 2020005053 | ISBN 9781476673363 (paperback : acid free paper) ∞
ISBN 9781476639512 (ebook)
Subjects: LCSH: Ruth, Babe, 1895–1948—Childhood and youth. | Ruth, Babe, 1895–1948—Friends and associates. | Boutillier, Martin Leo, 1872–1944. | St. Mary's Industrial School (Baltimore, Md.) | Baseball players—United States—Biography. | Xaverian Brothers—Biography.
Classification: LCC GV865.R8 M35 2020 | DDC 796.357092 [B]—dc23
LC record available at https://lccn.loc.gov/2020005053

BRITISH LIBRARY CATALOGUING DATA ARE AVAILABLE

**ISBN (print) 978-1-4766-7336-3
ISBN (ebook) 978-1-4766-3951-2**

© 2020 Brian Martin. All rights reserved

No part of this book may be reproduced or transmitted in any form or by any means, electronic or mechanical, including photocopying or recording, or by any information storage and retrieval system, without permission in writing from the publisher.

On the cover: Brother Matthias and Babe Ruth in front of the Cadillac that was a gift to Matthias from Ruth in 1927 (Xaverian Brothers)

Printed in the United States of America

*McFarland & Company, Inc., Publishers
Box 611, Jefferson, North Carolina 28640
www.mcfarlandpub.com*

Dedicated to everyone who works
with young people. You just never know…

Table of Contents

Acknowledgments   ix
Preface   1

1. Time for Reflection   7
2. A Farewell to Nova Scotia   16
3. St. Mary's   29
4. Birth and Rebirth   43
5. "He always built me"   58
6. A Star Begins to Twinkle   69
7. A Big Deal   82
8. A Homer for a Babe   95
9. Playing to Empty Seats   108
10. First Steps on the Big Stage   121
11. A Real Major Leaguer   133
12. Making History   148
13. The Peak and Past It   164

Epilogue   176
Appendix I: Brother Matthias Speaks   185
Appendix II: Statistics—Batting   188
Appendix III: Statistics—Pitching   189
Chapter Notes   191
Bibliography   205
Index   209

Acknowledgments

A book is the result of much digging and countless hours of research, of checking and re-checking information to ensure it's accurate. It was not a solo endeavor, by any means. I am indebted to many people who willingly shared what they knew, and documents they had or for which they were custodians, to help paint an accurate picture of Brother Matthias. The big man left little in the way of documentary evidence about his long association with Babe Ruth, so their help was vitally important. Apologies are extended to anyone who may have been overlooked in this list.

Fred B. Shoken, local historian, Baltimore, for his meticulous digging through census, archive, court and other documentation to provide an accurate picture of the Ruth family and its moves within Baltimore and the divorce of Babe's father. He has helped set the record straight where before only fog and conjecture prevailed. He was particularly helpful, and his work will benefit future scribes and historians.

David B. Stinson, author, researcher and historian, Baltimore. He operates the websites deadballbaseball.com and davidstinsonauthor.com and has written extensively about Baltimore baseball parks and Babe Ruth. David kindly provided an image of the building in downtown Baltimore, mere steps from Camden Yards, where Babe helped his father open a bar and outside of which George Sr. died. Today it is a strip club. David also connected the author with two descendants of the family of Brother Matthias, Jean Mor and Francis Xavier McGillivary.

Jean Mor, Stoughton, Massachusetts, descendant of Henry Boutilier, a brother of Martin Leo Boutilier, who was more widely known as Brother Matthias. She readily shared the family history she knew and kindly traveled to Danvers to take photographs of the headstones of Brother Matthias and Brother Gilbert in the Xaverian Brothers cemetery there.

Acknowledgments

Xavier McGillivary, fourth cousin, once removed, of Martin Leo Boutilier (Brother Matthias). He lives in Ottawa, Ontario. A dedicated researcher and family historian, he patiently and kindly shared details from his family tree and helped me understand the European origins of the Boutiliers and how they migrated to North America and became established in Nova Scotia.

Diana Copsey Adams, ancestry researcher and friend, Denver. She was always ready, willing and able to help unravel family connections and solve various puzzles as they crop up during research. She has such impressive investigative talents that the author has dubbed her "Sherlocka."

Harry Rothgerber, of Louisville, Kentucky, editor of *Young Babe Ruth*, published 1999. His book about Brother Gilbert of the Xaverian Brothers and the Brothers' connection to Ruth provided a mother lode of information. His kindness and willingness to assist me were exceptional. The product of an Xaverian Brothers education, he embodies the community's dedication to helping others.

Bill Nowlin, of Cambridge, Massachusetts, executive member and publications editor of the Society for American Baseball Research and a mighty fine historian. He is a valuable resource to any researcher and kindly makes time to help, no matter how trivial the request.

John Thorn, of Catskill, New York, baseball history guru and official historian for Major League Baseball. Despite his many and varied activities, he was invariably there to share his thoughts and expertise with a relative newcomer to baseball history.

Len Levin, of Providence, Rhode Island, SABR executive, baseball historian and retired journalist. His knowledge of his city and the time that young Babe Ruth spent there with the Grays was impressive, and he kindly shared what he knew.

Chris Tunstall, of Asheville, North Carolina, shared his theory that his great-grandfather J. J. Lannin, the one-time owner of the Boston Red Sox who signed Babe Ruth, was murdered.

Bernie MacDonald, a native of New Waterford, Cape Breton Island, and former city councillor in London, Ontario. He provided insight into life at the tip of Nova Scotia and helped the author in his bid to track down Boutiliers related to Brother Matthias still living there.

Jessy Wheeler, Research Department, Boston Public Library, for tracking down the only press interview that Brother Matthias gave.

Dale King, Maryland State Archives, for sharing a variety of

Acknowledgments

documents relating to the Ruth family in Baltimore and the divorce of George Ruth, Sr.

Shawn M. Herne, executive director, the Babe Ruth Birthplace and Museum, Baltimore.

Julia Ruth Stevens, daughter of Babe Ruth, Nevada. She passed away while this book was in its final stages of research.

Tom Stevens, grandson of Babe Ruth, Nevada.

Brent Stevens, great grandson of Babe Ruth, Georgia.

Stephanie Stricker, Mission Advancement Associate, Xaverian Brothers, Baltimore.

Brother Lawrence W. Harvey, Xaverian Brothers, Baltimore.

Kevin Cawley, Xaverian archivist, senior archivist and curator of manuscripts at the University of Notre Dame, South Bend, Indiana.

Christine Meadows, of *Our Sunday Visitor* magazine, for providing a helpful article from that publication.

Mike Kelly, licensing and permissions manager, *Toronto Star*.

Jacques Kelly, researcher and historian, Baltimore.

Andrew North, baseball historian, St. Marys, Ontario.

Bill Humber, baseball historian and author, Bowmanville, Ontario.

Don Murray, first-line editor, London, Ontario. The author's long-time friend and retired copy editor checked early drafts of the manuscript and provided many excellent suggestions for improvement.

John Horne, coordinator of rights and reproductions, National Baseball Hall of Fame and Museum, Cooperstown, New York.

Preface

It has been seven decades since Babe Ruth passed away, yet his hold on America and the entire baseball-loving world remains strong. He was a larger-than-life character, a man-child of terrible excesses in food, drink and women. Yet he loved children and his fans and they loved him back. He was the greatest ballplayer of all time but his engaging personality made him a true hero to everyone, sports fan or not. Ruth gave people something to believe in, demonstrating that regardless of one's circumstances, great success could be achieved despite the humblest of origins. Were he alive today, he'd be a pop culture star. Writer Robert W. Creamer, in his highly regarded *Babe: The Legend Comes to Life*, eloquently described Ruth as "a unique figure in the social history of the United States. For more than any other man, Babe Ruth transcended sport, moved far beyond the artificial limits of baselines and outfield and sports pages."

John Thorn, the official historian for Major League Baseball, has conceded that while there have been many great players, "Ruth was a culture hero in the way that others could not equal." Thorn is not alone in his respect for the icon. In 1969, to mark 100 years of professional baseball, the Baseball Writers' Association of America named Ruth the game's all-time outstanding player. And 30 years after that, the Associated Press conducted a poll that concluded Ruth was the best athlete of the twentieth century. The same year, *The Sporting News* declared him the greatest player of all time. His impact has not been forgotten, despite the passage of time, and in 2018 he was posthumously awarded the Presidential Medal of Freedom.

Ruth's beginnings were indeed humble. A first-born to parents who were unable to provide the attention he needed, young George Ruth was on the way to a life on the wrong side of the law and society. Although he spent the first years of his life in stable working-class neighborhoods, life deteriorated for him when his parents acquired a saloon not far from the docks of Baltimore. The bustling downtown streets became his primary school and the lessons he picked up there were converting him to a street urchin destined to clash with the authorities. He had no real father figure. George Sr. and his often-ailing wife, Kate, worked long hours in the saloon, leaving their boy to fend for himself and roam the mean streets in the city's core.

By the time he was seven years old, Ruth's parents had tired of his troublesome behavior and committed him to St. Mary's Industrial Training School for Boys. Located on the western outskirts of Baltimore, St. Mary's was owned by the Catholic Church and operated by a religious order known as the Xaverian Brothers. At times, as many as 800 boys were housed there. The Xaverian Brothers provided education and training in various trades for their charges, who were unable to leave school property without permission. St. Mary's was a combination of an orphanage and a reform school, but most importantly it was a home, despite the cells it reserved for the worst-behaved. Some boys lived there simply because their parents couldn't afford to raise them. Others, because the courts sent them. The Xaverian Brothers believed in fresh air and exercise. And baseball. Especially baseball. As many as 40 teams were formed within the school and St. Mary's varsity teams challenged other schools and acquitted themselves well on the diamond.

The head disciplinarian at St. Mary's was Brother Matthias, a man of intimidating proportions. He tipped the scales at more than 250 pounds and towered above the boys and staff, his frame reaching a full six feet six inches. Because of his size, Brother Matthias could bring order to unruly situations simply by appearing on the sidelines, triggering a buzz among the miscreants and a halt to proceedings when they realized he was watching. There was no need for him to raise his voice, which suited the soft-spoken giant perfectly. He spoke with his presence.

Brother Matthias had been at St. Mary's for several years when the Ruth boy, listed as "incorrigible," was admitted. As Ruth himself freely conceded in the opening sentence of his life story published in 1948: "I was a bad kid." He was one of the youngest boys placed at St. Mary's and he remained there until 1914. Ruth was granted several absences to live with his family during that time, but he invariably returned to what had become his real home and where he felt most accepted and comfortable.

For his part, Brother Matthias saw something that others had missed in the scrawny young left-handed kid. As his teacher and coach of one of the ball teams at St. Mary's, Brother Matthias felt there was potential in young Ruth and was the first to believe in the lost lad whose parents had given up on him. Brother Matthias became Ruth's mentor and the boy, later to become the Babe, never forgot St. Mary's or the man who turned his life around.

Brother Matthias was the man who taught Babe Ruth to play baseball. And much more. He shaped Babe Ruth into the man he became, much the same way a father would.

"It was at St. Mary's that I met and learned to love the greatest man I've ever known," Ruth said of Brother Matthias in his 1948 autobiography, his third and final telling of his life story. "He was the father I needed." He credited the big-hearted giant with teaching him to become both a man and a baseball player.

Despite the key role Brother Matthias played in his life, another Xaverian Brother was often credited with getting Babe his start in baseball. Brother Gilbert helped arrange Ruth's first professional contract, a fact Gilbert parlayed to great acclaim in the popular press. An outspoken and genial man, Brother Gilbert was often called upon as an after-dinner speaker at a wide variety of charity and other events. In all, he delivered more than 1,000 speeches, many of them featuring stories about the young baseball prodigy. The newspapers of the day ate it up, anointing Brother Gilbert as the "discoverer" of Babe. But Brother Gilbert's role was simple and limited, albeit pivotal. He drew Ruth to the attention of his friend Jack Dunn, the owner of the Baltimore Orioles of the International League. Dunn instantly liked what he saw, and offered the boy a contract. Brother Gilbert had never coached the promising youngster and was never posted to St. Mary's. Rather, he was coach for a very successful team at nearby Mount St. Joseph College, a Catholic high school. Brother Gilbert put Dunn onto Ruth because he didn't want to lose his own team's star pitcher to the talent-hunting Orioles owner, he later admitted. Brother Gilbert was a successful administrator at Mount St. Joseph, a private school for more affluent Catholics. Toward the end of his life, Brother Gilbert penned his memoirs, focused on his connection to baseball's first superstar. But Brother Gilbert, despite his key role, did virtually nothing to shape George Ruth into the man or ballplayer he became.

The self-effacing and mild-mannered Brother Matthias remained in the background for the most part, although Ruth praised him often and gave him tangible gifts as his way of thanking his beloved mentor. One of them, a brand-new Cadillac, is pictured on the cover of this book. It was one of two such vehicles he bestowed on Brother Matthias. Ruth did mention Brother Gilbert in his first autobiography, ghostwritten in 1928 by sportswriter Ford Frick, a future commissioner of baseball and hall of famer, saying: "I owe him a lot. More than I will ever be able to repay. It was Brother Gilbert who finally struck upon the thing to hold my interest and keep me happy. It was baseball." But Ruth made few other public comments praising Brother Gilbert, suggesting Ruth's memory was poor, that he'd had some sort of falling out with Brother Gilbert, or that Frick incorrectly connected some dots. Most likely, it was the latter. Regardless, little further praise came from Ruth for Brother Gilbert—and no grand gifts.

This book is an effort to tell the full story of Brother Matthias, a man who deserves more credit than he has received to date for shaping Babe Ruth into what he became. And to right a wrong, to a certain extent. Because of his humble nature, Brother Matthias shunned the spotlight that shone so brightly on his star pupil. He no doubt would be embarrassed by this effort to set the record straight. In the roughly 30 books written so far about Babe Ruth—and the three purportedly written by Ruth himself—Brother Matthias has been relegated to the role of a bit player, for the most part. He'd be fine with that.

So much myth surrounds Babe Ruth because sportswriters of the day were prone to further burnish his impressive accomplishments for a public that couldn't get enough of him. By 1920, when Ruth joined the Yankees, nearly 20 daily newspapers were competing in New York City and reportorial one-upmanship often led to embellishment. Ruth himself was complicit, sometimes willfully and sometimes because he couldn't recall names or details from his own life and didn't bother to correct the inventions of others. Baseball researchers rely heavily on contemporaneous newspaper accounts. Traditionally, they are considered to be the first draft of history and therefore valuable primary sources. But Babe Ruth creates special challenges for anyone documenting his life many years after the fact. His own words can't always be relied upon, even in the three tellings of his life story and the role of others in it, including Brothers Gilbert and Matthias. For instance, in his 1948 version he said his first wife Helen "Woodring" was from Nova Scotia. Her actual surname was Woodford and she was from South Boston, although her parents were from Newfoundland. Few of the books written about him and by him (ghostwriters, actually) provide footnotes or endnotes because they were written for the mass market, not for readers seeking the unvarnished, verifiable truth. Sometimes determining "true" facts is a daunting exercise. Kal Wagenheim, in his 2001 book *Babe Ruth: His Life and Legend*, referred to the slugger as "a mythmaker's dream." Like other authors and researchers, Wagenheim found sorting fact from fiction was exceedingly difficult. For instance, there was a dearth of information about Babe's difficult upbringing for the longest time. In Ruth's 1948 autobiography, which runs to 250 pages, slightly more than a single page is devoted to Babe's life at home before St. Mary's. Author Leigh Montville, who penned *The Big Bam: The Life and Times of Babe Ruth* in 2006, described the challenge of penetrating the "fog" surrounding the Babe. "The fog will make everything greater. That is the weird beauty of the fog. The fog will be part of the magic. The fog will be the beginnings of the myth."

Ruth biographer Creamer explained well the dilemma facing those who write about Ruth and the people connected to him. "Story multiplied by story becomes legend. Like all legends, Ruth's had a strong vein of truth in it—and an equally strong vein of baloney."

This book attempts to provide an accurate and long overdue account of the key character in the life of Babe Ruth. It focuses on Babe's formative years, his time spent with Brother Matthias and the beginning of his professional career when he blossomed thanks to the training provided by a quiet and kind Xaverian Brother. And later, when Brother Matthias was called upon for counsel when Babe was spinning out of control. For a comprehensive account of the entire career of Babe Ruth, the reader should turn elsewhere. Other writers have told the full story of the Babe well despite the minefield of baloney and fog out there and more books about his remarkable life are inevitable. Such is the ongoing fascination with Babe Ruth, more than 70 years after his death.

But for now, it's time to bring a modest Xaverian Brother to center stage, the man who made Babe Ruth.

1

Time for Reflection

On the ninth floor of Memorial Hospital in New York City, a barely recognizable Babe Ruth lay on his deathbed. Throat cancer had reduced the baseball legend, who had been so much larger than life, to a frail mortal slowly ebbing away at the age of 53.

Ruth was little more than skin and bone, presenting a picture that shocked old friends who stopped by and had known him as an overweight, barrel-chested six-foot-two bundle of energy. He could do little more than raise his hand a few inches off his bedsheets in greeting, his voice raspy and mostly lost to the disease that ravaged him.

For nearly two years Babe had fought back against the sharp pain in his head, neck and face, the fierce competitor determined to win his biggest fight yet.

"I honestly don't know who wants to live more than I do," he said in his then just-published autobiography *The Babe Ruth Story*. "I've got to stick around a long, long time."[1] And he battled to do so.

As he grew weaker during those hot days of August of 1948, he became serene. Ruth had only recently learned he was suffering from cancer, a fact from which he had been shielded by his wife, friends and doctors. An observant Catholic as a boy, he had lived a wildly indulgent adult lifestyle filled with food, drink and women. Facing his mortality now, he returned to God. His hospital room was described by one visitor as resembling "a religious articles store."[2] Perched on his nightstand was a statue of Blessed Martin DePorres, a famous lay brother who was a member of the Peruvian Dominican Order of Preachers. Holy pictures, medals and relics were also nearby, and so was Dominican priest Thomas Kaufman, 35, from St. Catherine of Siena Parish, which was located next door to the hospital. As a boy, Kaufman and his brother were sent to St. Mary's Industrial Training School in his hometown of Baltimore during a time of family crisis. It was the same orphanage/reform school to which Ruth had been sent at age seven and where he received his first religious training, was educated and learned to play baseball. Ruth called St. Mary's home for 12 years. Because of their shared experience at St. Mary's, the two men bonded.

On July 21, when Ruth's condition appeared particularly grim, Kaufman administered the last rites of the Catholic Church. But Ruth, forever unpredictable, rallied. Five days later, he and his wife Claire went to a movie. It wasn't just any film. They attended the world premiere of *The Babe Ruth Story*, which Hollywood producers had rushed into theaters because of the subject's worsening condition. The movie starred William Bendix, once a batboy for the New York Yankees when Babe played for them. Ruth was sweating profusely that evening and felt unwell, so he and Claire left the Astor Theater partway through the screening. Many who saw the film felt the Ruths didn't miss much. Great liberties had been taken with the truth in the screenplay, which was melodramatic and sappy. Bendix seemed miscast and his baseball skills were wanting. Critics blasted the cliché-filled tearjerker and likely wished they could have left early as well. *Time* magazine described it as "a mawkish tribute that left out everything that was robust about the man." In the *New York Times*, critic Bosley Crowther, opined: "...when all is said and done, [it] has much more the tone of low-grade fiction than it has of biography."[3] In the *Brooklyn Eagle*, Lew Sheaffer called it "a sorry botch" flawed by a "too preachy tone and hammering away at inspirational maxims." He concluded it was a "persistent attempt to milk the audience's tear ducts.... Chalk this one up as an error. The Babe rates something better."[4] Claire dismissed the film as an "obscenity" and a "ridiculous charade." Ruth's reaction is not known.

Brother Matthias, Babe's teacher and baseball coach at St. Mary's, was played admirably by Charles Bickford. His was a major role in the bad film, reflecting the significant part Brother Matthias played in the life of Babe. But, in Hollywood fashion, Brother Matthias's contribution was exaggerated far beyond reality. He was incorrectly credited as the man who helped Babe sign his first professional contract. And he appeared in Babe's sickbed scene toward the end, helping him decide whether to take an experimental serum that might save his life and the lives of others. The real Brother Matthias had been dead for four years at the time of the serum decision. "You'll make it," Hollywood Matthias assures the critically ill Babe as he is wheeled away for treatment to the rising strains of "Take Me Out to the Ballgame" and the movie mercifully grinds to a conclusion.

The remarkable story of the home-run king has been told many times. Separating fact from fiction has often been difficult, for writers, screenwriters, fans, readers and filmgoers alike. The 1948 screen version merely added to the myth-making. Some of the inventions are easy to spot in the film that some critics have described as among the worst of all time. In *The Babe Ruth Story*, two boys seem to recover from serious maladies because of Babe. He merely speaks to a crippled lad who can suddenly stand up, to the amazement of his father. Another boy seems to come out of a coma when the slugger promises and then delivers his "called shot" home run in Chicago. In yet another scene, Babe hits a boy's dog with a ball during batting practice and immediately rushes the injured dog and his master to a hospital where he demands a doctor operate on the pooch. The dog survives surgery, but Ruth is late for the ballgame and runs afoul of manager Miller Huggins.

An avalanche of mail poured in for the ailing King of Swat that summer of 1948. In all, 50,000 letters and telegrams were received during his time in the hospital.[5] Once it became known that Father Kaufman was at his bedside, the priest received notes from children thanking him for being with Babe, enclosing pennies for Mass along with rosaries and other religious items intended for their hero.

Babe found plenty of time to think, reflecting on a flurry of activity in recent months during which pain had loomed so large. Thinking of what the future held was not pleasant.

He would have recalled that fateful day late in November of 1946 when he finally agreed to check in to French Hospital in New York. For several months the Babe had complained of pain above his left eye and his voice had become quite hoarse. Friends and family finally persuaded him to seek medical advice. Doctors discovered a cancerous tumor had developed on the left side of his neck, wrapped around his carotid artery. As it grew, the tumor pressed on nerves that affected his larynx and throat. The doctors, Claire and his friends kept the cancer diagnosis from him and in early January surgeons tied off an artery and severed some nerves to relieve his pain. The tumor itself was inaccessible, so he received radiation treatment and was fed intravenously. Upon entering the hospital, Ruth weighed 278 pounds. Released three months later, he had shed 80 of them.[6]

While recuperating at his Riverside Drive apartment, Babe attended a press conference in early April at the Waldorf-Astoria Hotel, where it was announced he had signed a contract with the Ford Motor Company to promote their popular American Legion Baseball junior program. His doctors knew it would tax their patient but felt it would get his mind off his condition by keeping him active. It proved to be good therapy for the ailing slugger, who was happy to be back in baseball. In the following months, he, Claire and a nurse would travel about 50,000 miles across America making appearances on behalf of the program and speaking to children who adored him. Despite the strain, Ruth enjoyed reconnecting with youngsters. In one town, which closed its schools so the pupils could see their hero, Ruth laughed about his impact. He told Claire: "Even if they don't like baseball, they *gotta* like the Babe. Hell, I got 'em the day off!" Despite his pain and weariness, he still had some very good days.[7]

About the same time, he signed a deal with New York publisher E. P. Dutton for his autobiography, to be ghostwritten by acclaimed columnist Bob

Considine of the *Hearst Syndicate*. Ruth then sold film rights for the book to Allied Artists for a reported $150,000 and a cut of the profits.[8] That done, he was off to Florida for rest, fishing and golfing. Despite his weight loss and nearly constant pain, he was unwilling to slow down.

The new commissioner of baseball, A. B. (Happy) Chandler announced all ballparks would celebrate Babe Ruth Day on April 27, 1947, to mark the contribution of baseball's greatest player. The signature event would be at Yankee Stadium, known as the park that Ruth built. During the ceremonies there before nearly 60,000 fans, a tanned but gaunt Ruth appeared and spoke briefly, his hoarse voice amplified by the public address system. He thanked the fans for the day, noting: "You know how bad my voice sounds. Well it feels just as bad." He praised the game of baseball "as the only real game in the world," and how important it is for boys to begin playing it at an early age if they want to succeed in it. "There's been so many lovely things said about me," he said, concluding his off-the-cuff remarks. "I'm glad I had the opportunity to thank everybody. Thank you." With that, he waved to the crowd and walked slowly to the Yankee dugout, tears in his eyes and in those of his fans.[9]

Babe and Claire continued to travel, promoting the American Legion Baseball programs while Considine struggled to find time to get the subject of his book to sit still. Ruth's pain was constant and he blamed his teeth for his problems, still unaware he had cancer. Considine realized what was happening and was sympathetic. "Those who knew him best, Mel Lowenstein (his lawyer) and Paul Carey (his close friend) and Claire, believed that if he knew he had terminal cancer, it would destroy him. He'd go right out the window," Considine said.[10]

For his part, Considine struggled mightily to arrange time with Ruth for interviews. It was like trying to hit a moving target. The publisher was hoping to release the book in time for the lucrative Christmas trade, so Considine felt pressure to make progress, and was getting frustrated. "It was damn hard to work with a man who was dying ... dying as resentfully as Babe was. He was often in incredible pain." To help, Considine retained sportswriter Fred Lieb for a flat fee. Considine had little first-hand knowledge of Ruth because he was a general columnist, rather than a sportswriter, and he had arrived in New York toward the tail end of the slugger's career. Lieb, meanwhile, had covered Babe's exploits for several New York papers. He would play a significant role in writing the book and providing information and anecdotes when Babe didn't. Often, within minutes of sitting for an interview with Considine, the Babe would want to play some golf, go for a ride in his big Lincoln Continental or merely visit a driving range. Babe's power of concentration was poor and his need for activity incessant.[11] Considine had his hands full with the demands of his publisher and an elusive subject. He came to rely more

1. Time for Reflection

heavily than he expected on Lieb, who had written a series of baseball team history books for G. P. Putnam's Sons.

By late June, the effects of radiation had worn off, leaving Ruth with a sore jaw that made it difficult to eat even the softest of foods. He had agreed to be among the first human subjects to try a new drug called teropterin, which had shown some promising results in laboratory mice. (This was the serum from the movie.) It was a strong, synthetic version of folic acid which was injected daily for six weeks and which seemed to produce positive results. His hair, lost to radiation, grew back and the lymph nodes in his neck shrank. He could eat some soft foods again and gained some weight. Doctors were so encouraged by his improvement that they delivered a paper at the International Cancer Congress meeting in St. Louis describing what seemed to be a cure for his form of cancer. Babe felt well enough in July to fly to Dallas to speak to a convention of American Legion Baseball youth.[12] Around the same time, he asked his lawyer, Mel Lowenstein, to help him establish the Babe Ruth Foundation, whose goal was to provide funds for "the mental and physical education of underprivileged American boys."[13]

That September, the Yankees appeared in the World Series against the Brooklyn Dodgers. It went to seven games before the Yankees prevailed, taking their eleventh series title. They had won their first in 1923, led by Babe Ruth, the American League's most valuable player and home-run slugger. Among the attendees were Babe and Claire, and their comings and goings were closely watched, captured by television cameras, then making an early appearance in ballparks. Despite his obvious discomfort and gaunt appearance, Babe was gracious and posed for photographs with fellow old-timers Ty Cobb and Tris Speaker.[14]

Late in January, Babe was back in Florida, where he celebrated his 53rd birthday on February 6 at the Golden Strand Hotel north of Miami Beach. Refreshed by the warm weather and feeling better, he returned to New York in late March for a book-signing party for *The Babe Ruth Story*, attended by Considine and notables such as Ernest Hemingway and humorist Bennett Cerf. Considine had also written the screenplay for the movie version of the book and Babe had been retained as a "technical adviser." At the invitation of the producers, he and Claire and their daughter Julia traveled to Hollywood in late April to see some of the filming. But his appearance was little more than promotional for the film. He posed for photos with William Bendix, showing him how to hold a bat, and with the other stars for publicity purposes. Soon afterward, he was back on the road for the American Legion Baseball program, earning a reported $1,000 a month, plus expenses. On June 5, he was back east where he attended a Yale-Princeton ballgame where he met future president George H. W. Bush, captain of the Yale team. Babe also donated the book manuscript for *The Babe Ruth Story* to Yale. He appeared very thin, but spoke steadily and reasonably well despite the gravelly quality of his voice.[15] For a man who was wasting away, his schedule was hectic.

In 1948, Yankee Stadium turned 25 years old and team management decided to mark the anniversary on June 13 with a ceremony before a game with the Cleveland Indians. They invited members of the 1923 Yankees, including the man whose drawing power was credited with building the place and could still be counted upon to bring fans out. Ruth was delighted to take part, despite feeling weaker than he had in the past month or so. He was too ill to attend a banquet the night before the event and it was feared the rain that fell on the day of celebration might keep him away. But Ruth appeared in the locker room, accompanied by his friend of several years Paul Carey and nurse Frank Delaney, who helped him out of his street clothes and into his uniform. Ruth greeted his old mates with a croaky voice and big smile and happily posed for photographs with them. The crowd of 49,000 erupted when stadium announcer Mel Allen introduced the Babe. Unsteady, he leaned on a bat for support and spoke briefly about hitting the first home run in the stadium and how pleased he was to attend the event and see his old teammates again. That day, his uniform number 3 was retired. Chilled, and with tears in his eyes, Ruth left the stadium for the last time as a two-inning game of Yankee old-timers got underway.

Despite his pain and weakness, Babe visited St. Louis, Sioux City and Sioux Falls for Ford and the American Legion Baseball program before checking into Memorial Hospital in New York on June 23. Helped up the front steps, he recognized the place and asked: "This is Memorial, a cancer hospital. Why are you bringing me here?"[16] He was assured that Memorial was not exclusively for cancer patients. But the secret would soon come out. By July 3, the press learned he was receiving radiation treatments. Cancer had spread to his liver, lungs and kidneys and the old ballplayer finally learned the truth of his condition. Eighteen days later, Father Kaufman administered last rites when the end appeared near. But the old slugger bounced back, though he knew his cancer was terminal. When famed baseball manager Connie Mack came to see him, Babe reportedly said: "Hello, Mr. Mack. The termites have got me."[17]

Babe continued to sink and on August 9 he revised his will (his estate was later valued at nearly $361,000—roughly $3,860,000 in 2020). Claire had a room nearby in the hospital, while daughters Dorothy and Julia and his friends visited nearly every day. He was sedated and half asleep much of the time. The death vigil was underway. Two days later, on August 11, it was announced he was "critically ill." Hundreds of neighborhood kids milled around outside the hospital, sensing the end was near. More than 10,000 telegrams and letters poured in over the next two days. On August 13, the White House telephoned to say President Harry Truman sent his best wishes. On the evening of August 15, Babe kissed Claire and croaked: "Don't come back tomorrow, because I won't be here." The following day he was awake for Claire and was able to greet his friend Paul Carey and his nurse, Frank Delaney. At around 7 p.m., he fell into a deep sleep and by 8:01 p.m., the baseball legend was gone. "He said his prayers and lapsed into a sleep," Father Kaufman told reporters who relayed news of the death of the Bambino to the world.[18]

Baseball Commissioner Happy Chandler said he was shocked and distressed at the loss of "my personal friend…. His was the American story, the boy who came up from obscurity to learn the people's game and go on to be a great national hero. His deeds will be an inspiration for the children of the world who will try to emulate him."[19] In his 22 years as a major-league player, Ruth established 76 records, 62 of which still stood at the time of his death, including his 714 home runs. His hometown paper, *The Baltimore Sun*, saluted his life and said he "towered above all the rest. No other player has ever captured the imagination of the American public as did the Babe. From coast to coast his name has been a household word."[20]

Babe's body was taken to Yankee Stadium where the flags flew at half-staff. His casket and catafalque were placed inside the main entrance beginning August 17 and the crowds that filed by to pay their last respects were immense. That evening and during the entire next day, it was estimated at least 75,000 mourners had their last glimpse of the hero, who was dressed in a blue double-breasted suit with black rosary beads wrapped around his left hand. His funeral on a rainy August 19 at St. Patrick's Cathedral attracted a similar throng. His friend Francis Cardinal Spellman, the Archbishop of New York, presided over the Requiem Mass, while many mourners stood outside and endured the elements. George Herman Ruth was buried on a hillside in Gate of Heaven Cemetery in the town of Hawthorne, about 30 miles north of New York.[21]

The same day that Ruth died, his last words intended for public consumption arrived at a faith-based inspiration magazine founded by Norman Vincent Peale. Peale, a Christian preacher of the positivism gospel was known for his radio program, *The Art of Living*. A prolific writer, in 1952 Peale would publish *The Power of Positive Thinking*, which became a bestseller. In 1945, he founded *Guideposts Magazine*, a non-denominational publication in which celebrities and ordinary folk shared their inspirational stories with readers in a bid to provide hope and peace in their lives. As he prayed and reconnected with God, Babe had grown introspective and thankful for the life he had lived. In his public speeches he always encouraged others, children in particular, to aspire to great things. He may have received some encouragement to inspire others from what Francis Cardinal Spellman had told him in the dugout of Yankee Stadium on Babe Ruth Day. Moments earlier, Spellman had shared a prayer with the crowd for Babe whom he described as a "hero in the world of sport, a champion of fair play and a manly leader of youth in America." Spellman took Ruth by the arm and said: "Babe, you have been an inspiration to all creeds. You've always been an inspiration to me. Good luck and God bless you."[22]

It's unclear who suggested Babe share his story with *Guideposts*, a new and relatively small publication, subtitled *A Practical Guide for Successful Living*. Joe L. Brown, of MGM Studios, which had produced the "The Babe Ruth Story," helped Babe put it together. Also involved were his friend Paul Carey, a devout Catholic, and Ruth's lawyer, Mel Lowenstein. Given Brown's involvement with the movie and its intended uplifting message, the publicist might have seen this as valuable promotion within the faith-based community. Perhaps Peale himself had reached out to Babe in an effort to build circulation. The only writer credited for the piece titled "The Kids Can't Take It If We Don't Give It" was George Herman Ruth. And it was billed as "Babe Ruth's Last Message." The cover article ran to four pages in the October 1948 edition of *Guideposts*. An editorial note accompanying explained it was intended to deal with the problem of juvenile delinquency and was written by "a man who relearned what faith meant."

"Bad boy Ruth—that was me," it began, mimicking the "I was a bad kid" opening sentence of his 1948 autobiography penned by Considine and Lieb. "God had an eye out for me, just as He has for you, and He was pulling for me to make the grade." Babe described his "harum-scarum youth" when he didn't know the difference between right and wrong. He admitted he strayed from his early religious training, but never forgot it. "As far as I'm concerned, and I think as far as most kids go, once religion sinks in, it stays there—deep down. The lads who get religious training, get it where it counts—in the roots. They may fail it, but it never fails them."[23] Aside from promoting religious education for youngsters, Ruth spent a significant number of his 1,380 words praising the man who had been his own inspiration—Brother Matthias.

"I was listed as an incorrigible. I guess I was. Perhaps I would always have been but for Brother Matthias, the greatest man I have ever known, and for the religious training (at St. Mary's)…." Ruth continued: "I've seen a great number of 'he-men' in my baseball career, but never one equal to Brother Matthias. He stood six feet six and weighed 250 pounds. It was all muscle. He could have been successful at anything he wanted to in life—and he chose the Church.

"It was he who introduced me to baseball. Very early he noticed that I had some natural talent for throwing and catching. He used to back me in a corner of the big yard at St. Mary's and bunt a ball to me by the hour, correcting the mistakes I made with my hands and feet." Ruth described how Brother Matthias could toss a ball upward with his left hand and drive it 350 feet with the bat in his right hand. "I would watch him bug-eyed." He said

Brother Matthias played a role in helping him begin his professional baseball career with the Baltimore Orioles. And despite all his success in later years, he never forgot Brother Matthias, St. Mary's, "and the boys I left behind. I kept going back."

In his last public words, Babe wanted to set the record straight, knowing his days on Earth were numbered. He was making his peace with God and thanking the servant of God who had helped turn his life around.

2

A Farewell to Nova Scotia

For Brother Matthias, the long road to his key role in creating the legend of Babe Ruth began in the tiny community of Lingan near the northernmost tip of the Canadian province of Nova Scotia. The remote settlement was originally known as Barrachois when the French controlled vast swaths of territory in the colony they settled and named Acadia. Lingan (pronounced lin-GAN) is derived either from a corruption of the French word for the native, *l'indienne*, or from the River Lingan (today spelled Lingaun) near the southern Irish city of Waterford. The latter derivation seems more likely because the community that grew alongside Lingan in Nova Scotia is New Waterford.

Cape Breton Island, on which Lingan is situated, was originally explored by John Cabot in 1497 and claimed for Britain. On mainland Nova Scotia, the French established the capital of Acadia at Port Royal in 1605. The colony switched back and forth from French to English control as a pawn in peace treaties signed in Europe between England and France. Ultimately victorious, Britain renamed Acadia Nova Scotia ("New Scotland"), but the French retained Cape Breton Island, which they called Isle Royale. In 1758, the British captured the island one last time, nine years after establishing the colonial capital at Halifax. From 1755 to 1763, about 11,000 Acadians, whose loyalty to Britain was doubted by the government, were deported to far-flung British colonies in America and the Caribbean.[1]

Government officials in Halifax were anxious to populate their new capital and replace residents lost to disease or lured to other colonies. The local British authorities were impressed by industrious German and Swiss settlers and persuaded Britain to recruit more from various Protestant German and Swiss communities along the Rhine River. Prospective settlers were promised free farmland, a year's supply of food and the tools, building materials and equipment needed to work the land. Those interested but unable to afford passage across the Atlantic could pay off the cost by working on public structures such as forts and roads upon arrival in the colony. Between 1750 and 1752, about 2,700 such settlers came to Halifax, mainly from Württemberg,

Baden and Hesse-Darmstadt (in today's Germany), as well as from Switzerland and Montbéliard, France. The latter was a rare Protestant enclave within France, a tiny principality located 15 miles from the Swiss border.

Jean George Boutilier, a 60-year-old joiner who lived in the tiny village of Etobon just north of Montbéliard, somehow learned about the intriguing opportunity in the New World. He and members of his family traveled more than 40 miles from their home to Basel, Switzerland, to begin their odyssey. From Basel, they sailed down the Rhine to Rotterdam, where they boarded the British ship *Sally* in May of 1752. The Atlantic crossing took 120 days, during which time 40 of the 258 onboard died from disease, including Jean George, his wife Sarah, and the ship's captain, John Robinson. Upon their arrival in Halifax, authorities refused to let the *Sally* dock, fearing it might spread disease to the community. It was quarantined, forced to tie up at uninhabited St. George Island (now McNabs [cct] Island) in the harbor for three weeks before the newcomers were allowed to disembark.[2] The surviving offspring of Jean George and Sarah Boutilier were old enough to fend for themselves and began new lives in Nova Scotia.[3] In all, 431 residents of Montbéliard successfully made the crossing. Most of the new arrivals, who became known as the "Foreign Protestants," spoke German, but those from Switzerland and Montbéliard were French-speaking. About half of the newcomers became founding settlers of Lunenburg, established in 1753 along Nova Scotia's South Shore. Farmland in the area was good and it was granted to the newcomers as promised. Others remained in Halifax, working on public works to repay the British for their passage. Before long, those who settled in Lunenburg became self-sufficient through farming, fishing and shipbuilding. Within a few years, some of the settlers from Montbéliard with surnames like Boutilier and Dauphinee migrated a few miles east.[4] In 1808, many of the Boutiliers moved to the distant Bras d'Or Lake area of Cape Breton Island, not far from Sydney, where coal had been discovered nearly a hundred years earlier.

Soon after the "Foreign Protestants" arrived, local authorities began expelling the French-speaking Acadians, whose loyalty remained in question. Some Acadians went into hiding until the expulsions ended, while others escaped to Quebec.[5] French names and culture remain strong in the Maritime provinces to this day. While many Nova Scotians have French surnames, their mother tongue is English, the result of decades of assimilation. English pronunciation of French names is not uncommon. This is not surprising because when Acadians were sent to Louisiana, they became known as "Cajuns," a corruption of "Acadiens." Boutilier remains a rather common surname in the province, although it is most often anglicized to "BOOT-lear," rather than the original French pronunciation of "boo-TILL-eyay."

Not far from Sydney was the tiny oceanside settlement of Lingan, which, like so many others in the area, was tied to coal. Chunks of it were found in nearby cliffside openings along the Atlantic in the early 1700s and the French carted it off to their massive Fortress of Louisbourg, about 30 miles to the south. The first coal mine in Lingan operated from 1855 to 1886, when it became one of the largest in Nova Scotia, reaching peak production of 50,000 tons annually.[6]

The community around the mine remained small, consisting mainly of employees and their families. The first census for Canada was taken in 1871, following the federation of Nova Scotia, New Brunswick, Canada East (Quebec) and Canada West (Ontario) in 1867. Among the residents counted in Lingan were Joseph and Mary Ann Boutilier, aged 42 and 40. Joseph was born July 26, 1828, in Baddeck, on the shore of Bras d'Or Lake. Mary Ann was a daughter of Irish-born Patrick Howley, operator of *Howley's Ferry* on Little Bras d'Or Lake. The couple married in Sydney Mines on October 13, 1858. Joseph was listed as an engineer, or machinist, suggesting he probably maintained and repaired the mine's equipment as well as that of seagoing vessels. He acted as engineer on a schooner that traveled to Boston in about 1847 and he returned to Boston a year before his marriage to visit his brother Henry and his wife who had settled there.[7] Although Lutheran, Joseph converted to Catholicism because Mary Ann was of that faith. Listed as living with them in 1871 were their seven children: Nathaniel, 14; Eunice Mary, 11; Napoleon P., 10; Thomas Frederick, 7; Francis, 5; Henry J., 3; and Alice, 1. Two sons had died as infants. Three more children joined them: Martin Leo, in 1872; Joseph F., in 1875; and finally, Mary Margaret in 1877. Descendants of the family say the boys, who grew to be tall in stature, were known as being quite energetic and athletic.

There were many mouths to feed in the Boutilier household and as the mine began to play out, family breadwinner Joseph considered his options. His oldest son, Nathaniel, now 22, was also employed as a machinist, while 18-year-old Napoleon worked on the coal dock. Joseph's descendants believe he became overly zealous in his new faith and had some sort of religious argument at the mine that may have contributed to his departure.[8] He sought employment in Halifax, a bustling seaport, where he thought his skills would be in demand.[9] But his prospects weren't as bright as he'd hoped in a city whose population was approaching 68,000 because by the late 1870s, the Canadian Maritime provinces were struggling economically. The United States terminated a trade deal that had benefited the region and replaced it with prohibitive duties on imported coal. The lingering recession prompted thousands living on Canada's east coast to move to neighboring New England, attracted by its thriving economy tied to shipping and industry, primarily bustling shoe and textile factories. Atlantic Canada historians Margaret R. Conrad and James K. Hiller described the demographic phenomenon this way:

2. A Farewell to Nova Scotia

> The lure of urban jobs in factories, service industries, and emerging professions such as medicine, teaching and engineering drew young people like a magnet…. Since the Atlantic region lacked a major metropolis … they became part of what was described by contemporaries as the "exodus".… Out-migration was both an effect and a cause of the region's shaky economic performance. As early as the 1860s, the Maritimes began to suffer net migration loss, which reached a peak in the 1880s…[10]

By the 1880s, those emigrants included thousands from Cape Breton Island and Nova Scotia cities like Halifax, Digby and Lunenburg. The international border proved to be no impediment whatsoever. New England was booming and needed workers for its mills and factories. Boston was the destination of choice for Nova Scotians because of its bustling commercial and trade sectors. Nearly 30,000 Nova Scotians had settled in Massachusetts by 1880. In Boston, they tended to cluster in East Boston, not far from today's Logan Airport, where they were generally well received, and attracted good-natured nicknames like "down easters" and "herring chokers."[11]

Faced with poor prospects in Halifax, Joseph Boutilier sailed to Boston in late 1880. He liked what he found in the city of 362,839, a metropolis five times larger than Halifax. The Boutilier family settled in East Boston, first on Henry Street near the harbor, then on Saratoga Street. Their second youngest son, Martin Leo, had just turned nine years of age. He was still more than 20 years away from meeting Babe Ruth, by which time Martin was known as Brother Matthias.

Joseph Sr. and Nathaniel both found positions as machinists, the latter in a "sugar house," which supplied the sweet raw material imported from the Caribbean to local candy makers. Within a few years, Nathaniel landed a job at the Massachusetts State House, while Thomas toiled as a laborer. Napoleon and Henry became police officers, the latter rising to the rank of detective. Joseph Jr. became a firefighter. Francis (Frank) was employed as a lineman. Eunice married a successful electrician named John A. Kelly Jr. By the latter part of the decade, the Boutiliers had settled comfortably into the East Boston community, remaining close together. Several chose to become U.S. citizens.

Boston was firmly in the grip of baseball fever by the 1880s. If the Boutiliers had seen the game played in Lingan or in Halifax, it's unlikely they would have had much time for it.[12] It wasn't until several decades after the Boutiliers left Lingan that a very competitive Cape Breton Colliery League developed, pitting rival mining towns against each other for bragging rights on the diamond. As early as 1873, four baseball clubs had been organized in Halifax and the game was well established by the 1880s.[13] But Boston was far ahead in its attachment to baseball.

Researchers have found several references to games resembling baseball played in Massachusetts early in the 1800s. For instance, *Book of Sports*, a children's book published in Boston in 1834, described a game of "round-ball," which was likened to "base or goal ball." Even earlier, in 1791, the town of Pittsfield, in the Berkshires of western Massachusetts, outlawed the playing of "base-ball" or other ballgames near their newly erected meeting house.[14]

The Massachusetts (or New England) version the game did not have foul lines and the batter (striker) could hit the ball in any direction—forward, backward or sideways—with it remaining in play. This game featured a square infield with four bases marked by stakes. The batter (striker) stood between first and fourth base and tried to hit the ball thrown overhand from the center of the square. Teams had from seven to fourteen players, with a usual complement of eleven. While running between bases, a player was called out if he was "soaked" or "plugged" by the relatively soft ball thrown at him. The distance to first base was relatively short, so getting on the base paths, and then skillfully dodging thrown balls to reach fourth base and score a run, was a key part of the game. Final game scores could reach 100 runs or more. When one player was out, the team was retired and the other team took its turn at bat. The game differed from that played in New York, which more closely resembled the game of today, although the pitching was underhanded. By the 1850s the New York game prevailed, its rules having been codified and published far and wide.[15]

Boston was a charter member of the first professional baseball league, the National Association. The loop was founded in 1871 with nine members: Boston, Philadelphia, Chicago, New York, Washington, Troy (New York), Cleveland, Fort Wayne and tiny Rockford, Illinois. The Boston Red Stockings won 33 games and lost 22 that first year, to finish second in the official standings. Pillars of the team were brothers Harry and George Wright, the center fielder/manager and short-stop, respectively. Both had played for the Cincinnati Red Stockings of 1869–70, baseball's first professional team. The Wright brothers were born in England and had originally played cricket in the New York area before turning to baseball.

Once at the helm of the Boston franchise, Harry Wright decided it was time to show his homeland the American game of baseball at which he and brother George excelled. After all, British cricket teams had been visiting the United States for years, so he felt turnabout was fair play. He arranged for the Red Stockings and the Philadelphia Athletics to cross the Atlantic to play a series of games during July and August of 1874.[16] Some of the ballplayers tried their hands at cricket with sometimes surprising results, but were mostly unsuccessful at the game. The reaction to the baseball teams and their games was mixed, however, with fewer spectators than expected. Boston lost $700 after expenses on the tour, while Philadelphia dropped $1,800. When the teams returned to Boston, they were greeted by military bands playing "Yankee Doodle Dandy" and "When Johnny Comes Marching Home." The Red Stockings may have drawn a lukewarm response from the British, but to Bostonians they were conquering heroes.

2. A Farewell to Nova Scotia

The sometimes-shaky National Association expired after the 1875 campaign and was immediately succeeded by the National League, whose capitalist owners sought to put the game on a more businesslike basis than its player-centered predecessor. Boston was a charter member, fielding a team known as the Red Caps. Wright's nine captured the pennant of the new league in 1877 and 1878 as Boston remained in the top echelon of professional baseball. Boston and its fans were committed to the game. There was no denying the hold baseball had on America's fifth largest city.

The middle class was growing in Boston and city dwellers were beginning to find time to indulge in sport. There was golf, cycling and boxing, but baseball became the game of choice for Bostonians. History professor and Boston native Stephen Hardy described the rise of baseball this way:

> The source of expansion and enrichment, as all promoters knew, was the great middle class, of which so many Americans saw themselves as members. If there was a sport that tapped the interest of this vast constituency, it was baseball; and for this reason, baseball led the field in providing heroes for the city's masses. Moreover, the organization of the professional leagues nurtured the sense that the ball club was the representative of the city's fortunes.[17]

Baseball provided an outlet for civic pride and boosterism as America's growing cities vied with each other economically, politically and on the playing field. Many business and elected leaders attached themselves to baseball clubs and newspapers provided coverage of games to boost their readership. And nothing encouraged a strong following more than success. In August of 1883, when Boston was on its way to winning its third National League pennant in eight years, the *Boston Globe* explained baseball's popularity in Beantown:

> The hold that the game has in this city is well-shown by the fact that up to date almost 75,000 people have attended the games.... Unprecedentedly large throngs attend the games of all the associations, comprising youth of the tenderest ages, business and professional men, old men and ladies, in fact every class, every station, every color and every nationality will be found at a ball match.[18]

The Boutiliers couldn't help but get swept up in the baseball fever gripping their adopted home. Like other immigrants, they soon realized that following baseball helped them bond with their neighbors, old-timers and newcomers alike. It was all part of becoming American. Residents of East Boston had a longstanding attachment to sport, and as early as 1843 it was reported that a variety of games were being played "within a large fenced piece of land on Chelsea Street."[19] Baseball and other ballgames were among them. By the 1880s, baseball, boxing, rowing and yachting had become popular, although it's unlikely that working class families had the means or inclination to pursue rowing or yachting. The streets of working-class East Boston were often filled with men and children playing games while neighbors watched and cheered from their front porches and windows.

The Boutilier family had seven boys ranging in age from 6 to 22, nearly enough for their own baseball team. Nathaniel and Napoleon were the oldest and more concerned about entering the working world, unlike their younger siblings who would have joined impromptu neighborhood games. Thomas was 17; Francis, 15; Henry, 13; Martin, 9; and Joseph Jr., 6. It's a safe bet that the boys, all of whom would become big, physical men, joined games with their new friends. Martin, in particular, excelled in baseball, and he developed a passion for the sport. Quiet and reserved as an adult, Martin seldom spoke about his childhood, but given later demonstrations of his mastery of bat, ball and glove, he was likely in demand by local teams.

As in many large families of the Roman Catholic faith, parents often encouraged at least one of their offspring to consider the priesthood or to become a nun. Nathaniel, Napoleon, Francis, Henry and Joe Jr. felt no inclination to commit themselves to a religious life of poverty and abstinence in their exciting new surroundings, where the sky seemed to be the limit. But Thomas and Martin were more spiritually inclined, to the delight of their father. Both began to consider becoming servants of God in some capacity. Thomas was attracted to the proposition first. It is not known why. He may have learned about some charitable work underway in Jamaica Plain, southwest of downtown Boston. There, the House of the Guardian Angel, an orphanage and training school, was operated by a Belgian-based Catholic order of men known as the Brothers of Charity.

The Brothers of Charity were founded in Ghent, Belgium, in 1807. They took upon themselves a mission to tend to the sick, the poor, the elderly, the young, orphans and persons with mental issues. They established a beachhead in North America in 1865 when five Brothers opened the Brothers of Charity of Vincent de Paul in the Montreal area.[20] In 1874, at the request of the Boston archdiocese, the Montreal motherhouse dispatched seven Brothers to the House of the Guardian Angel in Boston. The Catholic Church had established the boarding school for boys in 1851, but its mandate expanded to accept orphans and destitute and homeless boys in response to growing social needs in the community. A new home was opened in 1872 and the Brothers of Charity were considered ideally suited to take over its daily operation from the Church.[21] By then, the Boston Children's Aid Society and the courts had begun sending them troubled and delinquent lads. Aside from providing a home for their charges, the Brothers of Charity educated the boys and provided training in trades, rather than encouraging the pursuit of higher education. It was a well-equipped industrial training school whose printing office published *The Weekly Bouquet* and, on a quarterly basis, *The Orphan's Friend*.[22] Thousands of Guardian Angel graduates readily found jobs as printers, bakers, book-binders and in factories thanks to the practical training provided by the Brothers of Charity.

Had Thomas Boutilier been impressed with the work of the Brothers of Charity and sought to join them, he would have been referred to their headquarters in Montreal. There, prospective members were trained at what was known as a novitiate. Thomas may have learned about the Brothers and contacted them through the Rev. Hugh Roe O'Donnell, pastor of St. Mary Star of the Sea church in East Boston, where his family attended Mass.

By the age of 26, Thomas Boutilier had decided to serve God and he moved to Montreal, where he studied with the Brothers of Charity from December 19, 1890, until October 7, 1891. He then returned to Boston, his failure to advance in the order attributed to his inability to speak the French language.[23] He left the Brothers on good terms, however. In a letter dated October 14, 1891, Father Candide of the Montreal novitiate confirmed that Thomas Boutilier had lived with the Brothers in Montreal for 10 months and was "honest, active and very obedient, in a word has given much satisfaction, therefore I recommend him…"[24]

In his quest to serve God, Thomas Boutilier may have shown Father Candide's letter to someone connected to the Congregation of the Brothers of St. Francis Xavier, another religious order founded in Belgium. But how that came to be is pure conjecture. Perhaps Father Candide or someone else in Montreal suggested Boutilier consider the Xaverian Brothers, who had established their North American motherhouse in Louisville, Kentucky. The Xaverian Brothers' operating language was English, so a referral there made sense. Upon his return, Thomas learned that his younger sibling Martin had already begun the lengthy process of becoming a member of the Congregation of Francis Xavier, where the Brothers appended the initials C. F. X. after their religious names. That may have prompted his choice. Regardless, two Boutiliers were soon on the years-long path to membership intended to ensure those who sought to join the order were truly committed.

The Xaverian Brothers, like the Brothers of Charity, are not priests and therefore unable to conduct Mass or bestow sacramental privileges. They are laymen who form a religious community approved by the Catholic Church. They do so in a bid to connect more closely to God. Like priests, the Brothers vow to dedicate their lives to poverty, chastity and obedience.[25]

The Xaverian (pronounced za-VAIR-ian) Brothers were founded in Bruges, Belgium, in 1839 to provide education and moral guidance for youths. In 1854, the Xaverian Brothers accepted an invitation to the United States extended by Bishop Martin J. Spalding of Louisville, Kentucky, to teach in Catholic schools in that city which has the oldest Catholic diocese in the United States. Ten years later, the Xaverian Brothers opened St. Xavier's College in Louisville. Bishop Spalding appreciated the work of the Brothers and when he was appointed Archbishop of Baltimore that same year, he asked them to help him. In his new city, Bishop Spalding was moved by the plight of indigent, homeless and wayward children in the wake of the Civil War. So, in 1866, the archbishop asked the Xaverians to assume operation of the new St. Mary's Industrial Training School for Boys, a diocese-owned facility he opened there. The Xaverian Brothers accepted the assignment and decided to move their motherhouse and novitiate to Baltimore.

The congregation found a 12-acre estate for sale on Frederick Avenue, about three miles west of the city core near Irvington and a bit more than a mile northwest of St. Mary's school. The property was purchased in 1876, to become their new American headquarters. Also on the site, the Xaverian Brothers established Mount St. Joseph College, to be led by Brother Dominic, who later transferred to St. Mary's school. Mount St. Joseph accepted its first student in February 1877, and within two years the quality of its education was recognized by the state of Maryland and it was conferred degree-granting status. A brick structure was built alongside the first frame schoolhouse the following year and students began to arrive in numbers from places as distant as Washington and Philadelphia. Another fine brick building was erected in 1885 to meet the demand for additional space for dormitories and classrooms on the lush and hilly campus that grew to 40 acres. The college continued to expand, with more classrooms, dormitories and laboratories, along with an outdoor swimming pool and athletic field.[26]

About 1890, Martin Boutilier connected with the Xaverian Brothers, possibly by learning about a new Catholic school in East Boston opposite The Church of Our Lady of the Assumption at Sumner and Seaver streets. The Reverend Joseph Cassin, with the assurance of help from the Xaverian Brothers, erected a substantial building across from the church that year. In January 1891, three Xaverian Brothers began teaching classes there. "The boys were wild and disorderly," a historian for the order later conceded. In Boston, Catholics were still considered second-class citizens and had no meaningful civic positions. Catholics did poorly in schools run by Protestants and they resented it, a situation understood by Cassin, who was determined to do better for them. "The boys, Catholic boys, finding themselves objects of dislike and suspicion, gave in turn what they received, and gave in good measure," the Xaverian account continued. "As a consequence, they became rough and unruly."[27] The Brothers had great success with their difficult charges, taking a deep interest in them, providing good basic education and instilling discipline by drilling them in a fife and drum corps. By 1893, the first certificates of graduation were issued to eight pupils. The success of the new school prompted Holy Redeemer Parish to open a school for girls and boys at London and Havre streets that same year. There, the Xaverians taught the boys, while the Sisters of Notre Dame instructed the girls. The Xaverian Brothers were making a difference in East Boston.

Martin Boutilier no doubt faced the same challenges as a young Catholic in East Boston and was impressed by the efforts by the Xaverians to improve young lives in his community. He may also have been encouraged to consider joining the religious community by his family priest, Father O'Donnell. Regardless, by the time he was 19, Martin was associated with the Xaverians and on May 31, 1891, he signed an "agreement of membership" with the Xaverian congregation. He accepted training by them, and renounced "all right to hold individual property, and in case my connection with said order should ever be terminated I agree to accept and be satisfied with whatever (if any thing) the superior of said order shall in his judgment decide reasonable to give me." His signature was witnessed by Brother Paul, whose legal name was Peter E. Scanlan, a trusted associate of Archbishop Spalding.

Applicants for membership were required to answer a series of questions about themselves. Queried about his occupation, Boutilier responded "electric business," suggesting he may have worked for his electrician brother-in-law for a time. He declared he was free from debt, that he could read with "correctness, ease and intelligence and that he could take dictation and spell correctly." He described his knowledge of arithmetic, grammar, geography, book-keeping and "mensuration and geometry" as "fair." He said he had been baptized and that he took holy communion and confessed on a weekly basis.[28] In signing the application with a flowing hand, he dropped the first "i" in his surname, to more closely approximate its pronunciation in English. He would do so repeatedly in documents he signed with the Xaverians. On July 13, 1892, two days after he turned 20, Boutilier signed as "Martin Leo Boutlier" while responding to "canonical" questions. One asked why he wanted to enter the religious state of the congregation. He replied: "for the salvation of my

Martin Leo Boutilier, a native of Cape Breton Island, Nova Scotia, became Brother Matthias when he joined the Congregation of St. Francis Xavier in the 1890s. He was posted to St. Mary's Industrial Training School in Baltimore, where the six-foot-six Brother Matthias taught and became head of discipline and a baseball coach (Xaverian Brothers).

soul and to help others." He said he understood the rules and obligations of the Xaverians and would observe them.[29] After spending two years at the novitiate, Boutilier applied to the Xaverians on June 14, 1895, to make his "final and perpetual vows to be admitted to the order." In March of 1900, he signed a "Formula of the Vow of Stability" at Mount St. Joseph College, witnessed by Brother Joseph, head of the college. He signed as Brother Matthias, no longer Boutilier, vowing to "observe poverty, chastity, obedience and stability."[30]

When Thomas returned to East Boston in late 1891 following his time in Montreal, he learned his younger brother was taking the initial steps to become an Xaverian. Mere days after his 27th birthday, Thomas applied for membership as well. His November 4 application was witnessed by Brother Paul, the same Xaverian who witnessed Martin's application a bit more than five months earlier. Thomas brought with him the letter of recommendation from Father Candide in Montreal and from his family priest testifying to his good character. In the questionnaire tied to his application, Thomas described his occupation as an engineer. He conceded he was unable to "read with correctness, ease and intelligence" and that he could not write from dictation with correct spelling. Asked about his knowledge of arithmetic, grammar, geography, book-keeping, geometry and other subjects, Thomas replied: "Division, not much Grammar or Geography and nothing in the rest."[31] Asked how often he took holy communion and confessed his sins, he said he did so once a month. His answers suggested Thomas had less formal education than Martin and that he practiced his faith less rigorously. He, too, soon began signing his surname as "Boutlier" in Xaverian documents. After two years as a novice, Thomas applied for membership.

While still novices, the Boutiliers were assigned to Xaverian schools, Thomas to Mount St. Joseph College, where he was given the name Brother Amandus, and Martin to St. Mary's Industrial Training School, where he became Brother Matthias. Their duties ranged from menial tasks, such as washing dishes or clerical duties, to assisting the Brothers in the school chapels, classrooms and athletic fields and in any other way needed.

In June of 1899, several members of the Boutilier family arrived in Baltimore and Thomas and Martin greeted them at Camden Station downtown. Their siblings Napoleon, Henry and Joseph, along with sister Eunice and her husband John A. Kelly, had been sightseeing in Washington, Newport News and Norfolk and wanted to see how their brothers were faring. The *Baltimore Sun* took note of the visit, which included meeting Brother Joseph, director of Mount St. Joseph, and his counterpart, Brother Dominic at St. Mary's. The reporter was apparently awed by the size of the Boutilier men. "Brother Matthias is 6 feet 4 inches tall, and his brother, Napoleon, an inch higher in stature."[32] His estimate was two inches less than the actual height of Brother Matthias and he failed to estimate the equally impressive height of Amandus. A few months later, on March 25, 1900, about nine years after they initially applied for mem-

2. A Farewell to Nova Scotia

St. Mary's Industrial Training School was at the westerly limits of Baltimore. A home for boys, it accepted orphans, young offenders sent by the courts and boys whose parents could no longer keep them. It housed as many as 800 boys and a staff that included about 30 Xaverian Brothers (Xaverian Brothers).

bership, both brothers Amandus and Matthias were invested with the habit of the order, thereby becoming full members in the Xaverian Brotherhood.

Brothers Matthias and Amandus remained at the schools where they were assigned as novices. Brother Amandus, about to turn 37, held a less demanding position at Mount St. Joseph than Brother Matthias because the students there were academically oriented and came from wealthier families who could afford tuition and board. About 115 students were enrolled at the college and there were 35 Brothers, 16 of whom were novices. Amandus became procurator at the school, an administrative position, and remained there until his death in 1938.[33] He may have been assigned the non-teaching role because of his weak grounding in academics. At Mount St. Joseph, Amandus worked alongside Brother Gilbert, who was posted there in 1908 after time at another Xaverian school in Louisville. Brother Gilbert, a native of Somerville, Massachusetts, was passionate about baseball, sharing his keen interest in the game with other Brothers, including Brother Matthias at St. Mary's. Brother Gilbert proved to be a skilled administrator and as a baseball coach helped bring statewide honors to Mount St. Joseph.[34]

Brother Matthias taught a number of subjects at St. Mary's and held the key post of school disciplinarian. With his towering size, Brother Matthias could bring order to an unruly scene merely by showing up. Soft-spoken and

At Mount St. Joseph College, not far from St. Mary's school, Brother Gilbert (top center) was a very successful baseball coach. Here, he poses with one of his teams. Brother Gilbert never coached Babe Ruth, despite often-repeated stories saying he did. Brother Gilbert simply introduced him to Jack Dunn, owner of the Baltimore Orioles, who signed Ruth to his first professional contract in 1914 (Xaverian Brothers).

mild-mannered, the giant from Cape Breton had a commanding presence, which belied his big heart and gentle soul. His colleagues called him Big Matt, but to the boys he was known as "The Boss." Discipline was important at the school, which at the time had about 500 boys and 30 Brothers to oversee them. The majority of the boys had been sent by court order and were often referred to as "inmates." The city and state paid the Xaverians about $80 per student annually to house, feed and educate them. Aside from his duties in the classroom and dealing with behavior issues, Brother Matthias also coached one of the school's baseball teams.

As he approached the age of 30, Brother Matthias was just getting settled into his simple life of choice when fate brought into his life a troubled young boy who, in time, the world would come to know.

3

St. Mary's

As the nineteenth century drew to a close, the city of Baltimore was booming economically as it reached a population of 500,000. With a fishing industry on its Atlantic doorstep and fertile farmlands in its backyard and around Chesapeake Bay, it became the world's largest supplier of oysters and the country's leader in canned fruits and vegetables. The fertilizer industry in the city was also significant, with 27 factories by 1890. Baltimore had become a world leader in the manufacturing of chrome, copper and steel products. The Pennsylvania Steel Company opened its ironworks in 1887, sourcing iron ore from Cuba and coal from western Maryland. Ready-to-wear garment production made the city a leader in the United States and by 1900 the banking and shipping sectors were major employers. Some 13 trust companies, 21 national banks and 9 local banks looked after the city's financial interests. By 1895, the year Babe Ruth was born, Baltimore was home to more than 200 corporations, a jump from 39 in 1881. Hundreds of passenger trains steamed into its 5 railroad stations on a regular basis while 13 shipping companies plied the Atlantic coast and 6 steamship lines linked Baltimore to foreign ports.[1]

Baltimore had become the fifth largest city in the United States, with just 60,000 fewer inhabitants than fourth-place Boston. It had been quite a century for Baltimore, the shipbuilding center which successfully defended itself from withering British attack during the War of 1812. The British had dismissed the city as no more than "a nest of pirates" because its speedy Baltimore Clippers, the fastest and most maneuverable ships in the world, created nothing but trouble for the British navy. Having occupied and burned Washington, the British attempted to take Baltimore by land and sea beginning on September 12, 1814. They expected the city to fall as easily as Washington, but at Baltimore the army and militia put up a spirited defense. Fort McHenry, guarding the entrance to the harbor, withstood a 25-hour bombardment by British guns. Realizing they could not take the well-fortified city, the invaders withdrew. Francis Scott Key, a lawyer and American negotiator held aboard a British ship during the battle, was inspired to see the American flag still flying the morning after hostilities ended and immediately wrote a poem about it. His "Defence of Fort M'Henry" was later set to the tune of an old drinking song and became "The Star-Spangled Banner."[2]

Because of its easy access and strong economy, Baltimore had attracted two million immigrants in the second half of the 1800s, making it the second busiest port of entry in the United States after New York City. Many arrivals promptly boarded trains of the Baltimore and Ohio Railroad for destinations in the west, but a good number remained in the city because of its prospects. Irish, German, Greek, Italian and Eastern European newcomers brought their language and culture to help diversify and expand Baltimore. By the 1890s, electric streetcars connected the city to its sprawling suburbs. City fathers paid little attention to dealing with industrial and human sewage, however, which ran off into local streams and rivers. The air was ripe every spring as privies and cesspools drained into watercourses like the Gwynns Falls and Jones Falls streams and Back Basin. Not surprisingly, Baltimore recorded the highest rate of typhoid in the country.[3] In his autobiography, Baltimore journalist and native H. L. Mencken, recalled that shortly before the turn of the twentieth century the city acquired "a powerful aroma every spring, and by August smelled like a billion polecats."[4] It wasn't until after a massive fire swept through downtown in 1904 that voters approved a plan to separate storm from sanitary sewers and to provide proper treatment for human and industrial waste.

Baseball was increasingly a part of the urban fabric in Baltimore. The game was brought to the city in 1858 by George Beam, a wholesale grocer. He had business with Joseph B. Leggett, a rising importer and exporter on the docks of Brooklyn, New York, and captain and catcher of the Excelsior Base Ball Club there. Once Beam witnessed an Excelsior game, he was hooked and organized a team back in Baltimore, borrowing the Excelsior name and becoming captain. The team played at a diamond they created in a former cemetery along a section of Madison Avenue that today is underwater at the west end of Druid Lake.[5] The Civil War put a crimp in expansion of the game, but by the late 1860s the Marylands and the Pastimes were among the top teams in the area. In 1871, seven talented local players from the Marylands, including pitcher Bobby Mathews, traveled west to Fort Wayne, Indiana, where they joined the Kekiongas, a professional nine named after a Miami Indian settlement. The Indiana team was a co-operative club and a founding member of the National Association, the first professional baseball league. But the Kekiongas folded before the 1871 season ended.[6]

In response to local demands that Baltimore join the new league, the Lord Baltimores, the city's first professional team, signed on the following year. They featured hometown pitcher Mathews along with fireball hurler Cherokee Fisher, formerly of the association's Rockford team, and other imported players who were paid handsomely by team organizer, Nick Young. Payroll for the club was reported at $12,700, one of the highest among professional clubs in the country.[7] The Baltimore nine were quickly dubbed the "Canaries" because of their uniforms, which consisted of yellow Saxony cloth pants, tight-fitting silk shirts and white hats. Their stockings were yellow and black plaid, while stitched on the left chest of their shirts was the coat of arms of Lord Baltimore, the English politician and colonizer George Calvert, for whom the city was named. For their first game, against the Mutuals of New York on April 22, their stockings were not yet available, so they borrowed red and black plaid ones usually worn by the amateur Pastimes. The gaudy, mismatched attire prompted the *New York Clipper* to report: "Although looking a little ginger-bready with their display of various colors, [they] played like Trojans."[8]

Indeed they did. The Canaries surprised the strong New York club, winning 14 to 8 at the just-opened Newington Base Ball Park on Pennsylvania Avenue, about two miles northwest of the city core. The game attracted a standing-room crowd of 2,500, and additional spectators watched from perches on nearby poles, trees and rooftops. Three days later, the two teams went at it again before an equally good turnout at the same park, but this time the still-visiting Mutuals prevailed, 13 to 11. Professional baseball was off to a good start in Baltimore. Referring to the fulsome accounts of the opening games that appeared in the *Baltimore American*, the *New York Clipper* said: "…we learn that the base ball fever has broken out very badly in Baltimore, the excitement occasioned by the visit of the Mutuals creating quite a stir even in the business circles of the city."[9] With a solid core of veterans and strong pitching, the Canaries had a fine inaugural season, winning 58 games and losing 35. They finished second in the pennant race of the National Association, 7.5 games back of Boston and a single game ahead of third-place New York. The Canaries led the league in hits and runs and their outfielder Lip Pike, with six home runs, had the most in the league.

The Canaries followed up their inaugural campaign with a third-place finish in 1873, with 57 wins and 34 losses. By 1874, a much-weakened club finished dead last in the eight-team league and struggled financially. It collapsed on October 15, unable to complete its schedule.[10]

Baltimore's next professional team, the Orioles, were founding members of the American Association in 1882. Sporting conservative gray uniforms trimmed in red with red stockings and belt, the team struggled on the field initially and at the gate as an outbreak of smallpox kept potential fans away.[11] The upstart loop permitted Sunday games and the sale of alcohol in the ballpark, with several owners associated with saloons or the brewing industry. The league intended to challenge the National League, which forbade both alcohol and Sunday games, prompting the upstart AA to be called "The Beer and Whisky League."[12] However, Baltimore had few top-drawer players and by mid–May was mired in last place. The Orioles finished the season with 19 wins and 54 losses, last in the six-team American Association and 32.5 games back of the pennant-winning Cincinnati Red Stockings. Baltimore remained in the Association until the loop expired after the 1891 season. Its best finish was third, in 1887, two years after brewer Henry R. Von der Horst took control of the team. His Eagle Brewery was among the largest of the city's more than 20 breweries and his ownership was a perfect fit for a league dominated by brewers and saloonkeepers.

For 1892, the National League accepted former AA members Baltimore, St. Louis, Washington and Louisville. In its new league, Baltimore finished last among the 12 teams, winning 46 games and losing 101, leaving the club a woeful 54.5 games back of the pennant-winning Boston Beaneaters. An eighth-place finish followed the next year before the Orioles found a winning groove, capturing the NL pennant in 1894, 1895 and 1896. Manager Ned Hanlon cleverly led the club with his knowledge of the game and offensive tactics that included bunting, hit-and-run plays, aggressive base-stealing and sacrifice hits. He didn't rely on big bats, rather he stressed what today is known as "small ball." Hanlon was a new kind of manager and, in some ways, revolutionized the game. "Hanlon's genius," it has been said, "lay in choosing players wisely, and allowing them to trust their instincts."[13] Baltimore finished second in the next two years. In 1899, Hanlon moved on to manage Brooklyn, taking five star players with him. Their absence was felt immediately. After the 1899 campaign, when Baltimore slipped to fourth and suffered dwindling attendance, the National League dropped the Orioles and shrank from 12 teams to 8. Baltimore sat out from major-league play in 1900 but joined the new American League in 1901. That year it finished fifth of eight teams. By 1902 it had slipped to the cellar.

After that dismal performance, Ban Johnson, president of the American League, sold the Orioles to some New York businessmen in a deal engineered by Baltimore manager John McGraw, who had gone to New York that July, along with four of his players.[14] The team was renamed the New York Highlanders with McGraw as manager. In time, the team became the New York Yankees.[15] For more than a decade Baltimore was out of major-league baseball. In 1914 and 1915, the Baltimore Terrapins competed in the Federal League with Ned Hanlon as its organizer and large shareholder. But following that interlude for baseball, Baltimore reverted to being a minor-league baseball city until 1954, when the American League's St. Louis Browns relocated to Baltimore.

After the 1902 season, former Orioles manager Ned Hanlon purchased the Montreal Royals of the Eastern League and moved them to Baltimore. In 1909, he sold the team to a consortium including Jack Dunn, a pitcher-turned-star infielder who had played for Hanlon in Brooklyn and was a member of the Orioles in 1901.[16] The AAA Eastern League was renamed the International League in 1912 to reflect the addition of Canadian teams in Toronto and Montreal. Dunn led the Orioles to fourth- and third-place finishes in 1912 and 1913 and was hoping to further improve the team with his sharp eye for talent and ability to develop players and sell his best ones to major-league teams.[17] Great things lay ahead for Dunn and for the Orioles under his watch.

As baseball gained a foothold and then a loyal following in American cities like Baltimore during the latter part of the nineteenth century, social problems were developing. A gap had grown between inhabitants who had the time, inclination and resources to follow baseball and those for whom mere survival was a struggle. The industrial revolution and urbanization were producing a class of urban poor in alarming numbers. Many Americans, long-time residents and newcomers alike, were being left behind as the country prospered. With limited funds and long hours, they struggled to find and keep jobs and raise their children, who they put to work as soon as possible. Difficult family situations were compounded by alcohol-fueled physical and mental abuse of spouses and children, leading to the growth of the temperance movement.

During the 1800s, orphanages began to appear in response to the increasing number of abandoned or runaway children, or those for whom a parent (most often a single mother) could no longer provide. The Civil War claimed many fathers and greatly increased the demand for orphanages, which were generally operated by religious or charitable groups rather than the government. Local municipalities contributed to the costs of running such homes, which were expected to provide children not only food and shelter, but also instill good character, self-reliance, sobriety and a good work ethic. By the 1870s, it was estimated that 150 children were abandoned each month and thousands more were simply left unattended, ill-fed and poorly clothed in unheated tenements. The least fortunate had to fend for themselves in the streets of their cities. By 1880, more than 600 orphanages had been established in America.[18]

In New York City, the nation's metropolis, the need to deal with the throngs of homeless children roaming the streets became urgent. In 1853, young Protestant minister Charles Brace Loring felt compelled to act. He established the Children's Aid Society, the first agency intended to improve the welfare of children. Loring established foster homes in which children were placed after being rescued from abusive families or from parents who were unable or unwilling to care for them. His CAS founded the "orphan train" program, in which orphans were sent by rail to live with Christian foster families in rural areas, primarily in the Midwest. The young transplants were provided food and accommodation by their host families in exchange for their labor on the farm, providing benefits for both parties. During the next 75 years, more than 150,000 children were sent west in the "orphan train" program.[19]

In late 1874, former diplomat Henry Bergh established the New York Society for the Prevention of Cruelty to Children. The plight of a young girl named Mary Ellen, a victim of cruelty in the Hell's Kitchen neighborhood of the city, had captured his attention and his heart. He enlisted lawyer Elbridge T. Gerry and on April 27, 1875, the two men incorporated the society. The object of the organization was not to punish offenders for cruelty but to try to prevent cruelty in the first place. This wasn't their first partnership. Bergh and Gerry had teamed up in 1866, shortly after the first laws were enacted to protect animals, to establish the American Society for the Prevention of Cruelty to Animals. At the time, however, no laws existed to protect children because governments were loath to interfere in family situations out of respect for independence, privacy and parental rights. But Bergh and Gerry were determined to act, both of them profoundly distressed that vulnerable children were being maltreated. One of the first steps taken by their new agency was to establish a telegraph link to city police headquarters to provide timely help for abused or neglected children. Another was winning authorization from the state and county attorneys general to act on their behalf in court proceedings. Once it had rescued children, The Gerry Society, as it became known, needed somewhere to place them. By 1880, a first shelter was acquired and quickly expanded. Thirteen years later, a new eight-story building was opened on East 23rd Street. The society expanded its role to enforce laws governing child entertainers and child labor laws, to transport children to court, to collection of child support payments and inspection of boarding houses and foster homes. By the end of the nineteenth century, the Gerry Society in New York had investigated 130,000 complaints, helped 370,000 children, sheltered 84,000 children and prosecuted 50,000 cases, with a conviction rate of 94 percent.[20]

The Gerry Society soon expanded to cities like Baltimore because the situation in New York was far from unique. Religious organizations like the Xaverian Brothers and the Brothers of Charity operated orphanage-type facilities in Baltimore and Boston in 1866 and 1874, respectively, but they did not have the activist agenda for intervention or the zeal that the Gerry Society displayed.

The Gerry Society picked children off the street if they deemed them abandoned, homeless or at risk. In about 1898, society members in Baltimore found 12-year-old Asa Yoelson aimlessly wandering the streets, more than 40 miles from his Washington home. Another account said the society found the boy working in a Baltimore bar. Officials were suspicious about his age and background but he steadfastly refused to cooperate or provide them his real name.[21] Regardless of where the agency actually found him, he was placed with the Xaverian Brothers at St. Mary's Industrial Training School. He and another son of St. Mary's, Babe Ruth, would go on to become two of the most formidable stars of popular culture of their times.

The Yoelson youngster was born in Seredzius, a village in Imperial Russia (now Lithuania) in 1886, a fourth child and the youngest of two boys, to Jewish cantor Moishe Yoelson and his wife, Naomi. Moses sought to escape oppression at the hands of the Czar and booked passage for America, finding a position as head of a synagogue in Washington, D.C. He brought his family to join him in 1894. Within a year, however, Naomi died.[22]

Asa Yoelson and his older brother, Hirsh, had a penchant for running away from their strict home life, made more difficult when Moishe remarried and started another family. Upon their arrival in Washington, Asa took to calling himself Al, and Hirsh became Harry. Al had a good voice and first sang publicly at his father's synagogue but had no interest in following in his father's footsteps. Rather, he and Harry became fascinated with Vaudeville shows and took to the streets of Washington, singing for applause and donations from passersby. When Harry left Washington to see the entertainment scene in New York City, Al followed him, anxious to see the bright lights for himself. Following one such visit at age 12 in 1898, when he stayed with a relative in Yonkers, Al was put on a southbound train bound for Washington. But the youngster detrained early in Baltimore, where he was soon apprehended and taken to St. Mary's.[23]

After his time at St. Mary's, and while performing with a partner in 1904, Al changed his last name to Jolson. It wasn't long before Al found great success on the stage as a singer, comedian and film actor. He became known as "The World's Greatest Entertainer" at the peak of his career. In 1927, he starred in an early talking movie, *The Jazz Singer*, which became a smash hit. Jolson often played in blackface and was exceedingly sentimental and demonstrative in his onstage performances. He became the highest-paid entertainer at that point in history and recorded more than 80 hit records. But all that lay in the future. For now, confined to St. Mary's and far from the footlights, the future may have seemed bleak for an independent-minded runaway of 12.

"I was a bad boy then, but not too bad," Jolson said, recalling his time in St. Mary's during a visit to the imposing gray-stone institution shortly before he died. He was in Baltimore to promote an emergency drive for funds to fight polio during 1949. Memories came flowing back as he was shown around by an Xaverian Brother, a reporter for the *Baltimore Sun* tagging along to record them. "I had run away from home. I gave my brother's name because he was supposed to be the black sheep of the family. After a few months, my parents came from Washington and took me home." He recalled the gates he now found wide open at St. Mary's had been shut and locked while he was held there. During the visit he reconnected with Brother Benjamin, the only brother still at St. Mary's.

Jolson, 63, was anxious to show the school to his attractive 26-year-old fourth wife, Erle Galbraith. Introduced to Benjamin, Erle was anxious to know if her husband really had been a "bad boy" during his time there as he claimed. "He was like other boys," replied the good Brother, diplomatically. "Some boys run away from Harvard, too, you know."[24]

Slim and dapper, Jolson marveled how St. Mary's had changed in 51 years. "I remember bars all around," he said, recalling one particular incident for Erle. "Once I hit a boy on the stairs, coming down from chapel, and they put me in solitary. Now that's bad enough, but to have to look through the window and watch the other boys playing outside—well, honey, I screamed and hollered until I ran up a temperature, so they had to let me out.

"I remember they put me to work making shirts [the same training George Ruth received just a few years after Jolson]." He recalled the boys weren't allowed to smoke, but he managed to get a plug of tobacco from the iceman during a delivery to the school. "It didn't taste so good, but a fella couldn't sleep right if he didn't pull some sort of fast one on the brothers," he laughed.

Young Al kept attempting to escape, which saw him lose privileges and be isolated from the other boys. He'd retaliate by refusing to work or study or by getting into fights. His time at St. Mary's came to an end when he learned at the infirmary his weak lungs indicated he had a predisposition to contracting tuberculosis. Al was familiar with what was also known as the "Jewish mumps" that had claimed many members of his faith and he panicked. He finally gave the brothers his correct name and address and it wasn't long before father Moishe arrived to take him home to Washington.[25]

The youngster hated being confined and found his time in the schoolyard, likely working in the garden, was a joy.

"I felt so good when I was working in the yard that I made up my first song," he told his listeners who hung on his every word. "I made a little money out of St. Mary's when it was published. I took the tune from Adeste Fideles and the words went like this," he said, breaking into song: "Don't mind the darkness, daylight will come. Shadows are bound to go by. Rosy dawn will kiss the sky." He stopped himself, confessing: "That's all I remember."

Jolson was rolling now, recalling other aspects of his time when bars may have kept him restrained physically but couldn't kill his love of singing or boundless optimism.

"They gave us marks, and if they were good, we were allowed out for a visit. I got plenty of marks but they were the wrong kind," he joked. At one point, the famous alumnus and his wife visited the spacious dining hall, its small tables neatly set for breakfast.

"Now this is something," Jolson exclaimed. "This looks like a night club by comparison to the old dining room. We sat at long tables. It was like a jail." Before leaving the dining area, Jolson noticed a painting of Babe Ruth, another famous son of St. Mary's, hanging on the wall. "Now, that's a fine thing honey," he said to his young wife. "I'll have to die before I get my picture up there." Babe had died the previous year. Their tour guide Brother Charles quickly assured the Jolsons that if they provided a picture, they would "hang it right away."

The special guests were taken to the school's assembly hall, where 135 boys eagerly awaited the singer. Jolson told them he was grateful for the positive impact St. Mary's had on him. "I have carried beautiful thoughts from those months all my life. I've had a measure of success, I guess, and I owe a great deal of it to the teaching of those wonderful Brothers," he said, adding good-naturedly: "I guess I am the only rabbi's son who was ever taught in a Catholic school."

With that, Jolson asked the gathered boys what song he could sing for them. "Mammy!" came the loud chorus. He obliged and delivered a full version of one of his signature tunes, complete with his famous exaggerated gestures and accompanied by his friend and pianist Harry Akst. Jolson followed with "April Showers" and "California, Here I Come" to the delight of his young audience. The Jolsons left for Washington about 8 p.m. by automobile and it was readily apparent the visit had touched the veteran entertainer deeply. "This was one of the happiest personal appearances I have ever made," he said before motoring off.[26] It was also among his last.

Jolson died of a heart attack 13 months later at the age of 64, shortly after returning home from an exhausting trip to Korea where he entertained American troops. Generously, he left 90 percent of his $4 million estate to charities—Catholic, Protestant and Jewish.[27] Perhaps inspired by his time at St. Mary's, he had decided to give back to them because of what was done for him at an important time of his life.

That same year, 1950, St. Mary's died. The institution had struggled for several years with a declining resident population, from a high of nearly 1,000 to less than 200, as the government introduced and expanded social services for young people and their families. But the death knell came when the state of Maryland withdrew its longstanding annual payment for boys who had been sent by court order. It was no longer deemed appropriate to direct public funds to religious-based organizations since the growth of non-sectarian social agencies. By then, Maryland had 14 state-run institutions for youths. Without state support, the Catholic Church could no longer afford to operate the large facility on its own. The decision to close did not come without deep regret. In its 84 years, St. Mary's had cared for more than 20,000 boys, including its most famous sons, Al Jolson and George Ruth.[28]

By the time the 12-year-old Jolson arrived at St. Mary's, living conditions had been improving, thanks to the enlightened leadership of Brother Dominic, superintendent since 1887. Brother Dominic sought to soften the treatment given the boys and shed the image of St. Mary's as a harsh penal institution. He did away with uniforms and a heavy reliance on cells for disciplinary purposes. The unarmed Xaverians had sometimes employed the cells to deal with criminal offenders who were prone to violence and who could be as old as 20 or 21. The stigma associated with being a student at St. Mary's was gradually dissipating and the school was receiving good grades following inspections by city, state and child welfare officials.[29] In practice, the city of Baltimore was segregated in its police force and racial discrimination was rampant. Blacks could not marry whites nor could they ride the streetcar, and they were barred from some neighborhoods and workplaces. By the 1902–03 school year, more than 10,000 students attended segregated black schools.[30] Not surprisingly, there were no black boys among the population at St. Mary's. Brother Dominic brought a sympathetic ear to the concerns of the boys who were accepted and to the Brothers who taught and lived there. For the latter, Brother Dominic hired night watchmen to patrol the student dormitories, relieving the teachers of that task. The Xaverian organization was impressed with the reforms brought by Brother Dominic and the extensive connections he developed with the business community. Because of his effective collaboration with potential employers, students at St. Mary's were provided training in various trades that helped them find work upon graduation. And the school found a market for the shirts and other consumer products it produced, helping to fund its operation.

In 1900, Brother Dominic was appointed Provincial, the senior post for the Xaverian Brothers in North America.[31] Despite his additional duties and required, Brother Dominic continued as superintendent of St. Mary's until his death at the school in 1907. His funeral Mass was held at St. Mary's and the 650 boys then at the school followed his body on foot nearly two miles to his grave for interment. Their respect for Brother Dominic was such that every one of them returned to St. Mary's that day, despite ample opportunity for escape.[32]

Since they welcomed their first students at St. Mary's, the Xaverian Brothers had focused their efforts on reforming them and providing guidance rather than correction. Boys sent from the juvenile courts of Baltimore and elsewhere in Maryland stayed for a year or two. Orphans, or those from broken homes, had to remain until they reached the age of 18 or 21. Parents sometimes sent children they could not afford or control and the duration of their stay could vary widely. By 1900, about half the boys at the school were placed there by parents who paid for them.[33] The Xaverians treated all boys equally, regardless of background, relying on suspension of privileges and peer group pressure, rather than corporal punishment. The approach

3. St. Mary's

worked. There were few desertions or escapes. Children from all denominations were accepted but all were expected to attend morning Mass in the school chapel. The boys were divided into four barracks-like dormitories, in wide-open spaces each with 200 beds arranged in rows. Off to the side were showers and toilets. The brothers had private rooms with windows from which they could monitor their charges. Generally, there were about 30 Xaverian Brothers on staff.

Each day started at 6 a.m., with the boys attending Mass in the 1,400-seat chapel before a breakfast of oatmeal or hominy. Milk was provided for the oatmeal and weak coffee was available. Then it was off to class, where the students used individual slate boards and chalk, rather than pencil and paper. Each Brother had 40 to 50 boys in his classroom. After a lunch of soup and bread and a short recess, it was back to the classroom for the younger students, while the older ones reported for training in the shops. Later in the afternoon, time was set aside for exercise and recreation in the large yards behind the school, with each dormitory having its assigned yard. Supper was again soup and bread. Bedtime was 8:15 p.m. Sunday was a day for treats, with hot dogs and baloney on the menu.[34] Basic education was provided for all, with an opportunity to learn a trade. In the shops, students were taught shirt-making, shoemaking, laundering, book-binding, carpentry, millwright skills, baking, electrical repairing, hair-cutting, glazing and typewriting. In season, students

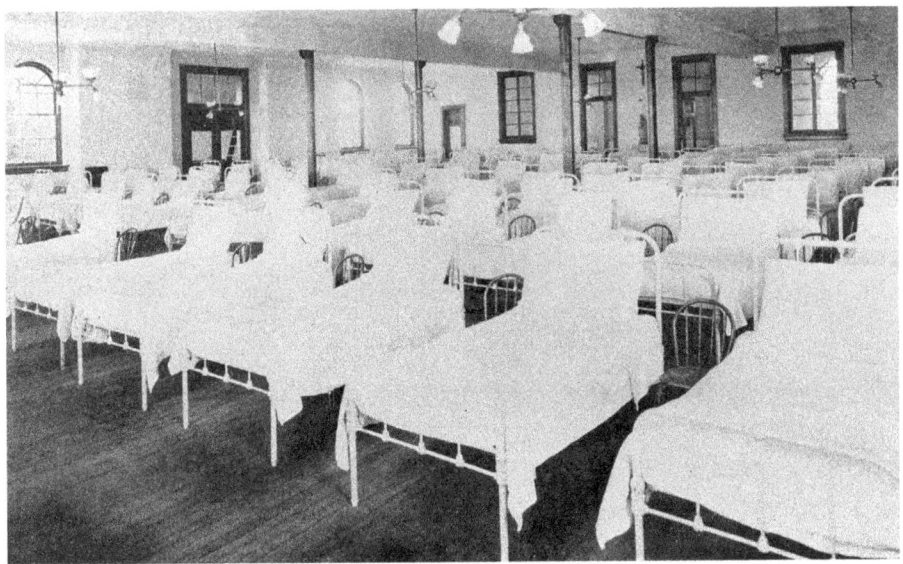

The dormitories at St. Mary's were spartan and privacy was impossible. The Brothers had tiny rooms and Brother Matthias, a big man, only fit into his once the door was changed to swing outward (Xaverian Brothers).

were assigned to the farm plots at the rear of the school where vegetables were grown. Some toiled in the school bakery, which produced hundreds of loaves of bread each day. Later, a printing room and garage were added to teach lithography and auto mechanics.[35] As in other institutions of the day, the boys were provided a solid basic academic education on the understanding that higher education was unlikely.

Physical education and culture were significant aspects of the St. Mary's experience. Boys took part in football, basketball, track and field and wrestling. And because Brother Benedict at one time had been a professional boxer, he taught budding pugilists the finer points of his favorite sport. But the single activity that consumed the school was baseball. As many as 44 intramural ball teams were formed and donned uniforms made in one of the school's two tailoring shops.[36] A few of the older and best players were selected for teams to compete against other schools, such as nearby Mount St. Joseph College. Several of the Brothers were accomplished baseball players and not only pro-

The Xaverian Brothers loved baseball and played it while wearing their heavy cassocks. Here, waiting for a pitch is an aging Brother Herman, while Brother Quentin acts as umpire. The catcher is unidentified. This image is from several years after Babe left St. Mary's, which continued to turn out baseball players (Xaverian Brothers).

vided first-rate instruction, but sometimes joined the boys on the field. Brother Alban, one of the youngest Brothers, was a particularly good athlete and played first base.[37] Also joining in was Brother Herman, who organized the teams into leagues. The Xaverians presented quite a picture when they did play, still wearing their long and heavy black cassocks, a cross atop the Sacred Heart of Jesus sewn on the chests and heavy rosary beads dangling from their belts. Baseball tournaments were held from March to September, pitting the various trades students or dormitories against each other. Aside from the physical benefits, baseball taught the value of teamwork and provided special events to which residents looked forward with great anticipation.

Apart from baseball, St. Mary's mounted theatrical productions on occasion and the school became famous for its bands. Three musical assemblages—the Little Boy's Band, and the junior and senior bands—all brought acclaim to St. Mary's and helped raise funds after a disastrous fire in 1919. Baltimore music teacher Albert Holland provided a good foundation for the music program. In the city, Holland led choirs and became conductor of the Independent Blues Band of the 1860s and 1870s. He was joined by other local music teachers in getting the school bands off to a strong start. He died in 1883, but the committee overseeing school operations saw the value in retaining the bands and by 1888 outfitted the musicians as young as six with uniforms made in the school's tailor shop. By 1890, the original band had grown to 32 members and four years later, a fife-and-drum corps was organized, doubling the number of musicians. The musical program expanded further when a 20-piece orchestra was established in 1896. Three years later, newly arrived Brother Pancratius took over responsibility for the various bands and orchestra and did so until his death in 1919. He was followed by Brother Simon, a master musician and conductor.

Over the years, St. Mary's musicians drew praise. One local music critic said at one point: "The technique of these young fellows was wonderful. Some of the selections were from operas, requiring skill and accurate reading."[38] The senior band played at Catholic celebrations held at the school and appeared widely in Baltimore and neighboring communities in Maryland. It was in demand at community fundraising events, fairs, civic receptions, service clubs and for University of Maryland football games and Baltimore Orioles ballgames. In its first 50 years, the main band gave more than 1,000 performances. One highlight came in 1913 when both the junior and senior bands were invited to Washington to march in the inaugural parade for President Woodrow Wilson.

Still more fame came to the school in 1928 when the 60-member senior band competed in the three-day National High School Band Contest in Joliet, Illinois, and won its division. St. Mary's was the only Catholic school in the competition that attracted 27 bands from 15 states.[39] Judges included acclaimed American composer and conductor John Philip Sousa. Afterward, the boys were treated to an American League baseball game between Chicago and Detroit as guests of White Sox owner Charles Comiskey.[40] The competition was not the first time the St. Mary's boys had played for Sousa. Several months before the competition, Sousa was invited to St. Mary's to see a rehearsal. He then led the band in two of his own marches and delivered a brief talk about choosing music as a profession.[41] At one point in their history, Sousa described St. Mary's as the best boys' band he had ever heard.[42] If Babe Ruth hadn't appeared at the front door of St. Mary's one day, it's possible the school's greatest claim to fame would have been its bands.

Teamwork and discipline, whether on the ballgame or in the concert hall, were among the qualities taught to the boys at St. Mary's by a team of dedicated and selfless men known as the Xaverian Brothers.

4

Birth and Rebirth

Babe Ruth seldom spoke about his childhood in Baltimore and researchers have struggled to penetrate the "fog" that Leigh Montville said in his 2006 biography permeates Ruth's life. In Robert W. Creamer's 1974 study of Ruth, that author said the problem is particularly acute for his first 20 years. Creamer lamented the "shifting mélange of elusive facts, supposition and unsubstantiated invention" and that the "mists of ignorance obscure concrete knowledge."[1]

Ruth himself was of little help dispelling those mists. Until he needed a birth certificate to obtain his first passport, he didn't even know when he was born. His first passport was issued in 1920, but another story says that was not until 1934. Regardless, for the longest time he believed he was born on February 7, 1894, but it was actually February 6, 1895. So Ruth spent many years celebrating the wrong birthday. And in his third and last autobiography, published in 1948, Ruth devoted fewer than 300 words to his formative years. It was almost as though he didn't want to remember them.

Despite some suppositions and inventions about his past, details of Ruth's early days are gradually emerging as more recent research has clarified his humble origins. It turns out he wasn't the total saloon rat that he described to biographers after all.

He was born in the Ridgely's Delight neighborhood in Baltimore, immediately west of Camden Yards, the huge terminal for the Baltimore and Ohio Railroad. Immediately to the west lies Pigtown, then a gritty working-class area so named because pigs shipped in from the Midwest were herded from the railway yard along neighboring streets to nearby stockyards and slaughterhouses. He was the firstborn for George and Katie Ruth. The birth occurred in the home of his maternal grandparents at 216 Emory Street, a narrow red-brick row house like so many others in Baltimore. It was a frigid February day, the coldest of the winter in the city. The temperature reached only 11 degrees Fahrenheit following an overnight low of a fraction of a degree above zero. Only two days had been colder in Baltimore in the 25 years since the weather bureau had been established, the *Baltimore Sun* reported.[2] The baby was delivered by midwife Minnie Graf, while Katie's mother Anna Schamberger sat nearby offering encouraging words in German, the language of the Schamberger household. At the time, Katie and George Ruth lived about two miles southwest of her parent's home, above a restaurant and saloon operated by George's parents, John and Mary Ruth. For her firstborn, Katie wanted to be with her mother. It proved to be a good decision because it was a difficult birth for the tiny woman. Her baby was a big boy and, in the Ruth family tradition, was named after his father.[3]

George and Katie were still newlyweds. He was Lutheran and she was Roman Catholic, a union that was not common at a time when religious divisions ran deep. Perhaps they had to marry, because the ceremony was a mere seven months before George Jr. was born.[4] They were married June 25, 1894, at West Baltimore Baptist Church by Reverend Ward. The groom, George Herman Ruth, a big, dark-haired man, was born in Baltimore in 1871. His parents were born in Maryland but his grandparents, Jacob and Catharine Ruth, were born in Germany. The name Ruth was an Americanized version of the original family name, variously spelled Rüdt, Rüd or Ried in Germany, Maryland genealogist Druscilla J. Null recently discovered as she delved into Babe's family history.[5] As Germans, they were not alone in choosing Maryland's metropolis as their home. Germans were the largest foreign-born group in Baltimore and by 1900, when it reached a population of half a million, the city directory contained more than 50 entries with the surname Ruth.

John A. Ruth, the grandfather of the future baseball great, was a tinsmith who established a lightning rod business in 1873. He was also an inventor, securing a patent for a lightning rod insulator in 1884 and four others between 1888 and 1896; one for a new type of wagon, another for a garment fastener and two for protective casings for oil and gas stoves.[6] Installing and repairing lightning rods was his primary occupation. He was a strong man and a good businessman, advertising his services extensively in the *Baltimore Sun* and eventually bringing his oldest son, John Jr., and next-born, George, into his operation. During 1873, his first year of business, he drew public attention, if not admiration, when he repaired a weathervane and lightning rod perched atop a building near Baltimore harbor. He erected a scaffold above a cupola 165 feet in the air to remove and fix the broken vane, which weighed fifty pounds. The *Sun* reported on the daring feat, which took some time, noting: "These aerial performances always draw crowds of spectators."[7] In 1880, Baltimore celebrated its 150th anniversary with a massive parade showcasing its industrial progress. The procession took five hours to pass any given point and attracted 300,000 spectators. The parade featured 20,000 participants, including John A. Ruth. He piloted a horse-drawn wagon displaying a steeple topped with lightning rods and images of Benjamin Franklin flying a kite during an electrical storm painted on its sides.[8] By 1890, sons John Jr. and

George were working with him at his shop and home on Frederick Avenue at Font Hill Avenue, on the edge of Baltimore about two miles southwest of the city core. In the house, the Ruths also operated a saloon connected to a social club in the area. It was here that Katie and George lived when their first child, George, was born.

Katie (Catharina, or Catherine) was born in Baltimore in 1874 to Pius and Joanna Schamberger, a couple whose families had German and Irish roots.[9] Both Pius and Anna were born in Baden, Germany.[10] Pius was an upholsterer like his father, and became vice-president of Woodworkers Union Local Number 6 after time spent as a grocer and saloonkeeper. Some biographers have insisted the Schambergers were Lutherans like the Ruths, but evidence suggests otherwise, such as their burial in Most Holy Redeemer Catholic Cemetery in Baltimore. Pius (Latin for "pious") was a name used by Roman Catholic popes beginning about 140 AD. The last, Pope Pius XII, passed away in 1958. It would seem unlikely any Lutheran (a follower of Protestant reformer Martin Luther—who famously broke with the Catholic Church) would be given that particular name.

Only recently it has been learned that George Jr. was baptized in the parish of St. Peter the Apostle Catholic Church in Baltimore on March 1, 1895, by Father Joseph O'Brien.[11] That baptismal record was apparently lost, so the record book at St. Mary's Industrial Training School listed the young Ruth boy who appeared at their door as a "convert." So, he was baptized again, just a week before his first communion at St. Mary's, on May 9, 1907. Regardless, members of the Ruth household were not churchgoers and at least one source says the marriage of George and Katie took place in Fulton Avenue Baptist Church.[12]

In all, George and Katie Ruth had eight children, but only one other child, Mary, survived past infancy. Five years younger than George, the survivor of twins was known as Mamie. Katie's many pregnancies and the deaths of her babies took their toll on the frail woman of four-foot-ten, who was called upon to help her husband when he entered the saloon business. It was a hard life for the young couple at a difficult time, regardless of how George sought to earn a living. A financial panic in 1893 led to the worst depression in American history, with failures of hundreds of banks and businesses. It lasted until 1897. Four million Americans were left unemployed, including half of Baltimore's industrial workers, many of whom were union members.

Babe and his parents lived with John and Mary Ruth until John died in January of 1897 and the house on Frederick Avenue was sold. George and John Ruth continued their father's business, moving to adjoining row houses at 339 and 341 South Woodyear Street, behind which they created their own lightning rod workshop.[13] The residential, working-class neighborhood consisted of 56 two-story row houses built in 1885, just west of downtown Baltimore and the Baltimore and Ohio Railroad's Mount Clare Yards, which employed many men from the neighborhood. It was a blue-collar area of single families, most of whom housed in-laws or boarders. Many of the family breadwinners were carpenters, laborers, boilermakers, craftsmen, cabinet makers, machinists, painters and marble cutters. Nearly half of the residents were of German descent, with some having Irish roots. Babe and his parents lived at 339 South Woodyear Street, where in 1900, his sister Mamie was born. Also living with them were George's sister, Annie, her teamster husband, Milton C. Brundige, and their daughter, Ellen, born in 1899. Next door, at 341 South Woodyear Street, lived his Uncle John and Aunt Mary, who had five children, three of whom were slightly older than Babe.[14]

Babe Ruth was surrounded by family in a bustling, working-class residential area of large families served by several corner stores. Just to the southwest lay Carroll Park, which provided ample opportunities for play for the neighborhood children. There were no saloons. Baltimore historian Fred B. Shoken meticulously dug into city directories and census records to track the Ruth family during Babe's earliest years and found a picture of his life that differed dramatically from that invariably painted by his biographers. Neither Frederick Avenue, where Ruth spent his first two years, nor South Woodyear Street, where he lived for the next four, were the rough waterfront neighborhoods from the legend of Babe Ruth. His homes were not "rooms over a bar."[15] If not idyllic, his first six years were reasonably normal in turn-of-the-century Baltimore.

The situation for the Ruth family changed dramatically early in 1901, shortly after Babe's sixth birthday (which he believed was his seventh). His father left the lightning rod business to his older brother and sold the family home on South Woodyear Street. The reasons are a mystery. Perhaps there was some disagreement between the brothers; perhaps the business could not support two families. Or maybe George had become restless and wanted to make his own mark on the world, somewhere with more action than he found in the blue-collar neighborhood. Regardless, by April the Ruths were living above a saloon they operated at 426 West Camden Street, a block from Camden Station downtown and the newly built Camden Yards Warehouse. The *Baltimore Sun* of April 13 reported George had applied for a liquor license for the establishment.[16] The new venture got off to a shaky start when on April 23, within days of securing the license, George was fined $10 and costs in court for allowing minors to play pool in the establishment.[17] One of them may have been his son, anxious like his father to try a new experience.

Life for Babe and his little sister would soon deteriorate. This was a tough neighborhood and operating a saloon was a hard way to earn a living. And it was a poor place to raise children. A streetcar ran in front of the saloon connecting downtown to neighborhoods in the southwest of the city. Neigh-

4. Birth and Rebirth 47

bors included meat packing and cold storage warehouses, a canning company, a chemical company, a delivery service and an undertaker. The Ruth's bar was at the northeast corner of Camden and Paca streets, seven doors west of 410 Camden Street, the newly established Baltimore branch of Jacob Ruppert's New York-based brewery. There was a fine irony in this. When brewery founder Jacob Ruppert died in 1915, his son, Jacob Jr., took over the entire brewing operation. That same year, the younger Ruppert became an owner of the New York Yankees and four years later, hired a new baseball sensation named Babe Ruth.

There were plenty of warehouse and other workers in the businesses surrounding Camden Yards and no shortage of places to quench their thirst. An African American citizen's group grew concerned about the proliferation of saloons in Baltimore as they sought better enforcement of liquor laws. In 1908, they counted 36 saloons then operating in a four-block area bounded by Camden, Pratt, Paca and Howard streets.[18] The saloon business was very competitive. The Ruths struggled.

Ruth biographer Marshall Smelser noted that saloon operators in Baltimore worked hard and for long hours to earn a living in the late 1800s. Typically, a saloon would produce net profits of as little as $5 to as much as $100 for a six-day workweek of 60 to 114 hours. He estimated George and Katie Ruth managed a joint profit of $15 to $20 each week, with each of them working about 100 hours. In a court deposition she made in 1906, Katie said by then their saloon was turning $30 a week in net profit.[19] That would generate an annual income of $1,560 for the young family. At the time, about half of Baltimore's wage earners made from $5 to $10 a week, so the Ruths were better off than many families. By 1900, the U.S. federal census pegged the average individual income of Americans at $449. In Baltimore, the competition among saloons was keen, Smelser noted, with one licensed seller of legal alcoholic beverages for every 105 Baltimoreans.[20] George and Katie worked hard for their money and reduced expenses by living above their saloon.

The Ruth family, Smelser surmised, could be described as being at the top of the lowest class, or toward the bottom of the middle class. That put them just a notch above the poor of Baltimore, whose scrapes with the law consisted mainly of disorderly conduct, assault and public drunkenness. Divorce, however, was extremely rare. By feeding and providing drink to laborers, longshoremen, sailors, teamsters and railroad workers, the Ruths earned their livelihood. And when his wife was ill or over-tired, which was often, George worked alone and sometimes angrily, worried about paying the bills. When his son got underfoot, Big George ordered him outside to play in the street.

German was spoken in the Ruth household and likely also on the streets of their new neighborhood. Many years later, famed sportswriter Fred Lieb, who was eventually tapped to help ghostwrite Ruth's 1948 autobiography, was chatting in German with Ruth's teammate Lou Gehrig on the Yankees. "Ruth got into the conversation," Lieb recalled. "He spoke it surprisingly well."[21]

The long hours in the saloon left little time for Big George and his diminutive spouse to care for Little George. The boy may have picked up that pet name because of his striking resemblance to his father, with his dark hair and skin, flat, wide nose and rather large lips. He joined the youngsters in his neighborhood, who easily found mischief in the busy cobblestone streets near the rail yards teeming with activity in the port city becoming known as "The Liverpool of America." His playground activity involved dodging cart drivers who plied the narrow streets with their cargo, taunting drunken sailors and pilfering from fruit stands, drawing the wrath of shopkeepers.

He told Bob Considine, the primary ghostwriter of his 1948 autobiography: "I was a bum when I was a kid." In that version, Ruth was reflective:

> I don't want to make any excuses, or place the blame for my shortcomings as a kid completely on persons or places. I might have been hard to handle if I had been born J. Pierpont Morgan V [a wealthy American banker and financier] ... Looking back on my early boyhood, I honestly don't remember being aware of the difference between right and wrong. If my parents had something I wanted very badly, I took it, but I must have had some dim realization that this was stealing because it never occurred to me to take the property of anyone besides my immediate family. I chewed tobacco when I was seven, not that I enjoyed it especially but—from my observations around the saloon—it seemed the normal thing to do.[22]

"I was a bad kid," he freely confessed in the opening sentence of the book, but said he was a victim of his circumstances. The streets were his primary school in the first innings of his life and he soon learned the language of "longshoremen, merchant sailors, roustabouts and waterfront bums." Young George was running with boys who were constantly getting into trouble in a rough-and-tumble part of town. "I hardly knew my parents.... I had a rotten start and it took me a long time to get my bearings." He had either forgotten the time spent on Frederick Avenue and South Woodyear Street, or simply didn't want to say more about his upbringing because of subsequent family turmoil.

There had been some good times, however, certainly before the move to West Camden. A photograph from a "family picnic" in 1896 or 1897, before the Ruths moved downtown, shows about 80 men, women and children, all smartly dressed in white shirts and dresses, the men in straw hats, in front of a large white building. Two men and a woman are holding guitars, although one man's may be a smaller stringed instrument like a lute or ukulele. The musical instruments suggest the gathering may also have been some sort of celebration. To the lower left can be seen a stern-faced Katie Ruth, her hair pulled up in a bun, blouse buttoned high, with Little George at her side. A few feet away, with two male companions seated on a step, is a bow-tied Big George, a pipe in one hand, glass of beer in the other.[23]

Life became a grind for the Ruth family with the move downtown. Mamie, who lived to age 91, recalled for a writer: "Mother was not a very well person." Tiny Katie was often pregnant and chronically ill, yet was still called upon to work long hours alongside her husband. Strains developed between Katie and George after their son was sent to St. Mary's and Katie likely developed a drinking problem.[24] For his part, George Ruth had no problem whatsoever with drink and found time for a social life as a member of the Bohemian Social Club, known as the Jolly Brothers Club. The third annual ball for the organization took place in November of 1901, a few blocks from the saloon at the Germania Maennerchor Hall. The *Baltimore Sun* noted he was on the dance committee for the well-attended event.[25]

Given the narrow city streets filled with commercial traffic that constituted his playground, it is doubtful Little George played much baseball. If he did so, it was in the most rudimentary way, likely without bats or gloves. There were too many vehicles, too many windows and too few open spaces in this older part of Baltimore. A lefty, the young Ruth developed a strong throwing arm, however, joining his pals in tossing stolen eggs and tomatoes at the heavy vehicles that traveled to and from the docks. The drivers would sometimes chase down the boys and try to lash them with their horse whips.

Later in his life, Ruth said he developed pretty good pitching control from that bit of mischief with those missiles.[26] And to escape a whipping, he required good foot speed that would later be useful on the base paths.

Ruth's 1928 autobiography, ghostwritten by sportswriter Ford Frick, provided further glimpses of life for the street kid, and his memories seemed vivid. This marked the second of what would be three tellings of his life story in all. A 1920 version for *United News Syndicate* was serialized in 12 newspaper installments published over the course of three months. It was cobbled together by sportswriter Westbrook Pegler. Eight years later, Frick learned how difficult Pegler's task had been to get Ruth to sit still for interviews. Frick had to guess at many aspects of Ruth's life and find alternate sources when his subject couldn't recall or wouldn't cooperate. Here is some color commentary by Ruth about his childhood on the streets of Baltimore, as channeled by Frick, who later admitted he'd spent little time with Ruth:

> Crowded streets they were too, noisy with the roar of heavy trucks whose drivers cursed and swore and aimed blows with their driving whips, at the legs of kids who made the streets their playground. And the youngsters, running wild, struck back and echoed the curses. Truck-drivers were our enemies; so were the coppers patrolling their beats, and so too were the shopkeepers who took bruising payment from our skins for the apples and the fruit we "snitched" from their stands and counters.

A rough, tough neighborhood, but he liked it.

There in those crooked winding streets I staged my first fight, and lost it, I think. There too I played my first baseball. There I learned to fear and to hate the coppers. Perhaps it was there, too, that I learned to control my pitches. For tossing over-ripe apples, or aged eggs at a truck driver's head is mighty good practice—although I don't recommend it to the boys of today.[27]

Little George was becoming known to the police officers who patrolled the streets he roamed. He and his running mates were occasionally apprehended for petty larceny and mischief and taken home. There, Big George would administer discipline with a horsewhip down in the cellar. It didn't do much good and the youngster continued to cause his family grief. In the family bar, Little George began to chew tobacco, steal from the till and finish beer and other alcoholic drinks left unattended. Upon being discovered, he was taken to the cellar and whipped yet again. Ruth later told the story that he once stole a dollar bill from the till and bought ice cream for himself and his pals. Busted by his father, it meant yet another trip to the cellar.[28] He was not responding to the harsh discipline dispensed by his quick-to-anger father. This was a dreadful environment for an impressionable and hyperactive youngster.

Ruth's parents may have hoped he would learn some discipline at school, but they were soon disappointed. His escapades merely expanded to include truancy. At age six, Little George was enrolled in school, but he preferred the familiar streets around his home to any desk. His sister Mamie explained many years later that he simply did not like school and that was a factor in later events.

By the late 1800s, children in poorer families often had little formal education and were sent to work in low-skill jobs to supplement the family income. They were seen as little more than income-generating units. Who can forget those gritty images of child laborers depicted in coal mines of the day, faces covered in soot, perhaps smoking and looking like hardened adults? Or those forced to work long hours in factories or textile mills? To their credit, George and Katie Ruth wanted some basic education for their wayward son, unlike many other parents. They hoped it would help him behave and get him out from underfoot. Education did not become compulsory in Maryland until 1902, and until then, a quarter of all white children did not attend school at all. But beginning that year, children aged 8 to 12 had to be enrolled. Also required in school were unemployed youngsters aged 12 to 16.[29]

By 1902, when he turned seven, Little George's parents were at their wits' end. Katie was caring for two-year-old Mamie and Big George was spending long hours in the saloon. It is not known precisely what brought matters to a head, but the Ruths finally concluded the time had come to find another way to deal with a boy who appeared destined for serious trouble. The situation was untenable. One story, often repeated, was that during a brawl at the saloon, some shots were fired by a patron and someone reported to child welfare authorities that a child was living there. This may have brought pressure to bear on the family to act.³⁰

"My father was a stern man," Ruth recalled in his 1920 autobiographical series. "He loved his family so well that it undoubtedly cost him many a sleepless night to decide on sending me away, young as I was, to St. Mary's."

> My father knew I needed the constant good example of the brothers, some discipline and close supervision. He would not flinch. After many conferences under the reading lamp after supper my mother consented for my own sake, although her heart was aching.³¹

Big George confided in his longtime friend, Harry C. Birmingham, a policeman who patrolled the streets of Ridgely's Delight where Little George and his pals roamed. It may have been Birmingham who suggested the family consider sending the youngster to St. Mary's Industrial Training School, just southwest of Baltimore on Wilkens Street. Birmingham knew firsthand that difficult or orphaned boys were often sent there by the courts. "I remember Babe was a little rascal," Birmingham told *Baltimore News-Post* sports editor and columnist Rodger Pippen several decades later. "Although he was not a bad boy—just mischievous, and no more so than other boys his age." Birmingham insisted that his friend's son "never gave the police any trouble. But his father decided to send him to St. Mary's because he just couldn't make him mind at home. Babe had a will of his own and was never one to take orders."³² As an aside, Birmingham said he'd never seen the youngster playing baseball in the streets he patrolled.

St. Mary's seemed to offer the sort of schooling and discipline their son so desperately needed. In 1882, the Maryland legislature had enacted legislation intended to relieve burdened parents of difficult offspring. Any justice of the peace was permitted to commit to St. Mary's "every such white male minor ... adjudged by such justice to be a proper subject for commitment to said Institution by reason of the incorrigible or vicious conduct of such minor, and because of such incorrigible or vicious conduct to be beyond the control of such parent, guardian or next friend."³³

Little George could not be described as "vicious," but it's clear his parents were unable to control him. Yet it's hard to understand how a boy of such tender years could be deemed "incorrigible" by anyone. But it was with that designation that a justice of the peace committed him to St. Mary's in June of 1902. "I was listed as incorrigible, and I guess I was," Ruth admitted in his 1948 autobiography.

June 13, 1902, marked a rebirth of sorts for young George Ruth. Unlike the bitterly cold day of his birth, Baltimore was in the midst of a heat wave. The temperature reached 94 degrees by mid-afternoon and five Baltimoreans had collapsed in the heat, one of them with fatal consequences. The city was one of the hottest places in the entire country. Towns in Maryland a few miles to the west were swept by damaging hailstorms, and by evening rain began to fall in Baltimore, providing some relief.[34] Nearly 600 miles to the northwest, in a much cooler Detroit, the Orioles shut out the Tigers 4–0 in an American League game that afternoon behind a strong performance by pitcher Charlie Shields. This was during the final season of major-league play for the Orioles.

In the stifling heat, police officer Harry C. Birmingham and George Ruth Jr. made the three-mile trip to St. Mary's, an imposing structure on a gentle rise where Wilkens Street intersected with South Caton Avenue. In Birmingham's 1947 obituary, it was noted that he was asked to take Babe to St. Mary's that day.[35] Their trolley stopped directly in front of the five-story gray-stone main building, flanked on its western end by a chapel and to the east by a large dormitory then housing 500 boys. In all, six imposing gray-stone buildings loomed behind large iron gates. A board fence completely surrounded the rest of the sprawling property. The institution was impressive to passersby but terribly intimidating for a fearful young boy about to become one of it youngest inhabitants.

Birmingham led Young George through the heavy entry gates and into an office where the boy began to weep and tell the Xaverian Brother who admitted him that he wanted to go home.[36] The scene had been repeated often in that office and the boy was lent a sympathetic ear. Paperwork was completed, which granted St. Mary's guardianship over the new admission until he reached the age of 21, the age of majority. After bidding Birmingham goodbye, Little George was shown to his quarters in one of the dormitories. It's not hard to imagine the feelings a young boy would have that night as he tried to fall asleep in a strange place, thinking he had been virtually abandoned. Outside, the skies opened up in apparent sympathy for a frightened and suddenly lonely lad. Rain lashed the windows of the dormitory. Babe's mind was racing and his heart was aching. He could have no idea how things would turn out. As biographer Smelser put it so well: "Against his will, young Ruth had found refuge from the kind of neglect that could have killed him, or worse."[37]

June was an odd time to send a boy off to school and George Ruth stayed only about a month before going home. He returned to St. Mary's in November, but was back with his parents for Christmas and didn't return to St. Mary's until 1904.[38] In his 1920 autobiography, he said discipline at the school was administered "the old-fashioned way," with lickings delivered for smoking and for chewing tobacco. Upon returning home, he said, he felt his father noticed some improvement in his behavior. "I think father was pleased with the change the Brothers had worked in me. It seemed that he and I had come to think alike; perhaps he had become a little more liberal. Probably it was a

4. Birth and Rebirth

little of both. At any rate, when we talked together we had an understanding which we had not had before."[39] It would seem logical to assume Big George and Katie had hoped for immediate improvement in the behavior of their boy, but change, if any, was not lasting. At St. Mary's, the term "parole" was used to explain absences that were granted to what were known as "inmates." The average stay of inmates, who ranged from age 5 to 21, was two years.[40] In all, young George Ruth would remain at St. Mary's for about a decade, finally released in 1914 to play baseball.

His mother and sister visited him once a month during his time at the school. And Birmingham would drop by. But Big George never came, other than to collect him for another ill-fated attempt to live at home. After Katie died, the boy had no visitors whatsoever. Sunday visits from family were considered the highlight of the week for most inmates. Lou Leisman, nicknamed "Fats" by Ruth, was sent to St. Mary's in 1909 along with his brother after their father died. Fats spent nearly five years with Ruth and decades later wrote about his time there. Leisman recalled that in 1912, when his own mother was ill, he commiserated with Ruth that he had not seen her in two years. "You're lucky, Fats," replied Ruth, who lost his mother that same year. "It's been 10 years since I have seen my father." It was clearly an exaggeration intended to make his chubby pal feel better. The comment stuck with Leisman, who said he never saw anyone visit Ruth. "Babe would kid me and say, 'Well, I guess I am too big and ugly for anyone to come to see me. Maybe next time.' But the next time never came."[41]

His cousin John Ruth, who had played with Little George on South Woodyear Street, explained the comings-and-goings this way: "His mother missed him when he was in the home and she would cry and ask her husband go get him out. Then when he came home she'd have trouble with him and hit him, and his father would put him back in again."[42] When autobiography ghostwriter Bob Considine confessed to his subject that he found the in-and-out routine puzzling, Ruth explained: "You know, I'd do things." Considine, unhappy with that explanation, pressed to know precisely what "things." Ruth replied matter-of-factly: "Drinkin'." At another point, he told Considine, testily: "What do you think? My old man had a saloon. For me, when he wasn't looking, the stuff was free."[43] His father, who had repeated scrapes with the law for selling booze on Sundays in violation of the blue laws then prevailing, didn't need further legal grief and possible license loss if underage drinking was detected on his premises.

Young George Ruth soon learned that religious instruction was not a major part of the formal curriculum at St. Mary's, despite the deep and abiding Catholic faith of the Xaverians. Inmates were required to attend Sunday Mass, were baptized, were confirmed and took their first communions, but religion was not emphasized in the classroom. Some, like Little George, became altar boys for the school chaplain.[44] The Xaverians preferred to deliver their religious lessons by setting an example for the boys entrusted to them. Such lessons were delivered on the spot, as necessary, explaining the difference between right and wrong. Correction was preferred to punishment. One punishment favored by the Brothers, however, was to take a young offender to the schoolyard and demand he collect 10,000 pebbles. If a Brother found the collection was too small at the end of the exercise, he would kick it, scattering it, and demand the collector begin again. The pile would be larger on another try.[45] Punishment was occasionally corporal, but most often it meant the loss of a privilege.

The Xaverians at St. Mary's accepted all boys sent to them by the courts, but were more selective about those who applied as boarders and for whom their parents paid a fee. Each type of boy comprised about half the school population by 1902. Regardless, the Xaverians treated all boys equally. Many of them were barely literate and others were lacking decency, hygiene and morals. Some found life at St. Mary's better than what they had endured in family homes which may have been dysfunctional because of drink, poverty, or violence. The Brothers took an eclectic mix of boys and provided them a sound basis of book-learning and vocational training. It proved to be a successful formula. By 1913, the St. Mary's student population had swelled to nearly 900, with boarders from 20 states.[46]

Inmates such as George Ruth were given plenty of choices. St. Mary's was not a place where different abilities or interests were ignored. Each boy could choose his sport, trade or choice of musical instrument in one of the school bands. It was ironic that many boys who had lost their freedom because of their behavior in the outside world were granted so much freedom within a facility to which they had been committed. The Xaverians thought of themselves as a substitute for family and took a sincere interest in the boys and young men in their care. They were available for counseling at all hours of the day. The board fence surrounding the school property was rarely breached, and when it was, it was more as a lark than a serious escape attempt. A grand jury inspected the school in 1905 and expressed surprise at the small fence and how seldom desertions or escapes were attempted.

Early in his days at St. Mary's, George Ruth was given a nickname. Not the famous one he picked up later, but another moniker. Just as Lou Leisman was dubbed "Fats" by Ruth, the boys gave George an unflattering name based on his appearance. He became known as "Niggerlips" during his time at the school. He didn't care for it, and fellow student Lawton Stenersen recalled: "Any time you called him that you could get yourself in a fight." Stenersen may have learned that firsthand. About 1930, Stenersen ran into Ruth before a boxing match held at Madison Square Garden in New York City. Ruth greeted Stenersen by his school nickname "Scoffer," picked up because he liked to eat.

4. Birth and Rebirth 55

But Ruth quickly warned him: "Now don't call me Niggerlips, or I'll break your arm."⁴⁷ Because of his dark complexion and facial features, a rumor would dog Ruth for much of his life that he had black ancestors, but there was no basis in fact for it. Nicknames were commonplace at St. Mary's and were often applied to some physical characteristic, mistake or failing. Boys could be cruel and the more a boy hated his nickname, the more it was used. Ruth heard it often, sometimes shortened to "Nig." To the Xaverians, he was always George, even long after the world had come to know him as "Babe."⁴⁸

Young Ruth adapted surprisingly well to his new surroundings. He was a big kid, loud, outgoing and constantly on the go. He was no shrinking violet. He made friends easily. A shy boy would have fared far worse in such a setting. There may have been a reason for his behavior. Without a medical assessment and from her vantage point of decades later, Ruth's granddaughter, Linda Tossetti, told biographer Leigh Montville: "He had ADHD, no doubt about it." That is the acronym for attention deficit hyperactivity disorder, a diagnosis often applied to hyperactive individuals. Tossetti explained that her own brother had the disorder and the signs were unmistakable. He was never able to sleep at night and played with his toys instead, she said. "That was the way my grandfather was. He always was moving. That's how he could eat so much, drink so much, and not be affected. He needed the energy. He would just burn it all off. That's why he would stay out all night."⁴⁹ Other Ruth descendants strongly dispute her opinion and note that Tossetti was born several years after Babe died. Because she never knew him, Tossetti was relying on her mother Dorothy's recollections. Tom Stevens, a grandson also born after Babe's death, rejected Tossetti's notion completely, saying his mother Julia knew Babe well and she described him as "very organized and orderly," as well as punctual. "These are very definitely not characteristics of someone with ADHD," insisted Stevens, relying partly on his wife, who, as a lifelong educator, was familiar with understanding and dealing with students suffering from learning disabilities.⁵⁰

One of the early decisions facing all new arrivals at St. Mary's was to decide which trade they'd like to learn. At the time, George could have chosen printer, brush-maker, bookbinder, carpenter, millwright, florist, launderer, knitter or shirt-maker. He tried carpentry before switching to shirt-making, apprenticing in the cutting department and then working his way up to the finishing section. In time, he became highly skilled and able to produce a perfect shirt collar.⁵¹ He was among 90 boys making clothing for inmates and uniforms for the school's baseball teams. For all boys learning a trade, the Xaverians paid them a token wage, which was credited to their accounts in the school savings bank. The boys were permitted to withdraw small amounts to patronize the candy store within the school. One of the buildings in which trades were taught was a four-story stone structure on whose first floor the laundry was located. The second floor was called Low City Tailor and the third was High City Tailor, where George worked. He and his fellow inmates were paid by the piece, with bonuses earned in extra playtime in the Big Yard or Little Yard (the younger boys used the latter).

"I was the best shirt-maker in the school," Ruth boasted later in life. "That's why you can't fool me about shirts to this day. I worked on an electrical machine that stitched the parts together; cheap shirts, those blue and gray cotton ones that in those days went for a dollar. Say, it's quite a trick getting a collar just right on a shirt." Work in the trade shops was Monday to Friday with another half day on Saturday. The hours in the classroom were reduced for older students as their time in the shops was increased. After work each day and following Sunday Mass it was off to the schoolyards where every boy was expected to take part in some team sport.[52] The sports offered were baseball, football, soccer, basketball, wrestling, swimming and boxing.

The tailoring shop was a going concern. All the stockings and underwear for the inmates were produced in a knitting mill at Low City Tailor, while about 1,000 shirts for all the boys were made at High City Tailor.[53] George was a good student in the shop, claiming later he could produce a shirt in less than 15 minutes. His specialty was collars. A skilled shirt-maker could earn $20 a week on the street, so the Xaverians taught him a skill from

The tailoring shop at St. Mary's where young George Ruth learned to make shirts. He excelled at collars and could have earned a living in the clothing trade if baseball hadn't worked out (Xaverian Brothers).

4. Birth and Rebirth 57

which he could earn a living, if other things hadn't turned out for him. Shirts were also sold offsite. One of George's fellow inmates recalled years later that the school received six cents a shirt from the Oppenheimer Shirt Company, an arrangement which suggested the operation produced commercial quality goods.[54] Outside sales also produced additional revenue for St. Mary's to run its multifaceted, complex operation and to acquire and repair necessary equipment and machinery.

The Xaverians had many arrangements with the business community in Baltimore to ensure the training they provided met the needs of businesses. As a result, the skilled young tradesmen St. Mary's produced found ready employment. One graduate said he felt the training school did so well because of the rigorous approach taken by the Brothers, which was instilled in all graduates: "Everything we did, we had to do well."[55]

At St. Mary's, expectations of doing well were not restricted just to schooling or trades.

5

"He always built me"

"My first day in school was the hardest," Babe Ruth recalled in the literary stylings of Westbrook Pegler, ghostwriter for his 1920 autobiography that appeared in 12 installments in daily newspapers.

It marked the first telling of his life story and readers could reasonably expect that his formative years would be clear in the recollection of a young man aged 25. But Ruth was hard to pin down for interviews and to provide the information Pegler needed, so the writer sometimes had to manufacture scenes to carry the story along. As a sportswriter, he was used to assembling facts for his readers. But when it came to the elusive Ruth, he took some license, possibly with the connivance of an editor anxious to disseminate a compelling and much-anticipated tale on a deadline.

The first installment described Ruth's introduction to St. Mary's and noted that by sundown of his first day, "I was a pretty homesick kid."

"I could see the family gathered about the table for supper and my chair empty, and I was wondering whether they missed me as much as I missed them. Nobody was paying any attention to me and I wanted sympathy," Ruth/Pegler wrote. "None of the fellows seemed to know what a time I was having with myself to keep back the tears, and I went to bed in the strange dormitory feeling as though I had been sold out by my best friends."

The pathos is palpable. The melodrama builds. Cue the strings.

> "What's the matter, Babe?" I looked up from my pillow in the darkness there, to see a great six-foot-six man standing over me. He said it in a whisper because he knew that one kid would be sensitive about having the others know him to be homesick. "What's the matter, Babe?" Brother Matthias whispered.

Ruth said the kindness made him melt.

> I don't remember having been called Babe before that. Perhaps that's where the name originated. Anyway, he told me he was coach of the ball club and advised me to come out and try for a place on the team. I knew I was going to like this kindly, understanding big friend.[1]

5. "He always built me"

What a lovely story. Unfortunately, it's pure fiction. Certainly the invention that Brother Matthias gave the name "Babe" to the visibly upset boy on his very first night at St. Mary's is. And it's highly unlikely Brother Matthias would urge one of the youngest boys ever to enter the school to try for a spot on "the ball club." The truth is Brother Matthias and the Xaverian Brothers always called him George. Many years later, Brother Gilbert called him Babe in his memoirs, which focused on the baseball star. It wasn't until shortly after leaving the school in 1914 that George Ruth picked up the nickname by which the world came to know him.

In this touching bedside scene, however, we can see the myth-making mischief about Babe Ruth is already underway. It continued in his 1928 autobiography penned by Ford Frick. In that telling of his first days at St. Mary's, Ruth said the first teacher who befriended him was actually the aforementioned Brother Gilbert, "a round-faced pleasant little man in clerical garb." The real Brother Gilbert stood more than six feet tall and was teaching a couple of miles away at the comparatively posh Mount St. Joseph College, not at gritty St. Mary's.[2] Ruth readily acknowledged in that recitation that he may been trouble for the Brothers, "but Brother Gilbert stuck with me. I owe him a lot. More than I'll ever be able to repay."[3] Brother Matthias was barely mentioned in the 1928 story. This emphasis on Brother Gilbert's role in shaping Ruth during his time at St. Mary's was widely accepted by sportswriters and appeared in their accounts for nearly two decades.

It wasn't until his 1948 autobiography that Ruth finally set the record straight:

> It was at St. Mary's that I met and learned to love the greatest man I've ever known. His name was Matthias—Brother Matthias of the Xaverian order.... I saw some real he-men in my 22 years in organized baseball and in the years since my retirement in 1935. But I never saw one who equaled Brother Matthias.[4]

Ruth then described the huge man who seldom raised his voice, a man so unlike any he'd known in his home life or on the streets. "I don't know why, but he singled me out when I first came to St. Mary's." Ruth gave proper credit to Brother Gilbert for alerting Orioles owner Jack Dunn to his pitching ability. Dunn signed Ruth to his first baseball contract. But it was Brother Matthias, in this final version of his life story, that Ruth praised as his friend, his coach in life and in baseball and his mentor.

In his early days at St. Mary's, Ruth tried his hand at boxing, a natural fit for a big boy from the streets who had endured his share of scrapes there. He noted "some pretty good boxers" attended the school. "I used to put on the gloves for exercise and a bloody nose now and then, but I was not much of a success as a boxer." He said he landed hard blows on his opponents "and I suppose I could have become a boxer if I had stuck to it."[5] But another sport beckoned.

Upon Ruth's arrival, there were 44 baseball teams formed among the 800 boys at St. Mary's, all wearing uniforms produced onsite by High City Tailor. Baseball was embraced by the brothers and taught to the boys and young men there. Ruth biographer Marshall Smelser aptly described St. Mary's as "a conservatory of the baseball arts." Many of the Xaverians had played the game as boys and Brother Herman and Brother Alban were still young enough to actively participate in games. "The Brothers were biased in favor of baseball," Smelser wrote. "Any game which combined so much popularity and fun must be good for people," they felt.[6] And while not a member of any particular league, St. Mary's acquitted itself well on the competitive diamond, winning its first city school championship in 1897. St Mary's developed and maintained a reputation for top flight teams, year after year.

Brother Herman was director of athletics and Brother Alban was head coach of baseball. Brother Matthias was the prefect of discipline and director of all physical activity and he and Alban ran a formal league among the oldest and best players at the school. They coached together, with Brother Alban often picking up a glove to take his favorite position at first base, while Brother Matthias tended to remain on the sidelines wielding a bat with one arm to drill the fielders. St. Mary's teams adopted the names of major-league teams, like the Red Sox, White Sox, Cubs and Giants. Tournaments were held from March to September, with dormitories, floors of dormitories and trades pitted against each other. Young George Ruth quickly demonstrated a natural aptitude for baseball and eventually found his way onto the Red Sox team managed by Brother Matthias.

Precisely when Ruth first met the massive man the boys called "The Boss" is not known. Brother Matthias was an imposing figure at six-foot-six with blue eyes and fair hair, rather sloping shoulders and a pear-shaped yet muscular body of more than 250 pounds barely disguised by his cassock. He was such a big man that he didn't fit into the tiny standard room assigned to him at St. Mary's. With his bedroom measuring six and a half feet square, the entry door had to be rehung so it opened outward. But Brother Matthias was a man of great humility and never complained or sought bigger quarters. He tended to walk with a slow shuffle, but when running, he was rather pigeon-toed and took surprisingly short steps for such a big man. Brother Matthias, called "Big Matt" by the other brothers, was invariably humble and soft-spoken. When he needed to bring discipline to an unruly situation, he merely needed to make his presence known and order would be restored. Years later, retired Brother Thomas More Page talked about how the boys were in awe of Brother Matthias. He recalled one day when a mini riot broke out among the older inmates in the Big Yard. At the time, Brother Matthias was attending a retreat at Mount St. Joseph College and was sent for. "When the boys saw Matthias at the head of the steps overlooking the yard, they immediately dispersed without his saying a single word," Page said.[7] Such was the power of the presence of The Boss. Even the toughest boys sent by the courts responded to his fair and consistent approach. One St. Mary's resident, Lou "Fats" Leisman, a chum of George Ruth's, later said this about Brother Matthias: "He was calm, considerate and gave everyone a fair break. But brother, if you ever crossed him you were in trouble."[8] Once discipline had been administered, however, Brother Matthias was willing to forgive and forget as though nothing had happened.

It's doubtful young George played baseball for Brother Matthias during his first days at St. Mary's in June of 1902. He remained at the school barely a month before returning home and teams would already have been picked by then. He was back in November and stayed until Christmas. Ruth remained at home for 1903 and didn't return to St. Mary's until 1904, at the age of nine, when he most likely would have picked up the game in earnest. His pal Fats Leisman didn't meet Ruth until he arrived at the school in 1909, but insisted Babe had played baseball in the streets of South Baltimore where he and his playmates broke many windows.[9] In Ruth's 1920 autobiography, he said he played ball instead of attending school in the year before he was committed to St. Mary's.[10] It is not clear to which year and to which committal he was referring. It's one of the few times Ruth mentioned playing the game before attending the school. But one of the Xaverian Brothers, Sebastian, who began at St. Mary's in 1896 and knew Ruth well, later insisted the boy "knew nothing whatsoever about baseball" upon his appearance at the school gates.[11] The difference in view is understandable. As suggested earlier, the game Ruth played in the streets may have resembled baseball in its most crude form, far below the level at which the boys of St. Mary's played it.

The streets of Baltimore may have been relieved of the delinquent-in-training in 1904, but the year began with a disaster for the city. Shortly before 11 a.m. on Sunday, February 7, as many Baltimoreans attended church or were about to do so, firefighters at Engine Company 15 received an automatic alarm that had been tripped at the John Hurst and Company wholesale dry goods business on the south side of German (now Redwood) Street. The building was at the westerly end of the downtown business district, where today's Royal Farms Arena is located. The blaze was believed to have been started by a cigarette or cigar that was flipped into a sidewalk grate and then rolled into the basement of the six-story building. Within minutes, a gasoline tank for an engine that powered the building exploded, sending flaming debris onto neighboring buildings and, fanned by winds from the west, set them on fire.[12] The blaze was soon out of control, with buildings along the narrow streets little more than tinder for the advancing flames. Firefighters were joined by those who arrived from Washington, Philadelphia and New York, but the new arrivals found their couplings were incompatible with the gauge found on the type of hydrants used in Baltimore and their impact was limited. Freezing temperatures also hurt firefighting efforts as more than 1,200 men battled the blaze. The Maryland National Guard was mobilized and another 2,000 soldiers and sailors were deployed to deal with crowds of spectators. Dynamite was used to knock down buildings and create a break for the advancing wall of flame that swept easterly in high winds, but it proved to be an ineffective strategy as many buildings withstood the blasts. The Baltimore and Ohio Railroad office was destroyed by flames, as were banks, major businesses and the offices of the rival *Baltimore Sun*, *Baltimore American*, *Baltimore Evening News* and the *Baltimore Herald* newspapers. They had to be printed in Washington and Philadelphia to share news of the destruction with their readers.

The fire raged for 31 hours, and finally halted at Jones Falls, well east of downtown, where firefighters found an abundant supply of water to halt the advancing flames. Most of central Baltimore had been destroyed, including many important businesses, about 1,500 buildings in all. Another 1,000 were severely damaged in the 80-block area. Fortunately, Baltimore's 1867 domed city hall had been spared, as well as the courthouse. Total loss was set at more than $100 million in that day's dollars, making it the second most destructive fire in United States history up to that time, exceeded only by the $200 million loss from the 1871 Great Chicago Fire.[13] In Baltimore, about 35,000 people were suddenly unemployed. They did not include George and Katie Ruth, who had moved from West Camden Street, which lay a block or two from the southernmost reach of the flames. The family was living at 712 Hanover Street, about nine blocks farther south. Four miles to the southwest, St. Mary's Industrial Training School was never at risk, although from the gentle rise on which it was built, an alarming view of the smoke rising downtown could be had by students and staff.

Originally, it was believed no lives had been lost, a miracle considering the extent of the conflagration. But on February 18, a badly burned body was recovered from the Inner Harbor near Bowley's Wharf, just east of Light Street. It was a 28-year-old black man, who, it was believed, had drowned when the wharf he was standing on to escape the flames caught fire and collapsed into the frigid water. He was never identified.[14]

Baltimore officials vowed to rebuild, and did so quickly. Narrow streets were widened and within two years a new city core rose from the ashes. A rigid building code requiring the greater use of fireproof materials was enacted in the city. The most important legacy of the fire was an effort to standardize firefighting equipment, hydrants and hose fittings to ensure compatibility when outside assistance was needed. That effort hasn't been completely successful. More than a century later the National Institute of Standards found that 48 major American cities had yet to adopt a national standard for the threads on fire hydrants and that even neighboring fire departments retain different hose threads, making mutual aid problematic.[15]

The year was off to a better start for young George Ruth. He was greeted back at St. Mary's with open arms, a welcome respite for a boy whose life at home was tension-filled, with his mother and father still working long hours, quarreling and drinking. Brother Matthias, about to turn 34, just like Babe's real father, ensured the nine-year-old a warm welcome. After expressing his mystification in his 1948 autobiography as to why Brother Matthias took a special interest in him during his early years at St. Mary's, Ruth said the big man must have picked up something indefinable in the new boy that warranted some extra attention. "It wasn't that I was his 'pet.' But he concentrated on me, probably because I needed it. He studied what few gifts I had and drew these out of me and amplified them. He always built me."[16] There was plenty of good to build upon. Ruth has been described as "a natural," someone who had good physicality and instincts for the game, but who needed practice to hone them to become truly great. As Ruth biographer Marshall Smelser noted, some skills can be learned without conscious effort or control, such as a baby learning how to say "Mama."[17] Brother Matthias needed only to channel and refine his young baseball prodigy, to build upon his gifts as Ruth himself said. As far as Ruth's young pal Fats Leisman was concerned, teaching didn't enter into it all: "My personal opinion would be that the Babe was born to play ball."[18]

Brother Matthias may have picked up on what scientists later determined to be his superior hand-eye coordination. In 1921, when Ruth was making his mark as a great hitter with the New York Yankees at age 26, graduate student researchers at Columbia University sought to see if there was some scientific basis for his outstanding performance. During a three-hour assessment at the university's psychological research laboratory, they subjected him to a series of tests shortly after a Yankee game played at the Polo Grounds. Ruth simulated his bat swing in front of electric wires intended to measure the power of his swing. He used a 54-ounce bat like the one he wielded on the field. A harness of rubber tubes was attached to him, which revealed that he held his breath during his home-run swing. He was asked to poke a small handle into holes in an electrified pegboard as many times as he could in a minute. Ruth was placed in a darkened cabinet and asked to tap a key the instant he detected flashing lights. At the end of the session, the scientists pronounced Ruth had recorded scores that showed his "co-ordination of eye, brain, nerves and muscle is virtually perfect," in fact, 30 percent higher than the average human. His left hand was slightly stronger than his right. His nerves were found to be steadier than 499 of 500 persons and his "attention and quickness of perception" were one-and-a-half times higher than the average human.[19]

The newspaper report of the findings may have been biased in favor of Ruth, but few modern researchers in psychology can find fault with the tests he was administered. The same tests were given to Cardinals slugger Albert Pujols in 2006 at Washington University in St. Louis. Like Ruth, Pujols was found to have better-than-average perceptual and motor skills. Pujols managed to swing his 31.5-ounce bat at 86.99 miles per hour, while Ruth had swung his 54-ounce club at 75 miles an hour. Washington University researcher Richard Adams studied Ruth's performance back in 1921 and concluded that while it was "not off the charts ... he was some amount faster or better than average."[20]

Brother Matthias required no electrical pegboards, rubber harnesses or flashing lights to know George Ruth was unexpectedly well coordinated for a boy so big for his age. He wasn't clumsy at all, like many boys who grow quickly. But Brother Matthias did detect something he didn't like—in the classroom. Like many teachers of his day, he didn't care for left-handers, thinking their writing technique looked awkward and produced poor penmanship. As a Catholic teacher he was not alone in knowing that Latin for left is "sinister" and that the devil sits on one's left shoulder. The right hand, by contrast, gives blessing and makes the sign of the cross. Many a left-handed pupil from Catholic schools can recall getting smacked on the offending sinister hand by a nun until the right hand replaced it. The discrimination against lefties was based on superstition and bias dating back to Roman culture. But the prejudice against lefties was never formally part of Catholic Church teaching.[21]

Brother Matthias allowed Ruth to remain a lefty on the ball field, even though one of the boy's favorite positions became catcher. In the classroom, however, he insisted Ruth use his right hand to hold his chalk on his slate board. To ensure he didn't slip, Brother Matthias placed him in the front row of the classroom where he could keep a close eye on him. The teacher's insistence paid off. Ruth developed a beautiful flowing script he later used to sign contracts and baseballs. Brother Paul, superintendent of St. Mary's from 1907 to 1925, confirmed it was Brother Matthias who forced the young lefty to switch hands to improve his writing. Years later, in retirement in Virginia, Brother Paul recalled Brother Matthias would crack Ruth's left knuckles with a ruler if he caught the student reverting to his left hand.[22]

Brother Matthias made no effort to convert the new boy to a right-hander on the baseball field, likely because he was so graceful. "Brother Matthias saw very early that I had some talent for catching and throwing a baseball," Ruth said in his 1948 life story.[23] Like a scout, Brother Matthias was able to discern a special something that set this particular youngster apart from the hundreds of others who played ball at St. Mary's. As a coach, Brother Matthias didn't like to pigeonhole his players, preferring to try them in a variety of

5. *"He always built me"* 65

A typical classroom at St. Mary's Industrial Training School. Brother Matthias is in charge. When young George Ruth was in his class, Brother Matthias ensured he sat at the front so he could keep a close eye on him. The school provided basic education and taught several trades. Graduates readily found employment (Xaverian Brothers).

positions. This improved his team by having experienced replacements when his players were hurt, disciplined or paroled and let the boys discover where their talents lay. In his 1920 autobiography, Ruth explained it this way, with the help of Westbrook Pegler's pen:

> Brother Matthias had the right idea about training a baseball club. He made every boy on the team play every position in the game, including the bench. A kid might pitch a game one day and find himself behind the bat the next or perhaps out in the sun-field. You see Brother Matthias' idea was to fit a boy to jump in in any emergency and make good. So whatever I have at the bat or on the mound or in the outfield or even on the bases, I owe directly to Brother Matthias.[24]

When he went behind the plate to catch, Ruth had to use a glove intended for a right-hander. It meant he had to catch with his left hand, quickly flip off the glove and with the same hand return the ball to the pitcher or make a hard throw to pick off base stealers. It was a cumbersome procedure that he described this way in 1948:

> You see, I thought of myself as a pretty good catcher. Brother Matthias and others at the school tried to explain to me that left-handed catchers just do not make sense. But it was the position I liked best and the only one I could play with any skill. We had no

catcher's mitt built for left-handers, of course. We were lucky to have any kind of mitt. I'd use the regular catcher's mitt on my left hand, receive the throw from the pitcher, take off the glove and throw it back to him left-handed. When I had to throw to a base, trying to catch a runner, I'd toss the glove away, grab the ball with my left hand and heave it with everything I had.[25]

Left-handed catchers are not common. The knock against them is that right-handed batters tend to get in the way of the catcher's throw to second or third base. But a lefty has an easier time catching a curve thrown by a right-handed pitcher if it breaks to the outside on a right-handed batter. Ruth biographer Marshall Smelser insisted there is nothing about baseball that makes life inherently more difficult for left-handed catchers. But there are few of them, for a reason. He cited Al Lopez, a right-handed catcher who spent 19 years in the National League with Brooklyn, Boston, Pittsburgh and Cleveland, who said if a left-handed catcher had a strong arm, he'd likely be converted to a pitcher.[26] Which is exactly what happened with Ruth.

Among the many eyewitnesses to this glove-juggling maneuver was Fats Leisman, who many years later recalled the first time he saw Ruth play. It was a game between Dormitory Three, which housed the younger boys, and Dormitory Two, the older boys. Ruth caught for the younger boys. "The most amazing feat to watch the Babe perform at that time was the way he could switch the catcher's glove from his left hand to his right, which was so fast that it was almost impossible for anyone to steal a base on him."[27]

Given the extra attention from Brother Matthias, Ruth thrived. He was never much more than an average student, but he was big, loud and outgoing, which helped him do well among his peers. When it came to baseball, he and the hulking brother spoke the same language. "Some men just have an ability to command respect, and love, and Brother Matthias was one of these. He could have been anything he wanted to be in life, for he was good-looking, talented and dynamic. Yet he had taken vows of chastity and poverty and shut himself out from the world."[28] Ruth may have understood the basis of their relationship. He needed love and attention and thrived when he received it. Brother Matthias may have seen himself reflected in the overgrown boy and gave him both, acting as a surrogate father figure. Perhaps Brother Matthias hoped to accomplish with this outgoing boy something he himself had been unable to achieve with his profound humility. A special bond grew between the two. As Babe's wife Claire put it in her 1959 biography of him: "When Babe Ruth was 23, the world loved him. When he was 13, only Brother Matthias loved him." She recalled the respect Babe had for Brother Matthias.[29]

Baseball was in Ruth's blood and he couldn't get enough of it. "At St. Mary's, I guess I gave more thought to the game when off the field than the other boys. I used to practice batting with a couple of kids pitching to me."[30] And because of the relatively mild climate of Baltimore, compared to other

5. "He always built me" 67

Young George Ruth (center) surrounded by fellow members of his baseball team at St. Mary's. He demonstrated natural ability on the diamond that was encouraged and improved upon by Brother Matthias. Brother Matthias insisted each boy learn all positions, although young Ruth preferred catcher. Baseball was a key activity at the school and the Brothers often joined the boys on the diamond (Xaverian Brothers).

cities in the Northeast, there was a long ball season, beginning in March and not ending until November or December. One Christmas morning, Ruth was so determined to play that he scraped the snow off the school diamond and recruited 17 boys for a game.[31]

Ruth recalled in 1948 that Brother Matthias was always willing to spend extra time with him to hone his baseball skills.

> He used to back me into a corner of the big yard at St. Mary's and bunt a ball to me by the hour, correcting the mistakes I made with my hands and feet. When I was eight or nine I was playing with the 12-year-old team. When I was 12, I was with the 16-year-olds, and when I was 16 I played with the best of the many teams we had in the school. All because of Brother Matthias.[32]

Claire Ruth said Babe felt lucky to have connected with Brother Matthias, with whom he shared a love of baseball. "For the next 12 years the Brother and the Babe spent what little time was free at St. Mary's working on the great talent the religious man saw in Babe."[33]

For his part, young George Ruth was in awe of Brother Matthias when he saw what the big man could do with a bat and ball. Ruth spoke about seeing Brother Matthias stand at one end of the schoolyard with a mitt on his left hand and bat in his right, toss a baseball up and belt it, sometimes more than 350 feet over the centerfield fence.

> I would just stand there and watch him, bug-eyed. I had never seen anything like that in my life, nor anyone who was even close to Brother Matthias when it came to manliness, kindness and grace. He became my ideal and I tried, in my feeble way, to do things as he did them.[34]

Brother Matthias ran with small steps and was somewhat pigeon-toed, as has been noted. Young Ruth began taking small pigeon-toed steps rounding the bases, mimicking his mentor. Brother Matthias swung the bat with a powerful uppercut, despite the prevailing wisdom that a level swing was more likely to produce line drives and create trouble for infielders and outfielders alike. Ruth developed a long swing with an uppercut that launched balls a long distance. At the time, the theory of batting was that a full swing could lessen a hitter's accuracy, providing an advantage to the pitcher. Most of the day's big-league hitters used a shortened, or "chop," swing, stepping forward to meet the ball. This approach helped the hitter keep his eye on the incoming ball and not get thrown off balance with a long, violent swing.[35] The prevailing wisdom was it was better to put the ball in play than swing for the outfield fence. The sacrifice bunt was often used and the home run was not a big part of the game in the early 1900s. In 1902 for instance, Socks Seybold of Philadelphia recorded 16 home runs to lead major-league baseball and set an American League record. His tally stood until 1919, when it was eclipsed by a player named Babe Ruth, who belted 29. It was the Deadball Era, a time in baseball marked by low scoring and an emphasis on defense and pitching. To improve scoring, the baseball itself was made livelier in 1911, but that made little difference initially. Nothing really changed until Ruth hit his stride in 1919 and the devastating spitball was outlawed a year later.

Brother Matthias's approach to hitting was unorthodox but effective. Ruth copied it and went on to revolutionize the game. "I think I was born as a hitter the first day I ever saw him hit a baseball," Ruth said in his 1948 life story, unable to forget the majestic fly balls Brother Matthias could launch with seemingly little effort.[36]

The chance meeting of a troubled boy from the streets of Baltimore and a humble giant who became his mentor in life and sport proved good for both of them.

And, as it turned out, historic for baseball.

6

A Star Begins to Twinkle

Young George Ruth wasn't the only student at St. Mary's who revered Brother Matthias for his decency and fairness—and for his talent with a baseball bat. Brother Matthias drew a crowd whenever he decided to hit some balls in one of the schoolyards. The boys would gasp at what The Boss could do. It became one of Brother Matthias's routines over the years to get a bit of exercise and it invariably drew rave reviews. Audiences assembled quickly when word spread that the big man was at his launch pad.

One boy who attended St. Mary's several years after Ruth had graduated wrote about the experience shared by every boy who watched Brother Matthias perform his longstanding ritual. The youngster, who became Xaverian Brother Thomas More Page, described the scene for a Brotherhood-sponsored publication later in life:

> What I think every boy at St. Mary's at the time will remember is the Sunday evenings after supper whenever the news got around that Brother Matthias would be hitting baseballs. Then every boy in the school from all the five yards would gather in the upper yard, over 500 of us, awaiting the occasion. He would stand at the bottom of the steps and, with what seemed like an effortless motion, hit the ball with the fungo bat in his right hand only. Up and up the ball seemed to soar, almost out of sight, and then when it came down there was a mad scramble for it. We knew the end was coming to this extraordinary exhibition when he hit one ball after the other in rapid succession, and the balls kept falling down like snow flakes over the entire yard.[1]

Perhaps inspired by the abilities of teachers like Brother Matthias, the boys couldn't get enough baseball. Whenever they found free time to themselves two of them would play "pokenins," a game to hone their pitching and hitting skills. As played at St. Mary's, one boy would wield a bat and stand three feet in front of a wall, which acted as a backstop. The other boy would pitch to him from the standard pitching distance used on the ball diamond. The pitcher sought to strike out the batter and when he did so, the players switched positions. Fats Leisman remembered the game was played often and he credited it with helping Ruth with both his pitching and hitting.[2] As long as he could find a willing partner, Ruth played pokenins by the hour.

Two other significant baseball influences on Ruth and his fellow inmates were Brothers Alban and Herman. Alban was born John T. Bannon in England in 1886. One of the youngest of the 30 Xaverians posted to St. Mary's, he was an excellent athlete and embraced the national pastime of his adopted country. He spent 27 years at the school, regularly appearing on the diamond as a star first baseman and as a coach. Brother Alban, whose name was often misspelled Albin, developed diabetes later in life, prompting the amputation of both his legs at the knees. Sadly, the once-gifted athlete spent the final 17 years of his life unable to stray far from his bedroom.

Brother Herman, born William Bahr in Fort Sanders, Wyoming, in 1879, attended Mount St. Joseph College and became an Xaverian novice at age 16. He was particularly athletic and worked closely with Brother Matthias as a baseball coach. He supervised the boys during recreation time in the yards and acted as director of athletics for the school. Brother Herman's record from the Xaverian archives notes: "As a young teacher and well into middle age, he was the object of awesome wonder at recess time when he handled a baseball." The record duly noted one of his "protégés" was the future baseball star, Ruth. Herman never sought any acclaim and his role in inspiring and developing a rare talent is not fully appreciated. Sportswriter H. G. Salsinger knew of Herman's influence, however, but exaggerated when he once wrote: "Brother Herman was the real discoverer of Ruth. He taught him and supervised his development."[3] Regardless of that overstatement, the teacher and student became close on the ball diamond. The good-looking and athletic Brother Herman was not only a role model for Ruth, but became almost a pal to him. As a sign of respect, young Ruth took "Herman" as a middle name when he was confirmed into the Catholic Church by James Cardinal Gibbons in 1907. His father's middle name was Herman, but the younger Ruth had been issued a birth certificate on which no middle name appeared. His baptismal certificate was the same.[4] Brother Herman remained with the Xaverians for six decades, his later years marked by arthritis, which greatly hobbled the former athlete.

By all accounts, young George Ruth wasn't much of a student, although he received a solid elementary education. He learned to read, write, do arithmetic and he studied grammar and geography. But the main goal of the Xaverians was to provide training in the trades. It wasn't until 1922 that St. Mary's began offering high school courses, but Ruth figured the 12 years he spent at the school had provided him the equivalent of a high school education.[5] He certainly had more formal education than most of his baseball peers and far beyond what could have been expected for a one-time delinquent from the streets of Baltimore.

Aside from basic education and baseball, the Xaverians also stressed the arts, particularly music. The school's bands were well known in the Baltimore area and were often invited to perform at civic events, celebrations and occasionally at Baltimore Orioles games. Music was a perfect alternative to baseball because it was largely an indoor activity that could be pursued in inclement weather. Yet it nicely complemented the game, with band-members in their own school-produced uniforms and learning teamwork through music. There is little known about how, or if, young Ruth played in any of the St. Mary's bands, although at various points it was claimed that he was a drummer or tuba player (the latter reference was likely inspired by a photo of Ruth posing with the band in later years while holding the stubby brass instrument). It was said he had a credible baritone voice, but neither he nor a member of any audience spoke about it. He did partake in music, it seems, at least to a limited degree. A newspaper clipping from 1908, when he was 13, said he appeared in a Thanksgiving minstrel show at St. Mary's called *One Thousand Smiles in One Hundred and Twenty Minutes*. The show was attended by the sisters of St. Agnes Hospital, priests from St. Joseph's Monastery and Xaverian Brothers from Mount St. Joseph College. Ruth was listed as one of about a dozen performers, but his specific contribution was not mentioned in the news account.[6]

Half an hour in chapel every morning was required for all boys at St. Mary's, while those who were Catholic were given an additional half hour of religious instruction each day. Ruth said the only days he missed chapel or religion class was when he was ill. Religion had never been part of his home life, his parents from different faiths, but in his surrogate home he became a practicing Catholic. In his 1920 autobiography he asserted: "For twelve years in St. Mary's I went to church every day and I have never missed a Sunday since I left the school."[7] In later years, we know, he strayed from the Church with his full-tilt hedonistic lifestyle, but he returned to it once he realized his days were numbered.

Young George instantly adapted to St. Mary's, where he discovered and thoroughly enjoyed what Ruth biographer Marshall Smelser described as "a postponed childhood." After years of neglect, he enjoyed the "family" the Xaverians offered him. It marked a sort of rebirth for the youngster and he appreciated the second chance that had been granted him. Unlike others, especially those who were forced to attend St. Mary's, Ruth praised the school whenever he had an opportunity. It helped make him the man he became. Despite being larger than most boys his age and having a quick temper, he was more inclined to a sunny disposition than to become a bully or resort to violence. He got along well with the other boys and preferred to be loved than feared. At school parties he was sometimes overlooked because outsiders thought he was an orderly or some sort of attendant because of his size. On at least one occasion, Smelser said a visitor realized what had been going on and made good by giving Ruth a large box of candies, just for himself.

While other boys generally stashed away such gifts to be savored later, Ruth immediately opened the box and shared its contents freely.[8] His friends appreciated and remembered his generosity.

Lou Leisman, in his story of life with Ruth at St. Mary's, said: "The Babe had a heart as big as gold." He told how boys at St. Mary's earned credits for various tasks they were assigned at St. Mary's and could cash them in at the little store within the school that opened for an hour every evening after supper. Treats like candies, cakes and peanuts were available. "Each evening when the store opened, he would buy a hat full of mixed candies and pass them around to the orphan boys, who had no parents or friends." Leisman said Ruth sensed how upset his chubby pal was when Leisman's widowed mother became quite ill and no one visited him. Ruth tried to make him feel better by joking that he himself was too big and ugly for visitors. And he offered something more tangible. "Each and every time when the little store opened, the Babe made sure that I got my share of the candy. However, it must be said that he did not show any partiality toward any one individual. He was kind and good to all the unfortunate boys."

Ruth carried his generosity into his later life. Years later, when he met fellow St. Mary's graduate Lawton Stenersen outside Madison Square Garden in New York and warned Stenersen not to call him "Niggerlips," Ruth asked about their former schoolmates. Stenersen said he'd recently seen "Congo" Kirby and "Dope" Flaherty. The latter, Stenersen said, seemed to be doing well and was operating a moving van with his name on it. Ruth winked at the news, bade Stenersen farewell and entered the garden. Stenersen encountered Flaherty a couple of months later and only then learned Ruth had lent him the money to start his business.[9]

Leisman also recalled Ruth's thoughtfulness. He said that one day he was trying to catch some of Ruth's pitches, only to hurt a finger rather seriously, not expecting such a hard throw. Ruth, he remembered, "sure was sorry about the whole affair, and after that he always asked me how my finger was getting along."[10]

Ruth was interested in the well-being of the other boys at St. Mary's, Leisman said, especially the less fortunate ones. It made him many friends. An eight-year-old boy named "Loads" Clark broke a window in the school laundry with an errant stone one day. Upset and fearing punishment, Clark was crying when Ruth saw him and sought an explanation. Upon hearing the reason, Ruth calmed the lad and advised him to "take it on the lam." Clark took the advice and disappeared. Leisman said: "The Babe? He took the blame and the punishment for something he didn't do. Any wonder we all loved him?"[11]

In his 1948 autobiography, Ruth said it wouldn't be surprising for someone like him, committed to a place like St. Mary's, "to look back on those

6. A Star Begins to Twinkle 73

days either with scorn or a wish to conceal the facts. I look back on St. Mary's as one of the most constructive periods of my life. I'm as proud of it as any Harvard man is proud of his school, and, to get crude for a moment, I will be happy to bop anybody on the beezer who speaks ill of it."[12]

Despite the bravado in that statement, Ruth wasn't prone to fisticuffs. Fats Leisman told the revealing story of Jerry DeLay, who tested the future baseball star. Leisman said two probation officers brought DeLay to St. Mary's by order of the juvenile court of Baltimore. DeLay was a rugged boy, who Leisman estimated at five-feet-ten and 180 pounds. School disciplinarian Brother Matthias had been warned to keep a close eye on the new arrival, who was seen as a troublemaker. DeLay was admonished by Brother Matthias to behave himself and then directed to the schoolyard. The new arrival looked at The Boss, mumbled something that could not be understood, and went to the yard. Leisman described the ensuing events:

> When it was thought that everything was O.K., all of a sudden there was a wild scramble down by the big yard shed.
> Like everyone else, when something like this happens, the boys all rushed into the big yard to find out what the trouble was. It seems as if the Babe had tried to be sociable with the newcomer and had asked him to have a catch. In return for his hospitality, Jerry had taken a swing at the Babe and told him to mind his own business.
> Of course, it was necessary for the Babe to defend himself and in so doing, he and Jerry got into a clinch. Then several of the other boys interfered in order to try and separate them. The consequences were that all six boys fell on the ground in a pile. Wherever he came from I cannot tell you, but the big hand of Brother Matthias reached into the pile, took a hold of Jerry and put him under his arm and carried him bodily up to the engine room. Then he stood him on his feet and told him to stay there until he could act like the other boys.
> This was the medicine that cured tough boy Jerry DeLay, as he was no trouble after that. It must be mentioned here that this is the first and only fight I ever saw the Babe have during his entire stay at St. Mary's. About two days later I was astounded to look over into the big yard and see the Babe and Jerry playing catch together.[13]

Ruth's good nature and unwillingness to hold a grudge had converted a foe into a friend. Given Ruth's size and outgoing nature, he could have been an aggressor and a bully. But conflict was not to his liking. His mentor Brother Matthias had shown him the best way to deal with others was by caring about them and forgiving them their trespasses.

Meanwhile, conflict between George Ruth Sr. and wife Katie was an ongoing fact of life for the couple, who gave up on the Camden Street saloon late in 1902. They moved three times by 1905 as they continued to pursue success in the saloon business. Their first stop was 712 South Hanover Street, a few blocks southeast of Camden Yards.[14] It is likely Babe spent Christmas of 1902 and all of 1903 there with his parents before returning to St. Mary's. The Ruths then moved to 527 East Clement Street, about a mile southeast of the rail yards, in what was then considered South Baltimore. They remained there only a short time before relocating in November 1905 to 406 West Conway Street, a block south of their former Camden Street saloon.[15] The location is in today's center field of Oriole Park at Camden Yards. During the moves, Katie bore and lost several children while caring for Mamie. The peripatetic lifestyle was particularly hard on her. And given all the instability, it is likely young George was better off at St. Mary's.

It would seem Katie found comfort in the alcohol that was readily at hand—and in the arms of other men. George had suspicions about her for some time.[16] George had tried to get Katie away from temptation by hiring bartender George Sowers with instructions he not supply his wife with drink, but she persisted. On March 12, 1906, things came to a head. That Monday morning, George descended from their living quarters to find Katie intoxicated. He demanded to know if she had been out and she replied she hadn't. George had seen Sowers in "close conversation" with her and in the bar demanded to know whether Sowers had let her have whiskey. Sowers denied he had done so, but said he had slipped into the back yard at some point and returned to see Katie take a "full cup" of whiskey.

George said he let the matter ride until the next day after closing the bar, when he confronted Katie in their bedroom about her relationship with Sowers. George bluffed his suddenly agitated wife, saying he had confronted Sowers downstairs and he had admitted to having sex with her. Faced with that supposed admission, Katie conceded they had done so on one occasion, the previous week. Angrily, George barged into Sowers's adjoining bedroom and dragged him before Katie, demanding a confession. Sowers denied everything. "I hit him once," George admitted, prompting Sowers to reply: "For God's sake don't him me again, and I will tell you everything. I was going to tell you before." Downstairs at the bar, Ruth made Sowers write a confession. The bartender complied, saying he had engaged in sex with Katie, at her request, on the dining room floor that very morning.[17]

The next day, Ruth went to the Western District police station and swore out a complaint that Katie had engaged in sexual relations outside their marriage, contrary to Maryland law. Both Katie and Sowers were arrested. Police Magistrate Daniel J. Loden issued the warrants and, after hearing from all parties, found Katie guilty and fined her $10 and costs of $1.70. Because she said she was struggling with a baby, the penalty was reduced to costs only. Katie had testified Sowers had taken advantage of her, but said she didn't want to press charges against him. Loden learned Ruth had a revolver when he confronted Sowers that night in his bedroom. Sowers testified Katie was constantly after him for sex, and if her husband continued to suspect her, he told her, she might as well do what he thought she was doing anyway: "When you make up your mind, I hope you will let me have the first crack at you," he testified before Loden.[18]

6. A Star Begins to Twinkle

Within days, George went to court to seek a divorce, a rare move in the day. He accused Katie of "unfaithfulness." Court files show how badly the marriage had soured. He fired Sowers, who promptly disappeared, and threw Katie out of their home. She moved in with her sister, Lena Fell. George also placed a notice in the *Baltimore Sun* saying he was not responsible for any debts incurred by Katie.[19]

In a deposition dated April 11, 1906, filed in support of his divorce application, George was asked how Katie had treated him. "Well, outside of her drinking, she was all right, but she was always drunk. The children were lousy, and she was lousy herself. When she got drunk she would lay [sic] in a stupor. Drink was the cause of it all." George insisted he cared for his family and invariably treated Katie well. "I never beat her up or anything of that kind. I was always kind and affectionate." He said he recently gave her $45 to buy clothes, "which put the business in a bad way."

He blamed his wife for all the recent moves from one place to another:

> I had sold out two other restaurants on account of the fact that I suspected my wife of being too familiar with the men who were hanging around. On the 12th of November, 1905, I moved to my present place of business, 406 West Conway Street, in this city, taking my wife with me. Early in February, 1906, I hired a bartender named George Sowers. I hired him so that I could keep my wife out of the bar, so that she would not continually be intoxicated.

George said he was convinced Katie was committing adultery during February and March with Sowers and others, whose names he did not know. Under cross-examination, George conceded he had a revolver on his person when he confronted his wife and her lover, but insisted it was in his pocket from when he closed the bar and he had forgotten about it. He said he did not brandish it and that Sowers confessed willingly. Sowers himself did not respond to a subpoena to appear in divorce court, despite repeated attempts to find him by George's lawyer, Frank V. Moale. On May 14, Circuit Court Judge Peregrine L. Wickes granted an absolute divorce, based on George Sr.'s assertion of "drunkenness and infidelity." The judge awarded him custody of George Jr., 11; Mamie, 6; and the Ruth's youngest child, William E., 7 months.[20] Katie had sought custody of them, but admitted she was "destitute," while George had promised to care for their children and give them a good education. A bit more than three months later, William died of infant malnutrition, mere days after his first birthday.[21]

Given the ongoing strife between his parents, it is doubtful that young George would have sought parole from St. Mary's to go home. Even less likely after the divorce as his overworked father struggled to raise two siblings. Baltimore historian Fred B. Shoken suggests Katie's drinking problem may have contributed to her poor health and loss of six of her eight children. And her husband may not really have cared for her or their children by forsaking the lightning rod business for the more lucrative saloon business, despite his wife's problems with alcohol. He also deprived his family of a relatively normal life in the stable neighborhoods where his oldest had spent six of his first seven years.[22] Saloons were no place for George Ruth's wife or his children.

It is not known how Babe reacted to the divorce, still a rare measure in its day. But based on his unwillingness, and that of his sister Mamie, to say anything publicly about their childhood, it must have been devastating for them. In the aftermath of the divorce, Babe remained with his stable "family" at St. Mary's.

Under Maryland law, formal education was required up to and including age 14. Once he turned 15 in 1910, young Ruth was able to enter the workforce. He had become a qualified shirt-maker by then and easily found a job in a Baltimore shirt factory. The Brothers operated a downtown hostel at Low and North High streets called St. James House, where graduating boys could find accommodations. Ruth moved in and the Xaverians treated him no differently than other graduates eager to enter the workforce and earn a living. The young men turned each week's salary over to the head Brother, who deducted funds for room, board, insurance and laundry. Spending money was provided and the balance deposited in each resident's bank account.

Ruth's leaving St. Mary's was a blow to the baseball program, one from which the younger boys feared the school would never recover. Their upset was short-lived, however. Within two months Ruth was back. The reasons were murky and involved him breaking some of the rules set by the Xaverians. It was generally thought he had fallen in with some "bad company."[23] Fats Leisman said he heard Ruth had been linked to a gang that was creating trouble.

Upon his return to St. Mary's that spring of 1910, Ruth was placed in Dormitory Number 1, which meant he was associated with the older boys in the big yard and all the activities there. "The day the Babe returned he was dressed in a grey [sic] suit and was wearing a black baseball cap," Leisman wrote. "I tried very hard to attract his attention as he walked down towards the big yard grandstand.... He walked very slowly with his head down and did not seem to hear the voices of the three or four hundred boys who were screaming 'Welcome Back, Niggerlips.'" Leisman said Ruth remained "low in spirit for awhile, but eventually snapped out of it and returned to his old self again."[24] There to welcome him back to St. Mary's was his big friend, Brother Matthias, who accepted him unconditionally and without passing judgment.[25]

About the same time, Ruth began to consider what his future might hold. He regarded Brother Matthias as his special friend and father figure. Emulating him in baseball had proven to be a good move. But perhaps there was more. He wasn't thinking about baseball as a possible career at that point. It was just a game. In her 1959 book about Ruth, his second wife Claire recounted the story that the man who would become the Babe talked to his mentor Brother Matthias about becoming a priest at some point. Brother Matthias was well aware of the young man's temperament and thought it an unwise direction for him. So The Boss "gently but firmly" talked him out of it, she said. "This is advice no Catholic man gives lightly to a Catholic youth," Claire wrote. "Brother Matthias would have much rather guided a young man into the priesthood than into a big-league job. But he saw no call."[26] Had young George Ruth ignored the advice of Brother Matthias, baseball history would not be the same. Nor would the priesthood, for that matter.

The timing of Ruth's return was propitious. Brothers Alban and Matthias were forming a senior boys league that spring. There were to be four teams, the Red Sox, White Sox, Cubs and Giants, their names derived from the big-league teams. Brother Alban arranged all games and took a position as first baseman for the Red Sox. Brother Matthias restricted himself to coaching and hitting high fly balls to the outfielders in practice. Leisman said Ruth was placed on the Red Sox team, while another outstanding player, Skinny McCall, was assigned to the White Sox. The best players at the school were distributed among the four teams. Ruth played every position for the Red Sox during the first year of the new league's operation, but his regular and preferred position was catcher. Leisman recalled that Ruth hit home runs in virtually every game he played.

There are two stories about how Ruth was converted from a catcher to pitcher that first season. The first is that the regular pitcher for the Red Sox, Congo Kirby, had violated some school rules and his punishment was being banned from play. This left the team without a pitcher. Brother Alban picked Ruth to replace him. The big lefty showed good speed and threw a two-hitter in the next game, shutting out the White Sox, 2–0. This was midway through the season and his appearances behind the plate grew fewer in number. Leisman said he thought Ruth won five of the six games he pitched.[27]

The other version of the tale of his conversion to pitcher was related by Ruth himself in his 1948 autobiography. He said he recalled a game in which one Red Sox hurler after another was faring poorly and his team was taking "a terrific beating." Ruth said he thought the situation was becoming funny. "When our last pitcher began to be hit all over the lot I burst out laughing at him. I guess I said a few things too."

This prompted Brother Matthias to confront his big catcher, who seemed to be enjoying himself far too much.

"What are you laughing at, George?" he asked me in his strong but gentle way.
"That guy out there—getting his brains knocked out," I howled, doubled over with laughter.
Brother Matthias looked at me for a long time.
"All right, George, *you* pitch," he said.

I stopped laughing.

"I never pitched in my life," I said. "I can't pitch."

"Oh, you must know a lot about it," he said, casually. "You know enough to know that your friend isn't any good. So go ahead out there and show us how it's done."

Ruth went silent. He realized Brother Matthias "meant business." He set aside his catcher's mask and mitt, borrowed another glove and walked to the pitching rubber, not knowing how to stand on it, much less how to deliver a ball to the plate. But he said he felt at home immediately, "as if I had been born out there and that this was a kind of home for me. It seemed to be the most natural thing in the world to start pitching...."[28] He said it worked out so well that Brother Matthias kept calling upon him to pitch for the remainder of his time at St. Mary's. It worked out well for Ruth and his team. In 1912, he led his Red Sox to the school championship.

Babe Ruth (top left) posing with his Red Sox team, senior champions of the school league, in about 1912. Ruth often played with older boys because he excelled at the game. Here, he is holding his catcher's mask and mitt. Brother Matthias made him play every position, including pitcher, where his talent drew attention and won him a professional contract (National Baseball Hall of Fame and Museum, Cooperstown, New York).

6. A Star Begins to Twinkle

A similar version of Babe's introduction to pitching came many years later from Brother Matthias himself. He recalled Babe was standing on the sidelines during a game of younger boys when the pitcher was "making himself ridiculous. George thought it very funny and laughed and laughed. Just to show him up a little bit I ordered him to go in and pitch. He mowed everything down and I concentrated on his pitching from that day on."[29]

Regardless of how he became a pitcher, it proved to be a watershed moment when Ruth took the ball. And it was in that position that he began attracting attention, although he felt that catching and hitting were the aspects of the game at which he excelled. In an interview of Ruth published in *Baseball Magazine* in February of 1918, the rising 23-year-old baseball star with the Boston Red Sox spoke about his final years at St. Mary's. By that time, he had four American League seasons under his belt and was the best left-handed pitcher in the game. He had hit only a total of nine home runs up until then, his focus on pitching rather than hitting. He described his baseball success during his final days at St. Mary's this way:

> I wasn't a pitcher in those days until I was pretty nearly through my course. My main job was catching, though I also played first base and the outfield. I used to hit .450 and .500. I kept track one season and found I made over 60 home runs. The last two years I pitched and got along pretty well, but I never lost my taste for hitting and don't ever expect to.[30]

Ruth certainly didn't. In that 1918 season he recorded 11 home runs, tying with Philadelphia's Tillie Walker for most in the majors. By October, *Baseball Magazine* dubbed him a sensation and "the greatest pitcher-batter the game has ever known." He told writer F. C. Lane: "I like to pitch, but my main objection has always been that pitching keeps you out of so many games. I like to be in there every day."[31] It was apparent Ruth was beginning to see himself as a slugger. It would take him a decade, but he would smash successive records for home runs, reaching 60 in 1927. His 60 home runs at St. Mary's came in more than 200 games when they were still a rarity, with a dead ball often kept in play until it disintegrated. And ballparks were cavernous.

During that 1912 season, Ruth continued to play several positions. The school newspaper, *Saturday Evening Star*, carried a box score from one notable game in which he played catcher, third base and pitcher. He hit one of three doubles recorded by his team, one of two triples and registered the only home run. Meanwhile, in the pitcher's box, he fanned six men.[32] George Ruth had become the school's baseball star and the biggest boy at St. Mary's, well on his way to a height of six feet, two inches and a weight of 150 pounds.

The baseball prodigy of St. Mary's was really coming into his own that 1912 season when his mother died suddenly. On August 11, Katie Ruth, 38, passed away at Baltimore's Municipal Tuberculosis Hospital, her cause of death listed as "exhaustion" and lung disease.[33] Katie had been living with her sister, Lena Fell, on Portland Street, and it was there that the funeral was held on August 14 before a Requiem Mass conducted at St. Peter's Church. Interment was at Holy Redeemer Cemetery, about a mile from St. Mary's School.[34] There was no mention of Katie's former spouse or her children in her obituary. Young George, now 17, whom she had visited frequently at St. Mary's with Mamie, was permitted to attend her funeral. Her grave remained unmarked for 96 years until 2008, when retired Baltimore lawyer and devoted Ruth fan Paul Harris led a campaign to erect a headstone to properly mark the resting place of the woman who gave birth to a baseball legend.[35]

Ruth couldn't get enough baseball, the activity at which he excelled and turned heads. The shirt-maker had more time for baseball in the big yard and beyond, playing two or three games some days. His talent and his size put him much in demand by amateur and semi-pro teams beyond the school gates and the Xaverians allowed him to play with them. He often played alongside boys who were two or three years older. Biographer Leigh Montville said the hyperactive Ruth "reached a point, somewhere in his teens, where he played more baseball, practiced more baseball, than a professional. He would return to the dorm most days with the shirt torn off his back after an afternoon of baseball and wrestling and running around."[36]

Press coverage of games at St. Mary's was scant, suggesting the Brothers were not keen on having the names of their students published for public consumption. Perhaps they felt it might be embarrassing for their charges, many of whom did not share Ruth's pride in attending the place. The Baltimore newspapers provided extensive coverage to amateur baseball and regularly provided game reports about Mount St. Joseph College. Their pitcher, a tall right-handed spit-baller named Bill Morrisette, another Baltimore boy, had begun attracting attention in 1912 when he struck out a dozen Washington College batters, carrying a no-hitter into the seventh inning. In the spring of 1913, he pitched a no-hitter against Georgetown, a one-hitter against Holy Cross and Western Maryland, a three-hitter against Bucknell and a five-hitter against Washington College. He struck out 15 Seton Hall batters in a game played at St. Mary's, where Ruth may have been among the spectators. Meanwhile, Ruth drew little coverage, even though his performance was superior to Morrisette's. In combing the papers trying to find a first reference to Ruth in a game report, at least one biographer confused him with a catcher for the Bayonne Athletic Club, Frank Ruth.[37] The mistake is understandable. Two catchers named Ruth in close proximity, not to mention another player named "Roth," whose name appeared in reports of amateur games of the day.

The 18-year-old George Ruth didn't lose a single game he pitched in 1913 and he batted .537.[38] He hit a home run in nearly every game he played. On June 8, the *Baltimore American* gave Ruth his first known mention in the report of a game between the "Stars" of St. Mary's and the White Sox, which

6. A Star Begins to Twinkle

the school's all-star team won, 10–3. No account of the game was provided in which Ruth caught for the all-star nine. It was played at St. Mary's and it may have been submitted to the paper by the Xaverians in a bid to find suitable competition for their star players. The brief item included an address for potential opponents to contact the school.[39]

In intramural play, Ruth had developed into an exceptional pitcher and hitter. On September 30, the *St. Mary's Evening Star*, the school paper, described his performance during a game at the end of the season: "Ruth, one of the Stars star slabmen, allowed but one hit, that being a two-base hit.... He also struck out twenty-two and issued but one pass." At the plate, he recorded four hits.[40]

His outstanding performance on the ball diamond was beginning to draw some attention outside the walls of St. Mary's. Within the school, he was already a source of pride, not just among the inmates, but for the Xaverians. Brother Paul, superintendent of St. Mary's since 1907, felt compelled to say something about the budding baseball star in his Annual Report for 1913. "One boy created a sensation by his excellent work," he wrote.[41] He wasn't talking about academics. He was talking about Ruth and baseball.

Biographer Marshall Smelser agreed that 1913 was "a spectacular year" for Ruth. He said any major-league scout would have been impressed, not just with his speed, his arm and his bat, but with the absence of "grave faults." Ruth's natural ability shone through and brothers Matthias, Herman and Alban had helped make that happen. The brothers could never have taught him how to hit a ball 425 feet at age 17, a distance claimed by Leisman. Or pick off a man at first base when Ruth wore a glove on his throwing hand while catching or pitching. On the latter point, St. Mary's ballplayers joked that he could pick off any runner at first who didn't have two feet planted on the bag.[42] Ruth was a natural. And by the age of 18 he had become the best amateur pitcher in the world.

In the closing days of that memorable 1913 season, the star of St. Mary's drew some attention that would change his life forever.

7

A Big Deal

While young George Ruth was finding success with his new "family" at St. Mary's, his now-single father continued to struggle with the West Conway Street saloon, and in early 1911 acquired a second liquor license, this one for 501 North Street, just northeast of the city core. To tend bar there, he hired William E. Sipes, a member of a family who had been neighbors of the Ruths (and likely customers) when they lived on West Camden. The Sipes family lived just around the corner at 403 South Paca Street. Big George likely found that adding a second bar was a financial stretch, so he returned to the lightning rod business to generate extra income. He began placing advertisements in the *Baltimore Sun* touting his 30 years of experience erecting and repairing lightning rods, providing his address at 406 West Conway.[1] He continued to advertise his sideline operation for several years.

George Sr.'s connection with the troubled Sipes family was not restricted to business. It also led him to his second wife. In late January 1908, Baltimore police officer Harry McCotter was dismissed by the city police board and charged with "acting improperly" toward 16-year-old Martha E. Sipes, a sister of bartender William. Two other officers were also charged, but exonerated, according to a sketchy press account.[2] It had been reported that another brother, Benjamin, accused McCotter of betraying Martha. Two days later, in a surprise move, McCotter married Sipes in the city jail where he was being held. McCotter had been committed to stand trial on two criminal counts, but the charges were dropped because a wife could not be compelled to testify against her husband.[3] The marriage, convenient as it was, did not last. By July 14, the McCotters had separated and in early September Martha applied for a divorce, alleging mistreatment at the hands of her spouse. By then, less than eight months after the "improper" incident that gave rise to McCotter's dismissal, a child had been born.[4] Four years later, in 1912, George Ruth was sharing his living quarters at 406 West Conway with the Sipes family. In April 1914, George Ruth and Martha were married.[5] Martha, was 20 years his junior—and just three years older than his 19-year-old son.

The year 1912 had proved particularly eventful for George Ruth. On St.

Patrick's Day, a Sunday, a suspicious police officer stopped a man leaving Ruth's saloon with a suitcase. Charles Dyson, a stevedore who lived nearby, refused to disclose what was in the suitcase and was taken to the police station where it was found to contain six bottles of beer. Police then raided the saloon, prompting patrons to flee upstairs and scamper across the roofs of adjoining buildings in a wild chase. Armed police eventually arrested the suspects and seized a bottle of partly consumed beer. Ruth and his bartender, George Strohmann, were charged with violating Baltimore's blue laws by selling liquor on a Sunday.[6] It was the latest in a long string of infractions accumulated by Ruth for selling alcohol on the Sabbath and he likely lost his liquor license as a result.

In July, a fire broke out at the West Conway saloon, and the *Baltimore Sun* reported Strohmann as its operator, with no mention of Ruth. The blaze was detected at 3 a.m. on July 10, and was attributed to rats gnawing on matches. The occupants, all members of the Sipes family, escaped safely. Dramatically, Thelma and Ethel Sipes, aged 3 and 4, were dropped from a second-story window into the arms of a patrolman, while their aunt, Martha E. Sipes, fought her way through dense smoke to reach the safety of the street.[7] Damage was not extensive, however, and the whereabouts of George Ruth at the time is unknown.

Four months later, Strohmann was again reported to be the operator of the saloon when it was raided for selling liquor on election day, November 5. It was one of six saloons charged by a flying squad of police.[8] Just a few days beforehand, George Ruth was in police news, but this time as a victim. He reported a thief had entered his home above 406 West Conway and had stolen a watch and chain from a dining room buffet. Ruth claimed his loss was $50.[9]

In 1913, after several years of struggle with the West Conway operation, and perhaps because of his license revocation, or merely for greater privacy, George Ruth and his new wife moved a block west to 552 West Conway. He no longer appeared in city directories as a saloon operator, and was listed as a co-owner of the Columbia Harness Company just around the corner at 521 Columbia Avenue, today known as Washington Boulevard. George continued to advertise his lightning rod business, now using the Columbia Avenue address, which suggests his continued reliance on a sideline because of ongoing money woes.[10]

Unlike his son, who had become the baseball star of St. Mary's, George Ruth was finding that success in life was elusive. He liked saloons and their clientele, but it was a hard way to earn a livelihood. Still, he preferred it to climbing onto ladders and roofs to fix or replace lightning rods, a lonely, dangerous occupation. Luckily, it wouldn't be long before his son helped turn things around for him and get him back into his preferred line of work. Ironically, just as things began to look up for George Ruth, his connection to the Sipes family proved fatal. But that was still a few years in the future.

By 1913, young George Ruth was a big man on the sprawling campus of St. Mary's, literally and figuratively. At 18, he was already more than six-feet tall and his build was solid and athletic. His hitting, pitching and catching had made him the school star and idol for the younger boys as he helped make St. Mary's a strong contender in local baseball battles. A rivalry developed between St. Mary's and Mount St. Joseph College for bragging rights about which school had the best baseball program and players. The latter invariably fielded strong teams because of the baseball knowledge and skilled coaching of Brother Gilbert. Born Phillip Cairnes, in Somerville, Massachusetts, in 1884, Brother Gilbert was trained by the Xaverians in Baltimore and given his first teaching assignment in Louisville, Kentucky. He was transferred to Mount St. Joseph in 1908 and quickly made a name for himself as a talented and successful coach. He developed a reputation as a perfectionist and strategist, urging his players to score runs in bunches and not rely on big hits. Brother Gilbert's teams often played some of the best collegiate teams in the northeast, including Boston College, Fordham, Holy Cross, Villanova and Maryland. In 1915, Mount St. Joseph won the Eastern College Championship. An outgoing character with Irish roots, Brother Gilbert made friends easily. He became a member of the local baseball community, which included Jack Dunn, another Irish Catholic and owner of the professional Orioles of the Eastern and then International leagues.[11] Brother Gilbert understood how Dunn operated and was always quick to alert him to talent. For his part, Dunn was constantly looking for promising youngsters he could acquire cheaply, develop and then sell to major-league teams. He acted as a sort of farm club for the majors and found success in that role.

During 1911, Dunn had tried to sign star pitcher Dave Roth from Brother Gilbert's Mount St. Joseph club. But Roth signed instead with Connie Mack and his Philadelphia Athletics, the city's American League team. Ironically, Mack then sent him to Baltimore for seasoning, where Mack's friend and business associate Dunn transferred him to Reading of the Tri-State League, feeling his delivery was too slow for the International loop. Roth did well there and Dunn recalled him toward the end of the 1912 season and he won seven games for the Orioles. Roth was sidelined by injury in 1913 after 39 games, and then offered a tryout by Chicago.[12] He never made it to the big leagues, however, and spent five years in the minors. The similarity of Roth's name to a young pitcher named Ruth soon to appear with the Orioles would later create confusion for some researchers. A catcher named Frank Ruth also played for the area's Bayonne Athletic Club in 1913 and 1914. He was occasionally mentioned in the local papers and sometimes mistaken for another catcher of the same last name.[13]

7. A Big Deal

By 1913, Brother Gilbert had an outstanding right-handed pitcher, 18-year-old Bill Morrisette, then in his fourth year at Mount St. Joseph. He was making a name for himself and getting positive press for his work on the mound, which featured a good fastball and devastating spitball that broke sharply. In an early outing that season, Morrisette held Georgetown University hitless for nine innings in a win for Mount St. Joseph, 3–1. Next up was Holy Cross College, when he allowed a single hit in a 7–1 victory. By the middle of May, he had recorded nine wins and three losses.

As Morrisette was leading his school team to victory after victory, Jack Dunn found himself beset by pitching woes on his Orioles. As early as mid–May, he was scouting around to boost what was described as his "wobbly" team and signed new arms released by the New York Giants and Cincinnati Reds, both members of the National League.[14] By May 15, the Orioles record stood at 14–11, good for third place in the International League. But Dunn wanted to do much better and a good prospect was right under his nose at Mount St. Joseph. Morrisette had already caught the attention of scouts from Washington, Detroit, the Boston Red Sox and the New York Giants, the latter reportedly offering him a handsome $400 a month.[15] But, on May 26, after lengthy negotiations, Morrisette signed with Jack Dunn and made his first appearance the next day in the eighth inning of a 9–2 Oriole loss to Newark. Despite the result, Morrisette got through his two innings of work without allowing a hit.[16] It was a good start.

He appeared in 16 games that year, winning 4 and losing 3. The Orioles finished the season in third place, well back of Newark and Rochester, and a half game ahead of Buffalo. Morrisette would have a future in the major leagues, unlike Dave Roth, his predecessor from Mount St. Joseph. After four years in the minors, Morrisette went on to three seasons of somewhat limited major-league duty for Philadelphia and Detroit.

Dunn, the talent scout, was on the hunt for pitchers, just as young George Ruth was making a name for himself as the outstanding all-around player at St. Mary's. Dunn himself had spent 8 years in the major leagues, where he won 64 games and lost 59 as a pitcher and proved to be a versatile position player. He really knew pitching and at one point early in his career had spoken about starting a school for pitchers upon his retirement.[17] How the Orioles manager learned about the young phenomenon at St. Mary's is unclear. There are many versions of how it happened. Once again, the fog of myth shrouds the truth, as in so many other aspects of Babe Ruth's life. Unlike the reasonably reliable account of his moving about as a child that can be gleaned from documents in registry offices, divorce courts and city directories, the story of his discovery varies depending on source. Even newspaper stories are difficult to rely upon, with sportswriters often guilty of trying to make a good story even better during an era of all-out circulation wars. Yet again, Babe himself was of little help in setting the record straight. That left the door open for inventive minds and pens. Biographers of Ruth have had their challenges.

In his 1948 autobiography, Ruth seemed to know about the sometimes conflicting stories. And he didn't seem to care. He put it this way: "There are half a dozen stories about my 'discovery.' Perhaps several of them are true...."[18] His excuse for not providing a definitive version is he was unaware of everything that was going on at the time. He seemed content to let sportswriters—and ghostwriters—have their way.

In the first telling of his life story, his 1920 serialized autobiography, he provided a very simple and brief explanation about his introduction to Jack Dunn. Ruth said he was playing outside at St. Mary's, sliding on a frozen pond one day during the winter of 1913–14, when he was unexpectedly summoned to the office of Brother Matthias, who introduced him to Dunn. After they exchanged a few words, Dunn asked Ruth to play for the Orioles for $600. A contract was signed.[19] At the time, that is all Ruth had to say about a moment that changed his life.

His 1928 autobiography provided another version. Ruth doesn't mention Brother Matthias at all as he described his meeting Dunn. He said Brother Gilbert (whom he incorrectly called his baseball coach) wrote a letter to Dunn saying what a terrific prospect St. Mary's had. Dunn came to St. Mary's, where Brother Gilbert joined him and introduced the player and coach. Dunn took Ruth into the schoolyard and caught pitches thrown by him for about a half hour. Back in the office, Brother Gilbert and Dunn conferred for another half hour privately before asking Ruth to rejoin them. "How about it

Jack Dunn, owner of the Baltimore Orioles, signed Babe Ruth to his first contract. Several stories were told about how he discovered the pitcher at St. Mary's school and how much he saw him perform before signing the prospect. Some of the stories may actually be true (National Baseball Hall of Fame and Museum, Cooperstown, New York).

7. A Big Deal

young man, do you want to play baseball?" Ruth said Dunn asked. Ruth replied: "Sure. I'll play. When do I start?" Brother Gilbert intervened to ensure Ruth knew he'd be paid $600 for the season. Ruth readily agreed to the terms, and the contract was signed.[20]

By 1948, Ruth shared even more, and said Dunn never saw him play baseball and signed him simply after witnessing his athleticism while skating on a frozen path at St. Mary's. Ruth added the new wrinkle that Dunn was actually trying to sign a lefty pitcher through Brother Gilbert named Ford Meadows. But Brother Gilbert wanted Meadows to finish his schooling and pitch another season for Mount St. Joseph. So, to retain Meadows and keep Dunn happy, Brother Gilbert suggested the Baltimore owner instead consider Ruth over at St. Mary's. (Meadows, from Frederick, Maryland, was eventually acquired by Dunn anyway and played for him in 1915 and 1916, but never reached the majors.) In this 1948 telling, Ruth was very clear about several details and provided some color (which may have been his ghostwriter's embellishment).

> Whatever the preliminaries, my first knowledge that I was going to be a professional ballplayer instead of a tailor came in the middle of February, 1914. I was throwing a baseball around the still-frozen yard at St. Mary's—dressed in tight-fitting overalls, by the way—when Brother Gilbert, Dunn, Brother Matthias and Brother Paul appeared. Brother Gilbert introduced Dunn to me.
> Dunn had "heard about me," he said, and, to my complete surprise, asked me if I'd like to sign with the Orioles. To me, it was as if somebody had suddenly popped up and asked me to join the U.S. Senate.[21]

Ruth said Dunn agreed to become his legal guardian until he reached the age of 21 and would pay him $600 for the 1914 season. Ruth said his jaw must have dropped when he learned he could not only play baseball, but be paid to do so. He added: "None of my later thrills ever topped the one I got that cold afternoon at St. Mary's when $600 seemed to me to be all the wealth in the world."

Babe's differing stories are charming, but many aspects of them are hard to accept. Why would a seasoned baseball manager like Dunn offer a nice contract to a young man who had just turned 19 without ever seeing him play the game? Dunn had a well-developed eye for talent, so why didn't he use it? Was he willing to commit to a boy based solely on the advice of an Xaverian Brother or two? And how did Brother Gilbert know so much about Ruth when he'd never been the star's coach and his exposure to him had been limited? As in many aspects of the Babe Ruth story, the truth is elusive. And good stories are not necessarily accurate ones.

Fortunately, there are other published accounts of what happened to which we can turn. In the hunt for elusive truth, they should be considered, because Ruth's varying recitations leave so many questions unanswered. In later years, both Dunn and Brother Gilbert wrote about events that led to Babe's historic first contract. And so did a young pal of Ruth's at St. Mary's who witnessed some of the events from the perspective of the schoolyard. Their stories may shed more light on a pivotal point in the life of the young baseball phenomenon.

In March 1923, the *Baltimore Sun* published a 15-part series by Jack Dunn about his long and distinguished baseball career, during which he won 10 pennants. In part seven, he described meeting Babe Ruth. "It was a raw and blustery afternoon in winter, when Brother Gilbert, my personal friend, then an instructor at Mount St. Joseph's College, called me up and said he wanted me to come out to St. Mary's Industrial School, on Wilkens Avenue, for he had a ball player for me," he wrote.[22] Dunn readily agreed and met with Brother Gilbert, bringing along New York Yankee Fritz Maisel, a Baltimore-area product and formerly an Oriole.

> When we got out there no Ruth was in sight, but Brother Matthias said he would have him looked up and we watched some of the little kids on an icy slide they had built, and they were having a rattling good time.
>
> While we were still looking, a big husky fellow in overalls put in an appearance and started for the slide. He took a flying leap and went down it, bowling over the kids right and left.
>
> Brother Matthias took one look at the bulky figure. "That's Ruth now," he said. Then Ruth came over and I asked him how he would like to play with the Orioles and go to spring training camp.

Dunn conceded he had been previously "tipped off that he could hit the ball a mile, pitch, catch and play the outfield." He didn't say by whom or when. Dunn said Brother Gilbert, a "mighty shrewd judge of baseball material, knew all about him, and assured me I was making no mistake in getting hold of his services." For his part, Dunn said he liked "the big fellow's looks" and agreed to become his guardian as part of the deal for his services. He continued:

> Ruth signed his contract without the slightest urging. Several of the school's players watched him as he penned his name to the paper, and one little fellow, who was peering in the door and didn't like to see Ruth leave, called out: "Well, fellows, there goes our ball club."

Dunn's telling shows amazing faith in Brother Gilbert. But it remains difficult to understand why the Orioles manager didn't demand to see Ruth perform on the diamond before offering the big lad a contract. Dunn was surprisingly willing to offer good money to an untested 19-year-old. Perhaps Dunn's need for additional pitching in the upcoming season and his imminent departure for spring training in North Carolina were at the top of his mind. Time was not his friend. It was the middle of February and Dunn had already told his pitchers to report to Fayetteville at the beginning of March.

7. A Big Deal

Brother Gilbert provided his own version of events in a seven-part series published in the *Boston Globe* late in 1928. In an introductory note to promote the series, an editor touted Brother Gilbert's credentials this way: "No other one man, except the Babe himself, knows more about his life than does Brother Gilbert."[23] The self-serving (and circulation-building) hyperbole overlooked others such as Brothers Matthias, Alban, Herman and Paul. Brother Gilbert's series appeared the same year Ruth's first full autobiography was released, in which he credited Brother Gilbert (for reasons unknown) with making him a baseball player and connecting him with Dunn. Very little mention was made of Brother Matthias. The net result was that Brother Gilbert was elevated in the public mind as the discoverer of Babe Ruth.

Brother Gilbert recalled that in the fall of 1913 a catcher for his Mount St. Joseph team named John Morgan "fairly begged" him to go to St. Mary's Industrial School to witness the hitting of a young player named Ruth. "With some misgivings, I finally went," he said. "Stories of great hitters and spectacular fielders are eternally current. Generally, however, these stories find their inception in the enthusiasm of youth ... [but] it was not so in this case." Brother Gilbert said he joined Morgan and Lewis Malone, shortstop for Newark of the International League, in the bandstand just behind first base one September day at St. Mary's to watch a game pitting Ruth's Red Sox school team against the Giants. He soon noticed the left-handed catcher for the Red Sox. "He is a fork-hander," Brother Gilbert recalled telling his companions, thinking that a left-hander behind the plate "is the equivalent of a bone out of joint, or a misfit in society." Morgan said not to worry, he had brought Brother Gilbert to see Babe hit, not catch. "Wait and see for yourself," Morgan advised. The opportunity soon arose. In the bottom of the first inning, Babe came to the plate after the Red Sox leadoff hitter singled and then advanced to third as the next two batters struck out.

"Clad in a baseball uniform that was a trifle small for him, there strode up to the plate one of the most graceful of big men that I have ever seen," Brother Gilbert wrote. "There was an ease in his manner, and confidence in his gait." Brother Gilbert watched the Giants pitcher gesture at his fielders to move back, but they were already doing so. The right fielder ventured about 280 feet from home plate onto the junior playground diamond near second base where a game was underway. When he did, the junior game stopped as the players realized Ruth was at bat on the big diamond. They wanted to see what their school hero would do. Once everyone was set, the pitcher delivered a curve ball to Ruth that Brother Gilbert said was low and inside.

> George Ruth, with an easy grace that portended the rhythmic muscular activity for which he has since become famous, took a lusty cut at that ball. There followed the usual resounding crash, and all eyes on the big campus followed the pellet as it fairly

screamed far over the right fielder's head, bounced against a wall with considerable force and caromed back into the junior yard.

Brother Gilbert said Ruth might have been held to a triple but the fielder played the ball poorly and both Ruth and his teammate crossed home plate. Brother Gilbert said Ruth belted two more home runs that memorable day. Brother Gilbert was sold. "I no longer doubted the word of John Morgan—George Ruth was certainly a great hitter. No great baseball acumen was necessary to recognize in Ruth a batter of remarkable promise. A 14-year-old boy could have sensed as much."

Brother Gilbert said he was also impressed with Ruth's catching. He could easily throw out base runners, even though he wore his catcher's mitt on his left hand and had to quickly flip off the glove and fire the ball with his now-bare throwing hand. "Though he was the best catcher in the school, the authorities did not see the necessity of providing him with a right-hand catching mitt," he noted. (One wonders if, had Brother Gilbert been his coach, Ruth would have been provided a proper glove.) Brother Gilbert described Ruth's throws to second base as like "a rifle shot." He told his companions: "Unless all signs fail, this young fellow will make a great pitcher." Brother Gilbert said he returned to St. Mary's some time later, accompanied by another of his players, and watched another game during which Ruth hit two more home runs. Later that fall, at Brother Gilbert's request during a visit to St. Mary's, Brother Alban introduced him to Ruth, a "great big, good-natured kid … free from guile and deceit of any kind." Brother Alban, he said, "was an ardent admirer of Ruth's batting prowess," and felt Ruth had the makings of a professional player. On another visit, during a walk with Brother Gilbert, Ruth confided a willingness to pursue the professional game, adding: "I'd be pleased to play just for the sake of playing."

Enter Jack Dunn in Brother Gilbert's recitation. Mount St. Joseph had a strong young pitcher for the upcoming 1914 season, Ford Meadows, in whom Dunn was interested. He said it was on March 1 when Dunn, accompanied by Fritz Maisel, the third baseman for the Yankees who lived nearby, drove up to Mount St. Joseph in Dunn's big red car and onto the playing field. Talk turned to Dunn's interest in Meadows, but Brother Gilbert resisted. "I could ill afford to let him go," he explained.

> To placate Jack Dunn, who has been my friend of long standing, I promised him, on condition that he would get off Meadows's trail, what I called at the time the greatest left-hand pitching prospect outside of big league folds.… Never having seen Ruth pitch, I was merely gambling, you will understand, on his possibilities as a moundsman. That statement, I hope, will not strip me of the glory that the press has duly attached to my name in connection with the Babe.

Brother Gilbert said he, Dunn and Maisel then went to St. Mary's, where they asked to speak to Brother Matthias. On the topic of Ruth and his abilities, Brother Matthias, never much of a talker, simply confirmed: "He can hit." Dunn was more interested in his pitching and pressed Brother Matthias about that aspect of his game. "Sure, he can do anything," came the response from the towering brother who had seen as much of Ruth's play as anyone alive. That was good enough for Dunn. School superintendent Brother Paul was sent for so they could discuss a contract and the guardianship issue. Soon afterward, Brother Gilbert introduced Dunn to Ruth, who'd been called from the tailor shop where he was making shirts. "That is the whole story," Brother Gilbert wrote. "The papers have told you that I found him. No, that is not so: John Morgan found him.... I merely brought Jack Dunn to sign him." Brother Gilbert, in his rare display of modesty, also credited two of his players who had vouched for the St. Mary's star.

The contract was signed that day. The press came to lionize Brother Gilbert as the discoverer of Babe Ruth, often erroneously saying he was his coach. Brother Gilbert reveled in the "glory" assigned him by the press and public. He shared no credit with brothers Matthias or Alban for taking a raw talent and coaching him to play the game he would revolutionize.

There is yet another version of that day when Ruth signed his first professional contract and the events leading up to it. It comes from Ruth's friend and fellow schoolmate Lou "Fats" Leisman, who was three years younger than his big pal. In 1956, Leisman self-published his recollections of his time with Ruth, whom he praised for being so good to the other boys at St. Mary's, especially the younger ones. Liesman wrote about a game played between St. Mary's and Mount St. Joseph he said was witnessed by Dunn. One would have thought Dunn and Brother Gilbert would have mentioned such a significant event in their recollections, had it occurred.

In his telling, Leisman said Dunn wanted to sign Morrisette, not Meadows, and Brother Gilbert alerted Dunn to the young phenomenon Ruth at St. Mary's, thereby "practicing the rule of self-preservation in order to keep his ball club together."[24] Leisman does not provide a year for this. If Morrisette was Dunn's actual target, it would have been early in the 1913 season. Dunn signed Morrisette in May. If Leisman confused Meadows with Morrisette, it would likely be late that same year. Regardless, Leisman said a game was arranged between St. Mary's and Mount St. Joseph and Dunn advised Brother Paul he planned to attend to see Ruth in action. How Leisman knew this background is unclear. Leisman said the boys at St. Mary's, where the game was to be played, were told about it a month in advance and anticipation ran high. About 10 days before the big game Ruth shocked everyone by disappearing. None of the brothers spoke about his whereabouts. It became known that Ruth had scaled a wall and escaped. "This was a terrible shock to the morale of the rest of the boys at the school." At the time, Leisman said he was mystified like the rest of his schoolmates about why their baseball star had slipped away, but later realized the strain must have been too great for the boy upon whom the hopes of the entire school were placed. Three days later, it was reported Ruth had voluntarily returned. As punishment, he was required to stand on the road separating the big and little yards from each other for five days during recreation periods. "After the five-day restriction period had ended, Brother Matthias sent for the Babe and handed him a ball and glove, with a warning to go down into the big yard and get in shape for the most important baseball game of his life." As always, Brother Matthias was inclined to forgive and forget. It would be understandable for the big man to be relieved, but if he was, he kept it to himself.

St. Mary's was scrubbed down in anticipation of visitors and the ball diamond put in top shape for the big game, Leisman continued. The grandstand was adorned with American flags and bunting and the crowd began arriving an hour early for the 3 p.m. game. A holiday had been declared at the school that day and many of the teachers were in the grandstand. Leisman said he saw brothers Matthias, Paul, Alban, Herman, assorted school staff—and Jack Dunn. He didn't mention Brother Gilbert, who was likely on the bench with his team. Ruth was the pitcher for St. Mary's, while Morrisette appeared for Mount St. Joseph.

> I do not remember every angle of the game, but I do know that it was very exciting and that the Babe got 14 strikeouts, which was enough to shut the Mount St. Joe club out, by a score of either six or eight to nothing. We were told later that after the game Brother Paul, Jack Dunn and the Babe were up in the school head office for about two hours, at which time Jack Dunn had decided to sign the Babe to a contract.

While his account differs greatly from those shared by Babe, Dunn and Brother Gilbert, Leisman said he was present at the "big game" and clearly recalled seeing Dunn in the grandstand when Ruth pitched. Leisman was just 16 at the time, and his memories from 43 years before may have been gilded by knowledge he gained later. But it's doubtful he would have invented such an important game—and Dunn's appearance at it—from whole cloth. Too many former St. Mary's students were still alive in 1956 and could contradict it, had it been untrue. Readers are left to judge Leisman's reliability.

Ruth biographer Robert W. Creamer related yet another story about Ruth's discovery. It echoes some of Leisman's account, upon which Creamer seems to have relied in part. Joe Engel, a Washington, D.C.-born player and a pitcher with the Senators, had attended Mount St. Mary's school in Emmitsburg, Maryland, Creamer wrote. Engel returned to his former school northwest of Baltimore for an alumni baseball game in the summer of 1913, and happened to see a preliminary game between the school freshmen and St. Mary's Industrial Training School. He couldn't help but notice Ruth; the young lefty had impressive speed. "This kid was a great natural pitcher," Engel recalled later. "He had everything. He must have struck out eighteen or twenty men in the game."[25] That night, on his trip south to Washington, Engel met Dunn on the train and told him about the left-handed prospect he had witnessed earlier that day. "Whether or not this was Dunn's first report on Ruth is impossible to determine," Creamer wrote. "In any case, it is likely that Dunn came to the big game at St. Mary's in 1913 to see Ruth and Morrisette pitch." Creamer concedes the game had a legendary quality, with the team from the snobby, richer school falling to the ragamuffins from an orphanage reform school. Creamer readily acknowledged other versions of the story in which Brother Gilbert alerted Dunn to Ruth in a bid to divert him from Meadows. Biographer Creamer also took note of comments made by Rodger Pippen, the long-time sports editor of the *Baltimore News-Post*, who was a young sportswriter in 1914. Pippen insisted that Dunn told him he had never seen Ruth play until his recruit reported to the 1914 spring training camp for the Orioles. Ruth shared the same assertion from Pippen in his 1948 autobiography.[26]

At the outset of 1914, stories filled the Baltimore newspapers about the arrival of the Terrapins, Baltimore's entry into the new Federal League, and Dunn's attempts to bolster his Orioles, focusing on pitching and the need for a hard-hitting outfielder. Dunn knew he needed a good club to keep drawing fans to the ballpark given the excitement that surrounded the return of a major league to the city after an absence of 12 years. The new competition would be right in Dunn's face, literally. The Terrapins built their $90,000, 13,000-seat Terrapin Park directly across 29th Street from his smaller Oriole Park (game reports often said 5,000 fans filled the older park to capacity). The *Baltimore Sun* reported on February 15 that Dunn felt he needed "an unusually strong team" for the upcoming season. Dunn, it said, "declares he stands ready to spend $20,000, if necessary, to give the local fans the strongest aggregation he has ever piloted." It continued: "The Oriole magnate signed another local player yesterday. The new bird is George H. Ruth, a pitcher, who played with teams out the Frederick Road. [The general area of Mount St. Joseph and St. Mary's School.] Ruth is six feet tall and fanned 22 men in an amateur game last season. He is regarded as a very hard hitter, so Dunn will try him out down South."[27]

How Ruth got to that point may remain the subject to some controversy, but the young man who excelled at baseball was turning a page. The shirt-maker was now a professional baseball player. Whether Dunn had ever seen him play doesn't really matter—the world soon would.

As with so much about Babe Ruth, the variations—even contradictions—are countless. Because Ruth was more interested in living in the present than recalling the past, he never bothered to set the record straight. He wasn't one to sit still and read much, so he may not have been aware of all the millions of words that were written about him. Questions linger. About the only thing we know for certain about Ruth becoming a professional ballplayer is that is that he signed that contract on February 14, 1914. Much of the rest is likely embellishment.

The young man was about to embark on a professional career that would become legendary. And despite the acclaim he received and the life he lived so large, Babe Ruth never forgot St. Mary's and the people who taught and studied there. He was proud of it all. Others who had been there may have preferred to forget the institution because of its stigma as an orphanage and reform school.

Not Babe.

8

A Homer for a Babe

For 19-year-old George Ruth, leaving St. Mary's for an uncertain future in baseball was a major step. He'd considered the school his home for more than half his life. Excitement was no doubt mixed with apprehension. But in his recollections, only his 1948 autobiography gets into this crucial turning point. Per usual, is it precious little. He said Jack Dunn picked him up at St. Mary's to begin his new adventure. "I'll never forget the ride to the railroad station, the day I left Baltimore. The whole thing still seemed like a dream to me. There were moments when my stomach turned over—wondering if I could make the grade and fearful that I'd fail, and be forced to come back to St. Mary's."[1]

The absence of detail about leaving the school and goodbyes shared with the boys and the brothers there who did so much to turn his life around is rather surprising. But, as with so much about Ruth, someone else filled in the blanks. Brother Gilbert later provided a fulsome account. At the time of his death in 1947, Brother Gilbert was feverishly working on a book about Ruth and had completed about 15,000 words of it.[2] His work was later discovered and turned into a book that was released in 1999.

In Brother Gilbert's telling of events, Ruth spent a day or two with his father before returning to St. Mary's on March 2 to say farewell to school superintendent Brother Paul. That evening, Ruth and some other Orioles were set to board a southbound train for training camp in Fayetteville, North Carolina. Brother Paul wanted to let Ruth say goodbye to the boys at the school. He took Ruth to the various dining rooms and school yards during the lunch hour. It is unclear if Brother Gilbert accompanied them as an invited guest, but the detail he provided suggests it. The lengthy and colorful comments attributed to Ruth and others during that tour raise some suspicions about possible embellishment, however. Brother Gilbert had a way with words and knew how to spin a story. In his prime, he was much sought after as an entertaining dinner speaker. He gave more than 1,000 speeches, many of them about his involvement with Ruth. So some invention is quite possible.

"I hate to say goodbye to the fellahs," Brother Gilbert said Ruth sobbed to Brother Paul before the pride of St. Mary's left the office to begin his farewell tour.[3] Brother Paul assured him he would be an inspiration and provide joy to the boys as a professional ballplayer. "Don't let them down," Brother Paul said, adding reassuringly: "You'll make good, my boy. Of that I am sure."

At one point, Brother Paul and Ruth entered the dining room for the younger boys, who went silent when their hero appeared. Brother Paul explained to them Ruth was leaving them for a career in baseball. Amidst the applause, Brother Gilbert said, one boy blurted out: "Don't let him go!" A similar scene was repeated in a dining room for the older boys. Reluctantly, Ruth acquiesced to repeated demands that he speak. "Fellahs, you're one bunch of swell guys. We've had lotsa fun together," Brother Gilbert quoted him. Ruth said he had been taught the value of fair play and he hoped other boys would have a similar chance to succeed. "And, hey, when I come back to Baltimore, I'll come right out to the school and tell ya about it. S'long fellahs!" He would be good to his word.

Brother Paul took his prodigy downtown and bought him a suitcase and some good clothes so he would make a good first impression on his new associates.

Brother Gilbert made no mention of Brother Matthias in his story. But what Ruth's giant mentor said to him that day was one of the few things Ruth felt important to include in his 1948 recollection. "You'll make it George," the taciturn giant assured him.[4] That boost of confidence from Brother Matthias would have meant the world to the uncertain rookie.

Departure day was a challenge. A blizzard had roared through the northeast the previous day, the strongest witnessed since 1888. On March 2, when the storm abated, the city was digging out from a foot of wind-whipped snow and assessing the damage to roofs, windows and other properties. The loss in Baltimore was initially set at $600,000, and one death was attributed to the storm. Telephone and telegraph wires had been knocked down along with a church steeple and its massive bell. Baltimore was at the southern edge of the blizzard and rail travel to the north was impossible.[5] Fortunately, trains were still running south to Washington and places beyond, like Fayetteville.

Because of the weather, only 12 of the 16 expected pitchers and catchers booked for the trip actually made it to Union Station for the 8:20 p.m. departure. Those missing included veteran catcher and team captain Ben Egan, who was stranded at his home in upstate New York. He was to have led the Orioles into camp. Taking over for him was Scout Steinmann, a coach, scout and general handyman who had been a ballplayer in his younger years. He was assisted by club trainer Doc Fewster.

Ruth remembered the excitement of the departure platform, many of the players confident as they renewed old acquaintances. Among them was Bill Morrisette, his former rival from Mount St. Joseph who was returning for his second year. "Few of them paid attention to me," Ruth recalled. "But that didn't matter. The important thing was that I was going with them to spring training camp, and going on a *train*. It was my first trip out of Baltimore—my first ride on a train."[6] Just before departure as scheduled, Jack Dunn took Ruth aside and slipped him $5 as an advance on his first $100-a-month pay packet. The rookie was stunned: "It was more money than I had ever had in my pocket before."

Ruth was as green as green could be. The older players readily spotted the wide-eyed innocence of the big rookie and decided to have some fun at his expense. They persuaded him the undersized hammock intended for clothes and other items that swung above his upper berth had a specific purpose for pitchers. They told him it was designed to rest his pitching arm while he was asleep. He didn't argue. "I held the arm up in this uncomfortable position all night, because I wanted to act like a pro. I wanted to be a complete part of this unbelievable break that had freed me from St. Mary's two years before my final release time and had brought me the promise of wealth and fame."[7] Needless to say, upon waking the next morning, Ruth's arm was stiff and sore.

The train arrived in Fayetteville at 7:30 a.m. and within hours of checking into the Lafayette Hotel on Hay Street downtown, Scout Steinmann led the players on a mile-long walk south down Gillespie Street to the Cape Fear Fairgrounds to lob balls around. At first, the players were greeted by sunny, spring-like conditions. Two workouts followed the next day at the fairground diamond as Steinmann had them bunting and chasing fly balls. Then rain appeared, forcing the players into the armory, the largest indoor facility in town. Captain Egan arrived and took over the training regimen from Steinmann. To break the monotony and because the wet ballfield was not yet fit for play, several of the Orioles played a game of basketball against the local high school team. The Orioles proved to be surprisingly good as they won the low-scoring contest, 8–6. The big youngster named Ruth was one of the stars of the game, along with veteran pitcher Ensign Cottrell and catcher Gene Lidgate.[8]

It wasn't until Saturday, March 7, that the weather cooperated and the fairground dried sufficiently for the Orioles to get on the diamond. Brisk winds and warm sun combined to improve both the field and the attitudes of the players who were tired of practice and anxious to show their stuff in a game situation. Egan and Steinmann decided a seven-inning game was in order and picked their teams. Egan's "Buzzards" included Ruth, whom he placed at shortstop with Egan holding down first. Frank Jarman pitched. Rodger Pippen, a young sportswriter for the *Baltimore News-Post* who had been a star player on several amateur Baltimore teams, was drafted to play center field. Steinmann's "Sparrows" used a pitcher named Cranston, while Steinmann played first and three other pitchers, including Morrisette, played outfield. Word spread quickly about the first game and a couple hundred locals were at the fairgrounds to watch. The Buzzards went to bat first and scored a run in the first inning, but the Sparrows replied with their own in the bottom of the first. With bases loaded in the top of the second, Egan belted a double to bring home three runs. Lefty Cottrell connected for a single and Egan scampered home. Next batter, the fifth in the order, was Ruth. In his second plate appearance that day he made history. He uncorked on a Cranston offering that carried over the head of right fielder Morrisette and into the cornfield beyond. In the story he filed about Ruth's plate appearance, Pippen said: "The next batter made a hit that will live in the memory of all who saw it. That clouter was George Ruth, the southpaw from St. Mary's School. The ball carried so far that he walked around the bases."[9] Ruth's first homer as a professional scored two runs and put the Buzzards up, 7–1. The hit was the longest ever seen by Fayetteville fans, Jesse Linthicum of the *Baltimore Sun* reported, noting it had traveled farther than a memorable one by former Fayetteville player and Olympian medalist Jim Thorpe, now playing outfield with the New York Giants.[10] After the game, Pippen measured Ruth's hit at 350 feet, making it 60 feet farther than Thorpe's clout.[11] Some tellings of the story say it flew more than 400 feet.

"I hit it as all the others, by taking a good gander at the pitch as it came up to the plate, twisting my body into a backswing and then hitting it as hard as I could swing," Ruth recalled in his 1948 autobiography. In the sixth inning Ruth went in to pitch, replacing hopeful John Messina, who had given up six runs and would soon be released from camp. Ruth threw effective fastballs with a sweeping delivery. At the plate, he had two hits in the game and scored twice, leading Egan's Buzzards to a 15–9 victory. Today, a marker along Gillespie Street near the spot of his blast commemorates the first professional home run by the greatest hitter the game has ever seen.

It was Ruth's fifth day in camp and he was beginning to attract attention. Veteran catcher Egan was among the teammates he impressed. "George Ruth, the Baltimore boy, has attracted Ben's attention, for the youngster looks like a real find," Linthicum reported in the *Sun*. "Besides hitting the ball to all corners of the lot, Ruth has shown up well in the [pitcher's] box. He has a world of speed and handles himself like a veteran, although he has no experience in the professional ranks."[12]

A couple days later, Jack Dunn made it to Fayetteville with the balance of the team. He was anxious to see the new recruits, Ruth in particular. Dunn was chatting with outfielder George Twombly as they entered the fairgrounds and the topic of Ruth had come up. Dunn said: "Wait until you see this kid," referring to Ruth.[13] Just then, the two men heard a terrific crack of a bat and saw a ball sail far over the heads of some outfielders. It had been launched by Ruth, they discovered. Dunn looked at Twombly: "What did I tell you?"

Dunn was also impressed with Birdie Cree, the former Yankee outfielder who regularly sent balls soaring beyond the outfielders. Partway through the 1914 season, Cree returned to the Yankees for 77 games and batted .309 for them. But the kid from Baltimore was a particularly pleasant surprise. "Frank Ruth, the Baltimore sand-lotter, was the other player to attract the manager's attention," said Linthicum in the *Sun*, not yet familiar with the newcomer's first name, or confused with the amateur by that name back in Baltimore. "At the bat he again showed his great hitting ability by smashing long flies into the cornfield. He twirled for a short time and Dunn watched every move he made. Ruth played shortstop while the regulars had batting practice [*sic*] and fielded the position as if accustomed to handling ground balls."[14]

Several more intrasquad games were played in the following days, pitting the "Regulars" against the "Yanigans." Ruth pitched well on whichever team Dunn placed him. He also was solid with the bat. He played shortstop when outstanding prospect Alvin Dove broke his finger on March 13, putting Dove out of commission for an extended period. Ruth had been on the mound and had struck out four batters before replacing Dove. At shortstop, he covered a lot of ground, easily handled hot shots, and took part in a double play.[15] Brother Matthias's insistence his players learn multiple positions was already paying off. The next day, Dunn announced some cuts. Ruth was one of nine pitchers kept, along with Morrisette. Dunn's pitching staff was his strongest in many years. The *Baltimore Sun* provided this assessment: "George Ruth has impressed Dunn most, and before he was at the training camp a week decided that he will be a regular whether or not he strikes his stride. The Oriole magnate predicts that Ruth will develop into a Rube Waddell, for he possesses every mark of a professional pitcher."[16]

From a man with the baseball acumen of Dunn, the comparison to Rube Waddell was high praise. As that comment was printed, Waddell was terminally ill with tuberculosis in Texas, and he died just a few days later, on April 1. He was 37. Waddell was one of the top left-handed pitchers that baseball had ever seen. He stood six-foot-one, but had the emotional maturity of a child. Waddell was prone to eccentricities, wild antics and irresponsible acts such as chasing fire trucks and marrying his second wife after knowing her for only three days. On the baseball diamond, he possessed a great fastball and curve, combined with pinpoint accuracy. Waddell won 97 games for Connie Mack's Philadelphia Athletics between 1902 and 1905 and recorded a long-standing major-league record of 349 strikeouts in 1904. He was inducted into the National Baseball Hall of Fame in 1946.[17]

A "rube," or hayseed, was what his fellow players in Fayetteville saw in gangly, wide-eyed George Ruth, a likeable lad completely free of guile or pretense. They took advantage of him with the "arm sling" during his first-ever train ride on the trip south. They themselves were left wide-eyed when they saw him eat. For the first time in his life, the always-hungry George could order whatever he wanted from a menu, and the team paid for his food. "Order anything you want, kid," one of the older men said, telling him the club covered the tab in spring training. Ruth couldn't believe his ears. On his very first morning at the hotel, he was nicely tucked into his third helping of wheatcakes and ham when he noticed he was being stared at. He barely paused, shrugged and continued to pour maple syrup over his pile of food. "I wouldn't have believed it if I hadn't seen it," said Pippen, the sportswriter who was his roommate.[18] Ruth's routine at St. Mary's had made him an early riser. So, he would get out of bed at the Lafayette Hotel in time to watch the 5 a.m. train steam through town and then hang around watching for more. He'd return to the hotel to be first in line for the dining room when it opened for breakfast and then tuck away vast amounts of the fare offered there.[19] Ruth could never remember names, including that of his roommate Pippen, and this quirk became a running gag in camp. He was a source of amusement for many of the veteran hands.

For Ruth, the hotel elevator was pure magic. He rode it up and down the way a child would play with a new toy. He watched carefully how it was operated and at one point slipped the operator most of the money remaining from the amount Dunn had advanced him to let him run it. Ruth would go from the top floor to the lowest, stopping at every level and poking his head out. One day, his curiosity got the better of him during his joyride and the elevator began to rise with its doors still open while Ruth's head was still sticking out, rubbernecking. "Suddenly a player screamed at me to pull my fool head inside, and I did—just in time to keep it from being crushed," he recalled.[20]

By the end of the second week in training camp, when Dunn and the veterans joined them, the big, goofy kid acquired a new name. In his 1948 autobiography, Ruth set the stage by noting manager Jack Dunn had a well-earned reputation for picking up very young players like him and developing their skills.

> Some of his older players used to kid him a lot about the baby-faced kids he concentrated on, and the first time they saw me with him—on the field—was no exception.
> On that day, Dunn practically led me by the hand from the dressing room to the pitcher's box. I was as proud of my Orioles uniform as I had been of my first long pants. Maybe I showed that pride in my face and the way I walked.
> "Look at Dunnie and his new babe," one of the older players yelled.
> Dunnie bawled me out until the stuffings ran out of me, and what he didn't say to me the older players said for him. But finally one of them took pity on me, shook his head and said:
> "You're just a babe in the woods."
> After that, they called me Babe.[21]

There are other variations on the story, but even though Ruth was poor at remembering names, one would think he'd recall how he picked up his

8. A Homer for a Babe

famous moniker. Several biographers credit Scout Steinmann with christening him.[22] One of them, Kal Wagenheim, acknowledged there are several versions and shared an interesting variation. In this telling, Steinmann and sportswriter Pippen were out for a walk one evening in Fayetteville, when they saw Ruth barrel by on a bicycle he had borrowed. "Rodger," Steinmann said, "Dunnie didn't get that fellow from St. Mary's, he got him from an infant asylum. We've got some real kids on this trip, and that Ruth is the biggest babe of the lot."[23]

Upon Ruth's death, Linthicum, by then sports editor of the *Baltimore Sun*, told readers Ruth that picked up his nickname immediately after connecting for his home run in Fayetteville. Linthicum said Dunn marveled at the blast and became "enthusiastic" about his power at the plate. "Walking back to the hotel that afternoon Dunn put an arm around Ruth's big shoulders and remarked: 'This baby will not get away from me!' Then and there Ruth acquired the nickname of Babe."[24]

Regardless, it wasn't long before Pippen and Linthicum were referring to the newcomer as "Babe" Ruth. His biographer Robert Creamer didn't specify who coined the name, but related another episode involving a bicycle to demonstrate Ruth was just an overgrown kid. Ruth made friends easily with the children in town, perhaps feeling he had more in common with them than the men in camp. He borrowed a bicycle from one of them and, while speeding around a corner, narrowly missed striking Dunn and Egan. He braked hard, collided with a hay wagon and was thrown to the ground. Uninjured, Ruth looked up at Dunn, grinning with embarrassment. Dunn was underwhelmed with the childish antics of his pitching star for whom he had great hopes and admonished him: "If you want to go back to the home, kid, just keep riding those bicycles."[25]

Brother Gilbert told the story of Ruth being impressed with some of his fellow players and their horsemanship and wanted to see what he could do in the saddle, even though he had never ridden a horse. To amuse themselves, some of the rookies began renting horses from a stable just outside the city limits, then ride into town and gallop past their teammates in the evening as they enjoyed some free time. Ruth managed to find the place, but as a novice was only allowed to rent a pony. During his ride, Ruth felt the need for refreshment and navigated his steed to a drugstore to buy an ice cream cone. Given his difficulty mounting and unmounting, Ruth rode right into the store and up to the soda fountain. "We don't serve horses here," said the clerk, who nevertheless sold Ruth the cone he wanted and then led the cowboy and his pony back onto the street. Brother Gilbert said his source for the tale was Pippen, the sportswriter/backup player in Fayetteville who later became sports editor of the *Baltimore News-Post*.[26] Brother Gilbert said in his memoirs anyone doubting the tale could easily confirm it with Pippen. The brother was quite familiar with Pippen, who would know firsthand the shenanigans of his roommate from Fayetteville.

Ruth was one of five pitchers in training camp younger than 21.[27] He wasn't even the youngest. Pitcher Lefty Caporel was 18. Outfielder Jack Dunn Jr., son of the manager, was also 18. Of all the babes Dunn brought to Fayetteville that spring, only one picked up the name. And Ruth, suddenly free of the regimented life at St. Mary's, was relishing his first taste of real freedom and sampling the delights it offered. Ruth was not the first baseball player to become known as Babe. At the time, Babe Adams, a right-hander for the Pittsburgh Pirates, was about to begin his sixth season as a major leaguer. George Twombly, the outfielder in camp, had a younger brother named Babe, also an outfielder, who later played two seasons for the Chicago Cubs. Other major leaguers who had been, or were about to be, given the name included Babe Doty, Babe Danzig, Babe Borton and Babe Ellison. But none of them did as much for the moniker as did Ruth.

After more than a week of watching Ruth on the diamond, Dunn was impressed with the newly christened Babe. He went so far as to say he was the most promising player he had ever seen on his club. "Ruth has all the earmarks of a great ball player," he told Linthicum of the *Sun*. "He hits like a fiend and seems to be at home in any position, despite the fact he is a left-hander." Brother Matthias, who made his players learn every position, would have smiled. Dunn said he expected to spend more time on Ruth than any other player in camp to refine his technique. "Naturally, Ruth is rough, but he will gradually lose some of the awkwardness, and I look for him to do so soon because he is a youngster who catches onto things quickly. He is a whale with the willow, and some of the drives he is making in practice [sic] would have cleared the right-field fence at Oriole Park."[28]

Ruth and the Orioles faced their first test beginning March 16 with a series of exhibition games arranged between the Orioles and the Philadelphia Phillies, the reigning National League champions and winners of the 1913 World Series. The games were to be split between Fayetteville and Philadelphia's new training grounds in Wilmington, North Carolina, along the Atlantic coast, about 90 miles to the southeast. The Orioles played like a well-oiled machine against a lineup of Philadelphia's regular players on their home field, Sunset Park. Baltimore won the first game, 7–2. For the Orioles, youngsters Bill Morrisette, Lefty Caporel and Frank Jarman pitched "superbly" and were supported well.[29] Ruth did not play. He stayed home with most of the Yanigans (rookies), who routed a team of cadets from Donaldson Military Academy by a score of 24–6. Ruth did not pitch, but played shortstop in that game and at the plate recorded a double, a triple and four runs.[30] The Orioles' second game against the Phillies was played March 18 in Fayetteville, and produced a 4–3 win for Baltimore. Brilliant outfield catches were featured along with Caporel's excellent control for the first three innings, when he let only two men reach base. Ruth then took the mound and also pitched well, but a fumbled infield drive by shortstop Claude Derrick allowed a run to score. Ruth struck out two and went 0-for-2 at the plate. The game was won in the ninth inning when Twombly stole home from second on a hard-hit single by catcher Gene Lidgate.[31] Modern scorers would give the win to Ruth.

The third game in the series was the next day in Fayetteville and Babe Ruth was outstanding as the Orioles won yet again, this time 7–6. Philadelphia took advantage of the first two Oriole pitchers, Morissette and Smoke Klingelhoefer, scoring four runs before Ruth was called in. It was 6–0 for the Phillies when Babe went to work. "His speed and benders put a halt to the merry-go-round," Linthicum of the *Sun* reported. Meanwhile, the *Wilmington Morning Star* also took note of the rookie's impressive performance, saying Ruth "pitched ball which ought to win any game."[32] Only four more Phillies reached first base, and none of them scored as the Orioles bats awakened and their fielding grew sharp. Ruth struck out two batters and again went 0-for-2 at the plate, still struggling with the first major-league pitching he was seeing. Curve balls seemed to give him the most trouble. Regardless, his work on the mound earned him another victory. Ruth's manager was not the least bit concerned about his batting woes. "Manager Dunn, after the game, said that the more he sees of Ruth the better he likes him. His showing today killed any doubt that he will not be retained during the season."[33] Attempts to play again in Wilmington on Friday and Saturday were canceled because of rain and poor field conditions. The Orioles had swept the series from the World Series champs and their new "babe" had been instrumental in that.

Bad weather, which included sleet and a bit of snow, idled the Orioles for several days and delayed their trip home to Baltimore, where Dunn learned that Oriole Park was not yet in shape to play. A couple more games were eventually played between the regulars and the Yanigans when the weather improved. In one memorable contest on March 24, the more experienced squad downed the rookies 9–1 in a game Jack Dunn called after six innings. He did so after a bizarre home run clouted by regulars' right fielder Bert Daniels. As he came to the plate, Daniels noticed Dunn's son, Jack Dunn Jr., had attracted some unwanted company in left field for the Yanigans. Some cows had begun grazing on his turf. The left fielder was preoccupied shooing them away and Daniels spotted an opportunity. He belted a hit down the left field line. Dunn was out of position and had no chance to make any sort of play, so center fielder Gus Schwarz sprinted to his right to retrieve the ball. By the time Schwarz fielded it, Daniels had crossed home plate.[34] Schwarz was released by the team a day or so later after committing a second offense of demonstrating his horse-riding skills for his teammates without permission from the manager.³⁵ Dunn Jr., formerly a star at City College, would make the final Orioles roster as a utility player, despite his bovine misadventure.

Manager Dunn contacted his old friend and silent partner in the baseball business, Connie Mack, to arrange a game for March 25 between the Orioles and Mack's Athletics at their training camp, which was also located in Wilmington. The Athletics were considered the best team in baseball, despite the recent success of the cross-town Phillies. In the previous four years, Mack's men had won three American League pennants and three World Series. They would again capture the league pennant in 1914, but lost the World Series to the Boston Braves. The Athletics featured slugger Frank "Home Run" Baker, a third baseman, who led the league in home runs the previous season with 12, and in runs-batted-in with 117. Baker was earning $8,000 for the season, the highest-paid player on his team, but well back of Ty Cobb of Detroit and Tris Speaker of Boston, who each took home $15,000. There was some Maryland pride in Baker, who was from Trappe, a small city about 70 miles southeast of Baltimore.

It has been suggested that picking Mack's Athletics for a game in spring training was part of Dunn's bid to test Ruth and also showcase him to the baseball magnate who might some day be interested in acquiring him for the Athletics.³⁶ Dunn, the talent scout, developer of talent and salesman, was always thinking ahead.

Ruth led the Orioles to yet another victory in a complete game, 6–2. "The victory was no fluke," reported Linthicum in the *Sun*. "The Birds played sensationally, hit the ball with men on bases and George Ruth, the phenomenal southpaw, who went the full nine innings, pitched brilliantly. Despite the fact that Ruth was touched up for 13 hits, he twirled a beautiful game. Not at any stages of the contest did he show any signs of nervousness.... Ruth was the real hero."³⁷ Frank Baker hit safely four times, pleasing the crowd of about 2,000. In the ninth inning, he made it to first for his fourth hit, but Ruth picked him off when he strayed too far from the bag. Babe fanned Eddie Collins and held him to a single hit. Meanwhile, Baltimore bats pounded starter Herb Pennock, who was pulled for Boardwalk Brown. The Orioles managed 10 hits and took advantage of four errors by the Athletics. In the sixth inning, Ruth recorded his first hit of the exhibition season, got to first on a sacrifice play in the sixth inning and was one of four runs to cross the plate to put the Orioles in the lead. He eventually scored. The loss for Philadelphia was their first in eight pre-season games.

Of Ruth, who proved himself to be a cool operator against the powerful Athletics, the local *Wilmington Morning Star* had this to say:

> Twirler Ruth, who handled the delivery end for the Orioles throughout the game, exploded several perfectly good rallies for the Athletics, once with the bases filled, when he deftly mixed 'em up for the batter in such a way that it was an easy out for that phenom left fielder, Twombly. Ruth, who by the way was playing back-lot baseball

in Baltimore this time last year, kept the hits of Mack's sluggers scattered throughout the game, only twice having allowed sufficient bunching to put runners across, and in other ways won the good graces of the assembled throng, striking out three men in the game. His only weakness was a slight wildness....[38]

Babe walked four batters and struck out three. He conceded later he knew nothing about the stars Baker and Collins when he faced them. "At St. Mary's we were too busy to read papers, or, if we did, to catch the significance of the sports pages. I was just beginning to find out there were two major leagues, the American and the National," he confessed in his 1948 autobiography.[39] Dunn was pleased with his star hurler. He penned a letter to Brother Gilbert in which he predicted: "This kid, Ruth, will become the greatest player of all time. Right now he is better than any youngster that I have ever seen." Dunn also asked Brother Gilbert a favor: to counsel Ruth to have nothing to do with the Federal League team that was being established in Baltimore and with which his Orioles would have to compete for players and fans.[40] Dunn had been stung when the Federal League team in Brooklyn successfully lured from him Danny Murphy, a second baseman and right fielder previously with the Philadelphia Athletics. It wouldn't be long before the Terrapins, Baltimore's Federal League team, would be after Ruth, he felt. He was right. In Ruth's 1948 autobiography, he said the Terrapins offered him a $10,000 bonus and a salary of $10,000 if he would jump to them. Ruth said he had been warned by Dunn and others that he stood the chance of being banned from major-league baseball for life if he did so.[41] So he stayed put. Dunn, his legal guardian, would have nixed a deal anyway.

On their return to Baltimore, the Orioles played a couple of exhibition games with Virginia League teams. On March 26, they defeated Portsmouth, 12–2, much to the dismay of local fans. Afterward, on their way from the ballgrounds to the ferry, a crowd of youngsters pelted the visitors with stones for a whole city block. Although several Orioles were struck, none were seriously injured.[42] In *Newport News* the next afternoon, a tenth-inning home run for the locals ended the winning streak of Baltimore. The final score was 4–3. Babe Ruth did not appear in either game. Manager Dunn was saving him for the return match on the 28th against the Athletics at Oriole Park. On game day, the *Sun* promoted the game with the headline "Baker Here Today," and in smaller type, "Ruth Will Oppose Champions." Home Run Baker was an established star of the American League and here was the kid from Baltimore sharing headlines with him. It had been a few days less than a month since George Ruth had left St. Mary's as a green, virtually unknown prospect. He was returning as Babe Ruth, a baseball star. March had been quite a month for the 19-year-old.

The crowd of about 5,000 that packed Oriole Park would be disappointed. The much-ballyhooed return match was a bust for the Orioles and their pitching prodigy making his first appearance as a professional in his hometown. The

Athletics were ready to administer some payback. The *Philadelphia Inquirer* reported: "The Athletics started in on Ruth as though determined to drive the juvenile off the rubber."[43] They pounded him for three doubles in the first inning and put two runs across the plate. Ruth was driven from the mound in the third inning, by which time the visitors had scored four runs. The Athletics won the game, 12–5, powered by the left-handed bat of Baker, who had four hits, including a double, a triple and two singles. Ruth could not solve him. Lefty Caporel relieved Ruth and fared even worse, surrendering six runs in the sixth inning. "Ruth was unable to strike his stride either in the box or at the bat," reported Linthicum in the *Sun*. He wasn't helped by three errors by shortstop Derrick, among five committed by the Orioles. At the plate he went 0-for-2. The Orioles left nine men on base, unable to get them across the plate in a generally lackluster performance for just their second loss of the spring. The game was called after eight innings because of darkness.[44] There is a reasonable chance that among those left disappointed in the crowd were his father, some boys from St. Mary's and likely Brothers Matthias and Gilbert. It was their first chance to see him with the "big" team in Baltimore.

Several exhibition games were canceled because of bad weather that lingered in Baltimore, but games against the Brooklyn Dodgers and the New York Yankees went ahead. Because of Baltimore's ban on Sunday baseball games, Dunn booked Back River Park, a field at a horse-racing track just east of the city limits, for an April 5 game against the Dodgers. About 3,000 fans caught the game played during cool, windy conditions. But they were rewarded when an aggressive Orioles squad came away with a 10–6 victory. Ruth, in one of his first outings in which he was called "Babe," was reported to look like "a million dollars" as he pitched a complete game.[45] His curve balls were particularly difficult for the Dodgers as he struck out six. At the plate, he was also effective. In his first appearance, he crushed the ball to deep right field, where 23-year-old Casey Stengel was able to collar it after a long run. Next time up, he was ready for Ruth and was playing 30 or 35 feet deeper. Babe hit the ball over his head this time, for a triple that scored two runs. Stengel, best remembered for managing the Yankees in the 1950s, when they won 10 American League pennants and 7 World Series, was an excellent fielder as a young man. He admitted many years later that he had underplayed the unknown batter Ruth. "When he hit that long fly I was embarrassed," Stengel recalled. Ruth's biographer Robert W. Creamer also penned a biography about Stengel and quoted Stengel as saying: "The kid beats us pitching and he beats us batting. That's when I first saw Ruth. I would say I was impressed."[46]

Several more games were arranged as the Orioles prepared for opening day. On March 31, the Phillies came to town and defeated Baltimore, 3–0. Ruth played the entire game April 5, leading his club past the Brooklyn Dodgers, 10–6. He struck out six and tripled. The following day, the Dodgers prevailed,

3–2. The Boston Braves downed the Orioles, 5–1, on April 9. On April 10, the Yankees—beginning their second season after changing their name from the Highlanders—came to town for a game at Oriole Park. The hometown bats were silent and errors were plenty as the visitors blanked them, 4–0. Ruth pitched all nine innings, gave up 11 hits, picked off a runner, walked 4 and had 1 strikeout. At the plate, he managed a single. For the Yankees, Fritz Maisel, the former Oriole and Baltimore-area native playing third base, was sharp at the hot corner and picked up three hits.[47]

The New York Giants of John McGraw, winners of three straight pennants in the National League, came to town April 11 for a three-game series in which Ruth saw limited duty. In the first game, which drew 5,000 fans, Ruth went in to replace his injured first baseman. The Orioles won, 2–1, to the surprise of many. The Giants came back to win, 8–2, the next day. Morrisette and Allen Russell pitched for Baltimore, while Ruth made one appearance at the plate and struck out. The third game was won by the Giants, 3–2. Ruth pitched in the final contest and did reasonably well, but he went hitless. His catcher Ben Egan would tell a story about that final game that would go down in baseball lore. Brother Gilbert shared it in his 1928 newspaper series, quoting Egan as claiming: "Babe wants to kill me every time he hears it." The Orioles were leading, 2–1, late in the game when the Giants came to bat. One man was out and there was a New York runner on first. Egan was anxious to throw out the runner he knew was a speedster. Beforehand, he had advised Ruth that if he clenched his fist in his mitt during the game, he wanted Ruth to throw him a "waste" ball so Egan had a better chance of gunning down the base runner. Ruth picked up the sign, nodded and delivered the ball right across the plate. The batter (some say it was Bob Bescher, others like Brother Gilbert claimed it was Red Murray) hit a towering drive that may have cleared the left field fence (or not, depending on the source). Hot and bewildered, Egan marched to the mound and confronted his rookie pitcher. "Didn't I signal you for a waste ball?" It was Ruth's turn to get lathered. "Yes, and that's what I gave you, a fast one, waist-high right in there, and you see the consequences of it, I hope. Get back in there and catch; I am sick of your second guessing." Ruth, the former catcher, paid little heed to Egan for the rest of the game. Later, Dunn took him aside and explained a "waste" pitch was a pitch out, and had nothing to do with a player's beltline.[48] It was all part of the steep learning curve for Dunn's babe.

With six days left until the Orioles home opener, Dunn took his crew on a quick road trip into New York and Pennsylvania, where about half the exhibition games he had arranged were rained out.

Opening day was April 21 and Baltimore continued to be unseasonably cold and wet. But the weather was the least of the worries facing Dunn as he fielded one of the most competitive teams he had ever assembled.

9

Playing to Empty Seats

It's doubtful any of the 3,000 fans attending the Giants-Orioles exhibition game on April 13, 1914, overheard the animated conversation between Babe Ruth and his catcher Ben Egan about that "waste" pitch. More likely, spectators would have heard the cheering from the crowd across 29th Street at newly finished Terrapin Park.

That same Monday afternoon, the Baltimore Terrapins of the Federal League attracted nearly 28,000 fans to their opening-day game against the Buffalo Blues. Given the park capacity of about 13,000, more spectators watched the game from their feet than from the seats. The throng was loud and happy that major-league baseball was back in the city for the first time since 1902. The Terrapins, who took their name from a turtle known as the diamondback terrapin, which is plentiful in Chesapeake Bay, began play at 3 p.m. Opening ceremonies included the governor of Maryland, Phillips Lee Goldsborough, Mayor James H. Preston of Baltimore and Federal League president James Gilmore. The crowd was reported to be the largest to ever attend a ballgame in the U.S. Northeast.[1] Stellar pitching by Jack Quinn, who had jumped from the Boston Braves of the National League, helped secure a win for the locals by a score of 3–2. Across the street, the game between the Orioles and the Giants began soon after the Terrapins took to the field. Orioles fans and Jack Dunn realized that 1914 would present a serious challenge to the minor-league franchise.

The Federal League, like predecessor rebel leagues, sought to break up the exclusive monopoly that professional baseball had become in its four decades. The first came in 1877 when the International Association was established, a year after the National League came into existence. The challenger failed four years later, partly due to predations by the National League, which scooped up its best teams. In 1882, the American Association was the next to fight league supremacy, effectively touting Sunday games and beer in the ballpark. It lasted a decade and Baltimore was a member for its entire run. Interloper leagues the Union Association and the Players' League each lasted a single year, 1884 and 1890, respectively. When the AA died after the 1891 season, Baltimore was among four of its teams picked up by the National League. However, the Orioles were dropped after their poorly attended 1902 season, by which time the American League had been established. The National League, weary of baseball wars, finally agreed to a peace treaty and let its latest rival survive. But a new battle loomed. The Federal League was founded in 1913 as a six-team minor-league loop. It expanded to eight cities for 1914, declared itself a major league and raided National and American league clubs for players. Federal League owners ignored the reserve clause tying players to their teams until their teams no longer wanted them, as well as rules that protected their designated territory from competitors to help create a virtual business monopoly.[2] In Baltimore, especially, the Federal League offered hope for a return to the big leagues. One of the key figures in the Terrapins was Ned Hanlon, the former Orioles manager who had led the Orioles to three National League pennants. Hanlon moved to Brooklyn, where he was manager until 1905. He then purchased the Montreal Royals of the International League and moved them to Baltimore, keeping the league affiliation and reviving the Orioles name. In 1909, he sold the Orioles and their ballpark to his former Brooklyn pitcher Jack Dunn. Hanlon wanted Baltimore back in major-league ball and he became the biggest shareholder in the Terrapins, Baltimore's Federal League franchise, who debuted in 1914.[3] The new league proved to be reasonably competitive, drawing respectable crowds and featuring a close 1914 pennant race. Aside from Baltimore and Buffalo, the other "Fed" cities that season were Indianapolis, Chicago, Brooklyn, Kansas City, Pittsburgh and St. Louis.[4]

For 12 years, baseball fans in Baltimore had resented the loss of major-league ball and the newspapers played on that sentiment to promote the Terrapins and their inaugural game. The *Baltimore Sun* said the new team provided a chance to right a wrong: "Baltimoreans are awake to the fact that their only hope to bring big league ball back to this city is to support the Federals. Organized ball has held a cold shoulder toward this city for several years and until the Federals entered the field the older majors declared Baltimore a poor baseball town."[5]

The opening series for the Terrapins was a three-day affair, but after their 3–2 win on April 13, rain delayed the second game with Buffalo until April 17, when 4,000 fans saw the Blues down the home nine, 4–3. The following day, a Saturday, 14,000 fans turned out to see the Terrapins lose again, this time 4–2. Attendance for the series stood at nearly 46,000, leaving team president Carrol Rasin, his fellow directors and Baltimore baseball lovers optimistic that major-league ball was back to stay.

Opening day for the Orioles came on Tuesday, April 21, against the Buffalo Bisons, and Mayor Preston and International League president Edward Barrow were on hand. Pitcher Dave Danforth "never pitched a better game," reported Linthicum in the *Sun* as the Orioles shut out the Bisons, 7–0.[6]

Unlike the extensive front-page treatment given the Terrapins opener, his report was relegated to page 8. Ruth did not play. Center fielder Birdie Cree and first baseman Ed Gleichmann, along with catcher Ben Egan, accounted for eight hits, one of them Egan's sixth-inning homer. No crowd count was provided, but the *Buffalo Commercial* newspaper reporter counted fewer than 1,500 fans in Oriole Park, the poorest opening day crowd ever recorded in Baltimore.[7] President Barrow "was apparently surprised at the skimpy attendance. He could scarcely believe his eyes." The Buffalo story added that "the teams seemed to be depressed by the slim attendance and the game was anything but brilliant."

Across 29th Street that very same day, the Terrapins drew nearly 3,800 spectators for a game against the Brooklyn Tip-Tops. The Terrapins trailed, 2–1, until third baseman Runt Walsh belted a ball over the left field fence to tie the game in the ninth inning. In the tenth, pitcher Jack Quinn, who had fanned seven Tip-Tops, put the first pitch he saw over the same fence for a walk-off homer and a 3–2 win. Delirious fans swarmed the field and hoisted Baltimore's new star player onto their shoulders.[8]

The following day, for the Orioles' second game in the opening series, Ruth took the mound. Fewer than 200 fans were there to see the local lad's first start as a professional. The signs were growing more ominous for Jack Dunn and his Orioles. This was the smallest crowd ever to witness an International League game in the city. Ruth was unfazed, however, and his play was outstanding. *Sun* sportswriter Jesse Linthicum didn't mince words: "Gilt-edge pitching by George Ruth, Jack Dunn's sensational southpaw, coupled with brilliant fielding by his teammates, enabled the Birds to apply another coat of whitewash to the Buffalo Bisons yesterday at Oriole Park, 6 to 0."[9] Babe struck out four batters, walked four and, although he allowed six hits, he buckled down and kept them from scoring. At the plate, he had two hits. The shutout was an auspicious start for the rookie. But it was barely noticed in the hometown. Meanwhile, Dunn released Lefty Caporal, leaving him with Ruth and two other left-handers, Dave Danforth and Ensign Cottrell. It's more than likely some of the boys and brothers from St. Mary's were in the tiny crowd to witness the debut of their star alumnus. Meanwhile, across the street, the Terrapins drew more than 4,000 fans who cheered a satisfying come-from-behind 9–8 victory over Brooklyn.[10]

The final contest of the Orioles series opener was April 23, when fewer than 100 fans saw the Bisons win, 5–3. Three errors by the Orioles helped the visitors score three runs while Lefty Cottrell was pulled after two innings, replaced by Frank Jarman and finally, Bill Morrisette. Buffalo pitcher Fred Beebe fanned 10 Oriole batters and didn't surrender a run until the eighth inning. In that inning, Ruth came in as a pinch hitter and tripled to deep center, scoring a run and then crossing the plate himself.[11] Across the street, the Terrapins defeated Buffalo, who were back in town for two more games, by a score of 4–3. Paid admission was 3,000. The following day, the Terrapins administered a 10–4 thrashing of the Blues to the delight of 2,000 fans.

After their April 24 win over Buffalo, the Terrapins hit the road for Chicago, Kansas City, St. Louis, Indianapolis and Buffalo. They were due back in town on May 14. Dunn and his Orioles were relieved to be the only professional baseball in Baltimore for more than two weeks. They hoped to do better at the box office. Linthicum of the *Sun* noted the breathing room the Terrapin road trip provided the Orioles. "Manager Dunn expects to draw well during the coming week. With the Federals on the road, the local magnate will give local fans an opportunity to see the best International League team that ever represented Baltimore in action against the other flag contenders. The attendance last week was unusually small, but Dunn looks for better support."[12] The next day, Linthicum was blunt in his own assessment:

> The following week will be a crucial one for Jack Dunn. The attendance in the first series with Buffalo was unusually small, fewer than 1,500 witnessing the four games played. With the Terrapins on the road, it will be determined if the Birds will be a drawing card here. While it was expected the invasion of the Federal League in Baltimore would cut Dunn's attendance, few fans thought the local magnate would be dealt such a blow.[13]

Babe Ruth was enjoying his first money from playing the game he loved. By the end of April, Dunn doubled his pay to $1,200, or $200 a month, for the six-month season.[14] Dunn provided further raises as his rookie hurler kept winning games so as not to lose him to other teams, particularly those in the Federal League. Given his sharply curtailed gate receipts, the added expense further hurt Dunn's bottom line. Back home in Baltimore, Babe lived with his father and paid repeated visits to his other home, St. Mary's "whenever time permitted," as Brother Gilbert later recalled.[15] Ruth found a ready audience of admirers at the school and awed the boys there with his tales of places he had been and things he had done.

One day soon after the Orioles began their season, Ruth took advantage of a rainout to purchase an Indian motorcycle for $115. At the time, the Hendee Manufacturing Company of Springfield, Massachusetts, was advertising its latest "motocycles" for anywhere from $200 to $325 new, so he likely acquired a used one.[16] That same month, the classified advertisements in the *Baltimore Sun* carried listings for used 1913 Indians at $115 for the four-horsepower unit and $140 for a seven-horsepower, twin-cylinder model.[17] Babe likely bought it at a bicycle shop, because exclusive dealers in the fledgling motorcycle industry were rare and many bicycle retailers had begun carrying them as a sideline. A biographer or two (including Babe himself in his 1948 life story) said his first purchase was a bicycle. Sears, Roebuck and Company, for instance, sold them for $12 to $24. But given his sudden wealth, his need for speed and perhaps after seeing one in a bicycle shop, Babe was soon astride the Indian, his first real possession. He couldn't wait to show the boys and Brothers Matthias, Paul, Alban and Herman at St. Mary's, and Brother Gilbert over at Mount St. Joseph.

Brother Gilbert clearly recalled Babe and his Indian. In his memoirs, Brother Gilbert said that once Ruth learned how to start his mechanical steed, the young man showed more interest in the throttle than its brakes, terrorizing others on Baltimore's streets. Babe made a particularly inelegant entrance to St. Mary's one day that Brother Gilbert described in detail. Brother Matthias was inside the gate and about to remove some "road apples" freshly deposited on the laneway by the mailman's horse. Up raced Ruth, who narrowly missed the equine souvenirs and awkwardly skidded to a halt. In so doing, he fell off his mount and into a puddle left by recent rain. Brother Gilbert quoted Brother Matthias as saying Ruth covered "three points of the compass with each revolution of the wheels" on his way up the lane. Brother Matthias offered to have Ruth's wet trousers laundered and dried, but the hell-driver was more interested in showing off his bike to the boys. In the schoolyard, play stopped and an admiring throng quickly surrounded Babe, with a torrent of questions and hands anxious to touch his mechanical marvel. "'Lefty' was back with a live bike … the surge was on," Brother Gilbert wrote. "No swarm of bees ever followed its queen in a more adoring formation." Ruth took some of the boys for short rides until interrupted by the supper bell. The show-and-tell ride resumed until 8:30 p.m., when the boys were summoned for evening prayers, some of them late reporting to chapel. Ruth eventually gave the machine to Brother Matthias for safekeeping and storage in a corner of the school's machine shop.

For Ruth, the motorcycle was the perfect way to express his newfound freedom. When he wasn't at the ballpark, he buzzed around city streets, instilling fear among motorists and pedestrians alike. He took others, including his sister Mamie, for rides around the block. Luckily, despite his rudimentary driving skills, Ruth survived. It didn't matter what he drove, he preferred to do so at a fast clip, a trait that saw him involved in several car crashes when he upgraded to four wheels.

St. Mary's was never far from his mind. It remained a touchstone for him and he was always thinking of the boys there. Early in his days with the Orioles, Ruth went into Dunn's office and asked for six passes to the next game. "What do you want with six?" Dunn asked. "I want to bring in some friends," Ruth explained. Sure enough, six boys from St. Mary's were the guests of their big friend.[18]

The Orioles welcomed Rochester for three games beginning with a double-header on April 27. Babe pinch-hit late in the first game, but failed to get a hit. Rochester won, 3–2. He pitched in the second game, shutting out the visitors for five innings. The Hustlers scored in the sixth and seventh and Baltimore replied with a single in the eighth, but fell again to the visitors, this time 2–1. Ruth struck out six men, walked two and allowed five hits. At the plate he was 0-for-3, his hitting woes continuing. The following day, Rochester prevailed, 5–2, to sweep the series. The next day, a new version of the Montreal Royals appeared at Oriole Park. This time it was Baltimore's turn to administer a three-game sweep. In the third meeting, on May 1, Ruth was called in to pitch in the tenth inning, when the clubs were locked in a 4–4 battle. He relieved Cottrell, who had replaced starter Morrisette. Ruth didn't allow a run in that inning or the next. In the eleventh, with Ben Egan on base, Ruth connected for a hard double to left field to bring Egan home and win the game. Linthicum in the *Sun* hailed Ruth as the game's "hero."[19] His bat had shown some life. The following day, another Canadian team was the opposition. A three-game series with the Toronto Maple Leafs began with a doubleheader, which attracted an unexpectedly large crowd of 4,000. Ruth pitched the first game in which the Leafs were downed, 8–3. He was a bit wild to start, but soon settled down to work. He allowed only five hits and struck out seven batters. Nine Toronto batters were left on base. At the plate, Ruth tripled in the second inning when Toronto was ahead, 2–0. His blast to left center field brought in two runs to tie the game. Only one more Toronto run crossed the plate while the Orioles plated six more. "George Ruth was again the hero," Linthicum wrote in the *Sun*.[20] Baltimore bats struggled in the second game, which Toronto won, 4–3. A Sunday exhibition game at Back Bay Park against the Philadelphia Athletics featured an exciting come-from-behind Baltimore victory, 8–7, a game for which Dunn rested many of his regulars, including Ruth. The next day, Baltimore shut out Toronto, 10–0, to take the series and conclude the season-opening home stand during which they won eight games and lost four.

The first road trip began May 6 in Buffalo and the experience was a real eye-opener for the Babe, a smorgasbord of new adventures. The big kid was on the road with his team for 29 days as they visited all seven other cities in the league. He saw Niagara Falls, then left the United States for the bright lights of Toronto and the charms of French-speaking Montreal before returning to Rochester. The Orioles then played Newark, Jersey City and Providence. Babe's world was expanding—and he couldn't be happier. In Buffalo on May 7, Ruth surrendered 8 hits but won the game, 5–3, in 11 innings. In Toronto four days later, only 500 fans braved unseasonably cold weather to see the Maple Leafs edge the Orioles and Ruth, 2–1. Babe had four strikeouts but went 0-for-3 at the plate. After a rainout, Baltimore swept the Leafs, 13–2, on May 14.

Montreal provided more than just another culture and language; it produced a terrifying episode for the Orioles. On the way from their hotel to

Atwater Park for the opener of a four-game series, a fire broke out in their streetcar. A fuse had blown in the older-style electric car along Windsor Street and passengers scrambled to get out. Pitcher Cottrell scraped his ankle and two other players had cuts and bruises. Dunn had planned to start Cottrell in the game, but instead sent Allen "Rubber Arm" Russell to the mound. The Orioles shook off the incident and won the game, 9–3. The following day, Ruth pitched, but was unimpressive, allowing five hits as Montreal won, 5–2. He went 0-for-4 at the plate. The Orioles won twice more in Montreal and, by the time they moved on to Rochester, were sitting atop the International League. They won two out of four games in Rochester before heading south to Newark. The series opened in Newark with a doubleheader and the well-rested Ruth appeared in both games, which attracted a total of 11,000 fans. In the first, he was relieved in the fourth inning with the bases loaded after giving up seven hits and striking out two. The Orioles still managed a 9–4 victory. Unfazed at his young star's poor outing, Dunn had him start the second game and Ruth shut out the Indians, 1–0, in 11 innings. He allowed five hits and collected one himself. On May 26, Newark edged Baltimore, 7–6, to salvage a game in the series.

The Orioles stayed in New York City when they played in Newark and Jersey City, most often at the Forrest Hotel on West 49th Street, just steps from Broadway. By the time he arrived in New York, Ruth was getting used to spending nights in train sleepers, checking in and out of hotels, tipping waiters, studying menus and enjoying a life far removed from the drab routine of St. Mary's. Ruth biographer Robert W. Creamer tells the story of how one night Oriole outfielder George Twombly returned to the hotel to find Babe sitting on the curb near a lamppost.

"What are you doing?" Twombly asked the 19-year-old hurler. "I'm waiting for a girl," said Ruth. "What girl?" Twombly pressed. "I don't know," Ruth replied, looking in the direction of Broadway. "I'm just waiting. The boys at the reform school said if you're in New York and you want a woman, all you have to do is wait for a streetwalker to come along." Twombly was stunned. "You better get in the hotel," he advised the testosterone-charged innocent. "You better not let Dunnie catch you out here waiting for a streetwalker."[21]

The Orioles moved on to Providence where they won two of four games and then to Jersey City where they won three. Babe performed unevenly. By the time the Orioles headed for home, despite having won 15 of their 25 road games, they had slipped to second place.[22]

At home, the Orioles hoped for better crowds. They drew well on the road and had become one of the top teams in the league. The Terrapins began a 22-game road trip on June 1, so their ballpark across 29th Street would be silent until the end of the month. The Orioles' home stand extended until June 29, four days after the return of the Terrapins. The Providence Grays, sometimes called the Clamdiggers or Clams, were the opposition on June 4, when fewer than 300 fans appeared at Oriole Park. Ruth pitched well, fanning seven batters and allowing five hits before the umpire called the game in the eighth inning on account of darkness. It was only 5:30 p.m., but it had started raining. With the score 2–1 for Providence, Manager Dunn protested, arguing a rain delay should have been called instead because within five minutes the rain stopped. However, the call stood. In the next two days, the Orioles won 7–6, then 3–2 and 6–2 in a doubleheader.

The Orioles made a quick trip to Jersey City for a doubleheader against the Skeeters on June 7 and took both games, 5–2 and 4–1. Ruth pitched in the second game, recording five strikeouts, and he singled and scored. Back in Baltimore, the same teams went at it again the next day, with the Orioles winning again, this time 3–2. Ernie Shore, making his debut on the pitching mound for the Orioles, allowed seven hits and fanned four batters. Dunn had discovered him during spring training in North Carolina. At six-foot-four, 23-year-old Shore was the tallest man on the team. On June 10, Ruth earned a 4–2 win, striking out four Skeeters and allowing eight runs. This was the ninth win in a row for Baltimore and when they defeated Newark, 6–5, the following day, they reclaimed first place. On June 12, Shore pitched his second win, downing Newark again, 3–2, before 5,000 spectators, many lured by a special promotion. Dunn admitted schoolchildren for free and pronounced the idea a success worthy of repeating. The next day, the Orioles extended their winning streak to 13 games as they took both ends of a doubleheader from Newark, 3–2 and 11–2. Ruth worked the first game and held the reigning International League champions to six hits, not surrendering a run until the seventh inning. He was 0-for-2 at the plate as his hitting struggles returned.

Rochester ended the Orioles' winning streak on June 15 with a 3–2 victory. Baltimore lost two more games and won one before the Hustlers left town. Ruth was pulled in the second inning of a 6–0 loss on June 17. He allowed three hits and five runs to score and was replaced by Shore. That same day, Jack Dunn warned that unless local fans provided greater support for the Orioles, he would transfer the team to Richmond, Virginia, about 150 miles to the south. Businessmen there had offered him $62,500 for 49 percent of the stock in his club, it had been reported.[23] In the meantime, Dunn was demanding organized baseball create a third major league consisting of the four strongest teams of the International and American leagues as a way to fight the Federal League. He also wanted the National and American leagues banned from drafting players from other leagues. Dunn said he would remain in Baltimore if the new league was created and the draft eliminated. If not, he was moving to Richmond.[24] He seemed to have won his case when the *Baltimore Sun* carried a news report from New York saying that the governing National Commission had decided to place the Orioles in a newly created major league.²⁵ The Commission was a three-member body that ran baseball before the commissioner system was introduced, comprised in 1914 of chairperson August Hermann, president of the Cincinnati Reds, American League president Ban Johnson and National League president John Tener. The paper celebrated with the headline "Orioles Celebrate Major League Debut." But the joy was short-lived and misplaced. *Sporting News* was dismissive of Dunn's threat to move the franchise, saying it was based on "assertions emanating from certain excitable scribes." The story, it said, was "a pure and simple yarn that originated by the opposition forces which would be tickled to death to scare Dunn.... While an alleged offer of $62,500 from a Richmond, Va. Syndicate may bear a semblance of truth, it can be taken for granted that President [Edward G.] Barrow [of the International League] will not allow a single change in the International League circuit."²⁶ Many months earlier, Barrow had threatened to seek major-league status for the International League and to buy out the financial interest major-league teams held in his league's clubs.²⁷ In late July, however, the New York State Supreme Court upheld the reserve clause of major-league baseball, ruling that the game was not trade within the meaning of the Sherman Act and major-league ball amounted to a benign monopoly.²⁸ The decision dampened enthusiasm to create another league. And International League owners rejected any move by Dunn to Richmond.

Montreal was next into Baltimore and won the first two games: the opener, 3–2, before fewer than 600 fans and the second, 6–3, dropping the Orioles to second place. The Orioles recovered to take both ends of a doubleheader on June 20 before a crowd of 5,000. The strong attendance that day may have been in response to Dunn's threats to bolt, talk of pending major-league status or, more likely, cut-rate ticket prices. It was said Dunn was losing $1,000 a day on the ball club by June and his losses were on track to exceed $20,000 for the season. He had borrowed $10,000 from Connie Mack of the Philadelphia Athletics to buy the team, coupled with his own life's savings, and repaying the debt was becoming difficult. Mack needed the money because competition from the Federal League in Philadelphia was hurting his operation. Dunn was growing desperate.²⁹ He was not a wealthy man, and the battle with the Terrapins to maintain the interest of Baltimoreans in the product he fielded was draining him. Dunn was actively exploring his options.

The first game of a series against the Toronto Maple Leafs was rained out, but on June 23 Ruth went to the mound and shut out the visitors, 3–0. He recorded nine strikeouts in what the *Sun*'s Linthicum described as "his most brilliant game."³⁰ Toronto managed five hits but six Maple Leafs were stranded on base. Ruth's hitting woes returned, as he went 0-for-3 at the plate. The same teams split a doubleheader the next day and on June 25 the Orioles overcame a seven-run deficit to win, 13–8. No attendance figure was given, but it was rumored to be just 20 paying fans.³¹ Ruth went to the mound in the fifth inning and allowed a single run and three hits the rest of the way. He struck out four and in his single plate appearance walked and then scored. The very next day, the Orioles squandered a seven-run lead and were edged, 10–9, by Buffalo. On June 27, the *Baltimore Sun* dismissed recent reports in New York newspapers that the games that day would be the last for the Orioles.[32] In the doubleheader Baltimore defeated the Bisons, 4–3 and 10–5. Ruth went hitless in the first game, but in the second, he recorded his second victory in a week, tossing a nine-hitter and striking out five.

Despite his dire financial straits, Dunn raised Ruth's salary to $1,800 during June, triple the amount Ruth signed for in February. Dunn was known for generous payrolls and treating his players well, so it wasn't out of character. The move brought his rookie's pay more in line with the money Dunn was paying his veteran players and might fend off feelers being extended by the Federal League.[33] For their part, the Terrapins denied they were after Ruth. "We have agreed not to touch any players under contract to Jack Dunn," said one official.[34] Besides, they had built Terrapin Park on land leased from former Oriole owner Ned Hanlon, the biggest shareholder of the Terrapins, and Hanlon had instructed Terrapin management not to tamper with the Orioles.[35] Dunn's concern lingered, and by July he further boosted Ruth's pay to $500 a month, or $3,000 for the season.[36] Besides, Dunn figured, if he had to conduct a fire sale of talent to stay in business, Ruth would be one of his most valuable assets. Ruth's play had been at times brilliant, but most often inconsistent—on the mound and at the plate. He'd been knocked out of the box as early as the second inning and pulled in the eighth after allowing 14 hits and blowing a 6–1 lead on June 1. By the end of the month he had appeared in 21 games and his record was 11–7.[37] At the plate, he recorded eight hits in 41 times at bat, with a double and three triples, for a batting average a bit shy of .200.[38]

On June 27, Baltimore fans faced a stark choice about which of its ball teams to patronize. Both the Terrapins and Orioles scheduled doubleheaders starting at 2 p.m. This was typical of what faced Dunn and his Orioles all season. The teams played home games on the same 18 dates between April 21 and September 26. For the June 27 doubleheaders, the Terrapins attracted nearly 11,000 fans as they defeated Brooklyn, 8–4 and 2–1. At Oriole Park, Dunn's club won both games, 4–3 and 10–5, but no crowd count was made public. The New York Yankees played a Sunday exhibition game against the Orioles the next day at Back River Park, which attracted about 1,500 fans. The score was 1–1 when the game was called after six innings on account of darkness. Ruth did not play. Two days later, the Orioles shut out the Bisons, 5–0, before the smallest crowd of the season, despite free admission for ladies. Again, no numbers were given. A quick trip to Jersey City on July 2 yielded a 12-inning, 3–0 shutout of the Dragons.

By Friday, July 3, Dunn had had enough and realized his only means of survival was to sell his stars. The proposed move to Richmond was off and he was staying put. The Orioles were sitting atop the International League, six games ahead of Rochester, and his top players, including Ruth, had drawn the interest of other teams. Outfielders Birdie Cree and George Twombly were terrific hitters, shortstop Claude Derrick was outstanding in his position and rookie pitcher Ernie Shore was quickly making a name for himself. "All eyes just now are on Jack Dunn, the manager of the Baltimore International League team," *Sporting Life* reported on July 4. "Dunn's business in Baltimore has got to the point where it is practically nil and it would not occasion any surprise if he sold out. He is quoted as saying he would sell his star players to the White Sox."[39] The publication went on to suggest if Dunn could not live up to his contracts with players, they could go wherever they pleased—including Federal League clubs. It suggested that Ruth, "said to be the best left-handed pitcher toiling in the minor leagues this year," would be a good fit with the Tip-Tops in Brooklyn. Meanwhile, a Cincinnati team official was seen at an Orioles game and the Reds were said to be interested in a package of players including Ruth.

Dunn knew Babe was his prize and he first tried to offer him to his business partner Connie Mack of the Philadelphia Athletics. At Dunn's invitation, Mack attended the June 13 games the Orioles played in Newark, when Ruth shut out the Skeeters, 1–0, after being pulled in the previous game. "He is everything you say he is," Mack reportedly told Dunn afterward. "In fact he's worth more money than you're asking." But Mack couldn't afford to add to his own roster, even at the $10,000 Dunn was willing to accept for both Ruth and Shore. Tough competition from the Federal League soon forced Mack to sell off his own players to stay afloat.[40] Mack was on his way to losing $60,000 in 1914.[41] J. J. Lannin, the new owner of the American League's Boston Red Sox, was interested, however. He had lent Dunn

J. J. Lannin, owner of the Boston Red Sox, acquired Babe Ruth and several other players in 1914 to improve his club and help financially strapped Jack Dunn, owner of the Baltimore Orioles. Dunn was struggling to compete against the upstart Baltimore Terrapins of the rival Federal League that year, who outdrew his Orioles. Lannin later decided he was too much of a baseball fan to be an owner and sold the team to New York theater impresario Harry Frazee (Library of Congress).

9. Playing to Empty Seats

$3,000 to meet his payroll the previous month and the two men got along well. On July 3 and 4, the Red Sox were 50 miles away from Baltimore for two doubleheader games in Washington. Lannin and Dunn agreed to meet at the Ebbett House Hotel in Washington to see if they could strike a deal.

On July 2, the Orioles visited Jersey City, winning 3–0, and returned home for a July 4 doubleheader against Providence. Ruth pitched in the first game that morning, before 5,000 fans. He notched the win as the Orioles edged the Grays, 4–3. He struck out seven and hit a double. At some point, Babe asked Dunn for the rest of the day off. Dunn, his mind preoccupied with potential transactions, agreed, but wanted to know Ruth's plans. "Oh, I'm going out to St. Mary's to play a little ball," came the reply. "It's just an amateur game." Dunn was somewhat startled, but still able to joke about the unusual request. "Amateur?" he scoffed. "They're a lot of professionals out there!"[42] Dunn understood how important Ruth's former schoolmates and teachers were to him. Ruth was in the school's big yard that afternoon playing the game he loved, in the place he loved, with the people he loved. Now filled out to 183 pounds, he also gave the boys a talk about the importance of staying in good condition for an athlete. Ruth said he had promised Brother Paul he wouldn't smoke much. "At first I smoked, but soon I cut it out entirely." He had a rapt audience among his young admirers. Likely some the Brothers listened in and smiled. It had been just four months since he said goodbye to everyone and walked out the big iron gates at the school. Ruth had a fine time.

Newark was the last team to visit before the Orioles left for another road trip. By July 6, rumors swirled around Baltimore that the New York Yankees had offered Dunn $25,000 for Ruth, outfielder Birdie Cree, first baseman Ed Gleichmann and third baseman Ezra Midkiff. Dunn insisted the story was "without foundation."[43] But the next day, it was learned that Dunn sold Cree back to the Yankees, his former team. Dunn declined to reveal the sale price, which included an outfielder from New York, but the *Sun* said it was $5,000.[44] Cincinnati was looking at Derrick and Twombly and Boston was interested in Ruth, Shore and Gleichmann, the papers said. The *Sun*, despite being a booster of the Terrapins, expressed sympathy for what Dunn was going through:

> No one can blame Dunn for selling any of his players who will bring him money enough to tide him over this season. The year is a bad one in baseball, to begin with, and the Federals have hit organized baseball a terrific blow. Of course, organized baseball does not like to admit that the Feds have caused the slightest damage, but they have, just the same. Dunn, a part of organized baseball, has lost a great deal of money at the gate through competition with the Terrapins. His attendance has been very poor and his payroll has been larger than during any previous season.

Twombly and Derrick were sold to the Cincinnati Reds shortly before noon on July 8, but still played that day in the Orioles' 1–0 loss to Newark.

Paid attendance was 231. Neither Twombly nor Derrick managed a hit. The sale of the first three Orioles had produced $23,000 for Dunn, with $8,000 of that amount paid for Cree.[45] The loss of the latter from Dunn's payroll helped because he was believed to be the highest-paid player in the minor leagues. Cincinnati was expected to trade Derrick to the Chicago Cubs.

On July 9, only a "few fans" saw Newark edge the Orioles, 7–5. Ruth played in left field as Dunn shuffled his lineup to deal with the loss of outfielders Cree and Twombly. Ruth doubled and scored.[46] The following day, Newark shut out the Orioles, 8–0, and Ruth was again in left field. His bat was silent. It marked his last appearance with the Orioles. That night, Ruth, Shore and catcher Ben Egan were sold to the Boston Red Sox for $25,000 (some reports said $20,000, others, $30,000). Dunn's talks with Joe Lannin in Washington had borne fruit.

Babe Ruth had been a minor leaguer for less than three months. He had shown some flash as a pitcher, but he remained inconsistent on the mound and at the plate. His only home run was in Fayetteville during spring training. And his hometown had virtually ignored him.

All that would change before long. Ruth would become the greatest slugger baseball had ever seen and a terrific gate attraction wherever he went as he helped rescue baseball from some very dark days that lay ahead.

10

First Steps on the Big Stage

Babe Ruth was dumbstruck when he learned he'd been sold to Boston that summer of 1914. The revelation came in Dunn's office on July 9 as the owner explained the transaction to Ruth, Ernie Shore and Ben Egan. Dunn said they were to report to Boston on July 11 and they'd be accompanied on the train by Orioles secretary Bill Wicks, who was to ensure they were not intercepted by any Federal League team operatives. Dunn said he was counting on the players to help him complete the deal without complications, noting he had treated them fairly and asked for the same in return.

Sensing the young man's bewilderment, Dunn kept Ruth behind after dismissing Shore and Egan and wishing them good luck. Dunn explained that his financial situation forced him to sell off players. Hadn't Babe noticed the poor attendance, he asked. In a bid to cushion the blow for his greatest find, Dunn explained he was in line for a nice raise. Ruth had started at $200 a month, was boosted to $350 soon after the season began and most recently had been earning $500. He'd be paid $625 in Boston, Dunn said.[1] The manager expressed confidence his prodigy would do well in the major leagues and that further pay increases lay ahead.

At age 19, Ruth was already earning far beyond anything he could have imagined while toiling in the tailor shop at St. Mary's. In the Baltimore classifieds at that time, tailors were being sought for $60 a month, a sausage maker about the same. Across the northeast, unionized carpenters were earning from $20 to $25 a week.[2] In Boston, he'd earn 6 to 10 times that amount. Baseball had already produced good money for Babe, and if he continued to do well, untold wealth could be his.

Money was not something he cared about as much as his friends and his home base at St. Mary's, however. His roots were in Baltimore. Aside from playing for the Orioles, he still played games for the school, sometimes on the same day. Brothers Matthias, Paul, Alban, Herman and Gilbert were among his touchstones. Ruth knew nothing about Boston and had never been there. He was apprehensive and far from happy at this turn of events.

That same evening, Babe shared the news of his departure with the

Brothers at St. Mary's and spoke to some of the boys before heading to his father's place downtown, where he began packing his things.³ Other players would have rejoiced at becoming a major leaguer, but he was terribly conflicted. On Saturday morning, July 11, the threesome and their keeper detrained in Boston at Back Bay Station and, after checking in at the Brunswick Hotel, went for breakfast at nearby Lander's Coffee Shop. The story goes that their waitress that morning was pretty, dark-haired, 17-year-old Helen Woodford, from South Boston. She caught Babe's eye instantly. She was the third oldest of 10 children born to Michael Woodford and Joanna Brien (sometime spelled Breen), who immigrated to the United States in 1888 from their native Newfoundland, Britain's colony that wouldn't join Canada until 1949.⁴ Her father was a laborer. Whether it was love at first sight or something that developed over a short time, the always-hungry ballplayer became a regular and he and the waitress soon became an item. Babe had his first girlfriend.⁵

At Fenway Park, Ruth, Shore and Egan were introduced to hard-nosed Red Sox manager Bill Carrigan. The solidly built, red-haired catcher from Maine was only five-foot-nine, and the newcomers, all more than six feet tall, soon realized he was all business. He was known as Rough Carrigan for his aggressive play, and as manager he was demanding, but not demeaning. He engendered respect among his players and the newcomers appreciated the quiet authority he exercised, especially the undisciplined Ruth. "Carrigan was nice to me and told me early, 'I hear you like to step out, Babe. But you play fair with me and I'll play fair with you,'" Ruth recalled in his 1948 autobiography.⁶ In the 1928 version of his life story, Ruth dubbed Carrigan "one of the finest chaps I ever knew, and one of the best coaches of young pitchers there is in the game. With the Red Sox I really began to learn a little baseball."⁷ Many years later, Ruth went even further, saying Carrigan was the best manager for whom he ever played.⁸

The Red Sox were in sixth place when Ruth, Shore and Egan met the 31-year-old Carrigan, but only five and a half games behind the American League-leading Philadelphia Athletics of Connie Mack. Right away, Carrigan wanted to see what Ruth could do. He told the new lefty he would pitch that same day against the Cleveland Naps. Carrigan would catch, having been alerted that Ruth would need a steady hand to guide him. Babe got off to a good start, showing his baseball smarts in the first inning and wowing the crowd of 11,000. Leadoff batter Jack Graney managed a single off Ruth and advanced to second on a ground ball collected by Steve Yerkes, who threw to first baseman Hal Janvin for the out. The next batter was right fielder Shoeless Joe Jackson, who singled to short center field just in front of Tris Speaker. Speaker, who had a strong arm, collared the ball and fired it toward home. Graney saw the incoming throw and held up at third, as Jackson rounded first and headed for second. Ruth cut off the throw and fired the ball to Yerkes.

10. First Steps on the Big Stage

Jackson retreated to first as Yerkes threw to Carrigan, who tagged out Graney at the plate. It was an exciting play and the rookie pitcher had contributed like a veteran. Soon after, Ruth picked off Jackson, who was "napping" at first base to get out of the inning without a run.[9] Ruth demonstrated an alertness to what was happening around him on the base paths that was unexpected in such a young player. His baseball instincts first noticed and honed by Brother Matthias at St. Mary's were on full display. Ruth didn't allow a run until a single tally in the fourth inning. He gave up five scattered hits while recording one strikeout, but went hitless. In the seventh, he faltered, as Cleveland connected for three singles and scored two runs to tie the game, 3–3. He turned the ball over to lefty Dutch Leonard, who kept the Naps from any further scoring. Speaker drove in Scott in the bottom of the seventh for the winning run and Ruth was credited with the win. In the *Boston Globe*, Tim Murnane, a former first baseman in the National League and the first pro player to become a sportswriter, called Ruth "a natural ball player…. He has a natural delivery, fine control and a curve ball that bothers the batsmen, but has room for improvement and will undoubtedly become a fine pitcher under the care of Manager Carrigan." A sub-headline on his story read "Southpaw Displays High Class." In his game notes, Murnane said when Ruth first came to the plate, he "received a perfect ovation." Overall, it was an impressive start for the young man from Baltimore.

Years later, Carrigan recalled that first outing for his new hurler in an interview with *Boston Record* writer Joe Cashman. "If I remember," Carrigan said, "Babe was crude in spots. Every so often he served up a fat pitch or bad pitch when he shouldn't have. But he showed a lot of baseball savvy…. Anybody could see he'd quickly develop into a standout with a little more experience. He had a barrel of stuff, his speed was blinding, and his ball was alive."[10]

Ernie Shore picked up a 2–1 win over Cleveland the next day, throwing a two-hitter. On July 16, Ruth again started, but was knocked out after three innings in a 5–2 loss to Detroit. Shore's second start came July 22, a 6–2 win over the St. Louis Browns in which he struck out five and allowed seven hits. Right-hander Shore had earned the one open spot in the Red Sox rotation while Carrigan's other righties, Rube Foster, Hugh Bedient and Joe Wood, were battling injuries and inconsistency.[11] Dutch Leonard and Ray Collins, the other starters, were both lefties, so Ruth was the odd man out. Shore also had fewer rough edges in his game than Ruth and was four years older. Shore continued to impress his manager while Ruth was relegated to the bench.

During the 11 games he played in Boston before the Red Sox went on the road, Ruth was miserable. For the first time on the baseball stage he was an extra, not the star. And he was lonely. His friend and surrogate minder Egan never played for the Red Sox and was traded to Cleveland within two weeks.[12]

No one seemed willing to take over Egan's role as mentor. Upon arriving in Boston, Ruth boarded in a house, but soon moved into Putnam's Hotel on Copley Square. It was at the hotel that he received his first—and only—fan letter that season. "You're doing fine, George. I'm proud of you," said the note from Brother Matthias.[13] The message came as great comfort and Ruth biographer Wilborn Hampton said he kept it for the rest of his life.[14] His connection to St. Mary's helped sustain the 19-year-old during some dark days. One of Ruth's former teachers, Brother Bruno, traveled in from Somerville, where he had been posted. Bruno was particularly sensitive to the needs of those who felt neglected and Babe appreciated his counsel. Ruth confided in Bruno that he hated being idle. He was in Boston to play the game he loved but he was warming the bench. Bruno lent a sympathetic ear and wondered if his former pupil was biting off more than he could chew. Perhaps the professional game was not for him, Bruno suggested. Ruth would have none of that—he was never one to doubt himself.[15] While the reminder of his roots helped him deal with his feeling of emptiness, he was finding even greater comfort by courting young Helen. And he was enjoying money, spending it as fast as it came in.

Loud, brash, naive and irreverent, Babe managed to irritate the older players in the Boston clubhouse. He himself later recalled his early days this way:

> When I went to the Red Sox I got the same kind of rough treatment I had experienced in the training camp with the Orioles. Someone must have told them I was a fresh kid who didn't have much respect for big baseball reputations, and I guess some of the old guys let me have it. I suppose I did talk back, but not because I was fresh. I just wanted to show them I was as good as any of the other pitchers Bill Carrigan had.[16]

Rookies were expected to be quiet and deferential, so the veterans responded to the kid in their midst. He wanted to take batting practice every day, but they viewed him as a pitcher, so why would he want to hit? They gave him the cold shoulder and warned him away. But Ruth was persistent and paid a price. "One day I came to the park and found that all my bats had been neatly sawed in two," he recalled later.[17] Tris Speaker, a future hall of famer, was particularly annoyed with the behavior of the newcomer. And Smokey Joe Wood, Speaker's pal and roommate, didn't like the nonchalant behavior sometimes displayed by Ruth. To them, Ruth became "the Big Baboon." Ruth disliked the name intensely, as much as Niggerlips from his school days, and at one point grew so upset at being taunted with it that he challenged the entire team to a fight. "Nobody was so dumb to take him up on it, so that put an end to that," outfielder Harry Hooper said later.[18] "He was such a rube that he got more than his share of teasing, some of it not too pleasant."

Babe and Helen picked up the pace of their relationship as his troubles continued with the Red Sox, the couple often double-dating with Myrtle

Durant, another waitress at Lander's Coffee Shop, and her boyfriend, Parker Hatch. They skated at Boston Arena, listened to the latest hits on the Victrola, enjoyed the movie serial *Perils of Pauline* and tried to learn the tango, the popular dance craze. "They got along real nice," said Hooper, a future Hall of Famer. "They used to call each other 'hon.'"[19]

Just as Babe had some rough edges to his pitching, he was a crude character socially. His years at St. Mary's had produced no refinement in his social graces and table manners. Ernie Shore, four years older than Babe, was much more finished on the pitching mound and in daily life. A college graduate, he had benefited from a more traditional family upbringing. Shore was an early roommate for Ruth, but didn't last long. Ruth himself said: "I guess it would have been all right if I had been a little more careful about using Ernie's things.... He said it was bad enough for me to use his toothbrush but when he complained about it I had said innocently, 'That's all right, Ernie, I'm not particular.'"[20] In another version of the story it was a shaving brush, not a toothbrush, that drew Shore's ire.[21] Shore was appalled by other habits of his roomie; the toilets he never flushed, his pride of flatulence and the exaggerated belches. Ruth had a propensity to wander around their living quarters naked, was constantly in motion and was unwilling to go to bed. Ping Bodie, a later roommate of Ruth's with the Yankees, said he often had their hotel room all to himself because Babe was constantly out on the town. "I don't room with him," he said, succinctly: "I room with his suitcase."[22] Manager Carrigan complied with Shore's request and found him another roommate.

Babe was constantly eating. Biographer Leigh Montville colorfully described his voracious appetite this way: "He ate every day like a man released from prison."[23] The analogy was apt. After the simple fare he'd consumed for a decade at school, this was a time of indulgence for Ruth. In his first months out of St. Mary's he began packing on weight. He liked his steaks large and uncooked. During train stops in the night with the team, he'd order loaves of sandwiches and quickly pack them away. Montville noted that Ruth ate before, during and after games. At one point, manager Carrigan banned food on the players' bench to stop him, but Ruth found a way to smuggle food into the clubhouse.

"Lord, he ate too much," recalled Hooper. "He'd stop along the road when we were traveling and order half a dozen hot dogs and as many bottles of soda pop, stuff them in, one after the other, give a few big belches, and then roar, 'OK, boys, let's go.' That would hold Babe for a couple of hours, and then he'd be at it again."[24] His loud, carefree ways and lack of discipline rubbed veterans the wrong way. He was seen as too casual during practice and was dismissed as a mouthy kid.[25] If he hadn't found Helen, things in Boston would have been far worse for him. He embarrassed players and their wives at restaurants. Aside from wolfing down vast amounts of food, he was obscene. "Excuse me,

I have to piss," he'd announce, only to be told by a teammate that was inappropriate language around ladies. He'd return to the table to say he was sorry "for using the word piss."²⁶ The Xaverian Brothers at St. Mary's provided a good basic education and training for trades, but with so many boys in their care, table manners and social graces hadn't received close attention.

Babe rode the bench for nearly four weeks in Boston as Shore continued to pitch well. The *Boston Globe* noted on August 3 that veteran Dutch Leonard and the rookie Shore were the most effective pitchers for the Red Sox at that point. Shore had four wins and one no-decision in five appearances and stood atop the list of American League pitchers in the winning percentage.²⁷ That story may have jinxed him. The next day, Shore suffered his first loss, 2–1, to St. Louis. Babe's annoying behavior and being outshone by Shore likely combined to keep him off the field. On August 12, after the Red Sox returned from a western road trip to Cleveland, Chicago, St. Louis and Detroit, in which they won 10 of 15 games, he finally saw some action—in exhibition games. He won both and was heartened to be playing again, albeit in the shadow of Shore.

The 1914 version of the Red Sox made a good run for the American League pennant, but by the beginning of August, the Philadelphia Athletics had an insurmountable lead and it was doubtful Boston could catch them. To give Ruth more playing time and experience, team owner J. J. Lannin and manager Carrigan decided to send him to the Providence Grays of the International League. At the end of July, Lannin purchased the Providence franchise from the Detroit Tigers for $75,000, to act as a sort of farm team. The Grays were one of the top teams in the minor loop, where many teams were struggling with low attendance because of growing competition from the Federal

After his first few weeks with the Boston Red Sox, Babe was sent to the Providence Grays, a farm team for Boston, for more playing time. He turned heads with his pitching, but his bat was slow to make its mark. He belted his first homer in a professional game when the Grays appeared in Toronto late in the 1914 season (National Baseball Hall of Fame and Museum, Cooperstown, New York).

10. First Steps on the Big Stage

League. By this time in the season, Baltimore had fallen back in the standings because of Dunn's fire sale of players. Lannin was a relative newcomer to baseball and was willing to invest heavily in the game he had come to love. The wealthy hotel owner had bought into the Boston club with partners in 1913 and became sole owner the following spring. Lannin was determined to ensure his team was a winner. Buying top talent and creating a feeder team to develop his own players seemed to make sense to the self-made millionaire.

Lannin was the second Canadian to play an important role in the baseball career of Babe Ruth. And like Cape Breton native Brother Matthias, he caught baseball fever in Boston during the 1880s and 1890s. Lannin was born April 23, 1866, just north of Quebec City to Irish immigrant parents in a farming community then known as the Waterloo Settlement (today, Lac Beauport). He was the ninth born in a family of 10 children. His father died when he was young, and then he was orphaned at age 14 when his mother passed away from tuberculosis. Like many others in his economically challenged region, Lannin looked south to New England for opportunity, where commerce, textiles, shoemaking, shipbuilding and shipping were thriving. And just like the Boutiliers of Nova Scotia (Brother Matthias's family), he joined thousands of other Canadians who migrated south in search of greener pastures. Lannin made the 410-mile trip to Boston entirely on foot, following the well-worn steps of fur traders. In Beantown, the ambitious boy soon found a job as a bellhop at the Adams House Hotel. There, he toiled for $3 a week and impressed his employer with his work ethic and attention to detail, eventually becoming the hotel's head waiter. A veritable sponge for information, Lannin paid close attention to the well-heeled guests, who discussed real estate and other investments, and he began to invest his spare money. One guest offered him a position at a new hotel, where traits such as his attention to detail immediately shone and he was soon named manager. Lannin lived frugally and did well, investing in the coffee market and in real estate.[28] Some time later, the owners of the Great Northern Hotel in New York lured him away and he began putting his money into hotels and other ventures, including golf courses and even an airfield, in Boston, New York and on Long Island. His Lannin Realty Company was headquartered in Boston.

Lannin retained a passion for sport as he became a wealthy man. He had played lacrosse when he was younger and in 1886 was a member of the South Boston Lacrosse Club, which won the championship of New England. He became a noted checkers player and avid golfer. At one point, Lannin bought 35 shares in the Boston Braves of the National League, which was owned by his friend James Gaffney. In 1913, Lannin acquired a half interest in the American League's Red Sox and sold his interest in the Braves. By early 1914, he was sole owner of the Red Sox, a team conservatively estimated to be worth $700,000 and doing well on the field and at the box office.[29] Lannin wanted a winning team and was willing to pay for it. He had the highest payroll in baseball, believed to be more than $100,000.[30] After three years as owner of the Red Sox, however, Lannin sold out to theater impresario Harry Frazee and an associate. Lannin said he sold the club after winning back-to-back World Series because he was "too much of a fan to run a baseball club. I found it interfering with my health, as I have always had more or less trouble with my heart."[31] During 1915, Lannin purchased the struggling Buffalo Bisons of the International League, a team he retained until late 1920. In 1915 and 1916, when the Red Sox won the World Series, the Bisons were champions of the IL. But the Buffalo team lost money for four of the six years he owned it.[32] He sold the Providence Grays after the 1915 season for $30,000, so once he disposed of the Bisons he was out of the business of baseball entirely and able to revert to his preferred role of simple fan.[33]

Lannin died tragically in 1928 when he fell from a ninth-floor window of the swank 16-story Granada Hotel in Brooklyn he had recently purchased. He was 62. Police thought it might have been suicide, but found no note. Lannin seemed to be in good spirits that day and his financial affairs were said to be in order. A hotel staffer said the boss came to the hotel about 10 a.m. and wanted to inspect some new plastering in Room 915. Lannin apparently suffered a heart attack when he opened the French windows and fell out, landing on a second-floor roof. Lannin's lawyer James J. Dooling told the *Brooklyn Eagle* that Lannin had been subject to heart attacks and dizziness in recent times and that his condition likely led to his death. At the time, Lannin was estimated to be worth $6 to $7 million.[34] A medical examiner ruled out an accidental cause, however, because of Lannin's broad shoulders and the narrowness of the window opening. So mystery shrouded the case. Murder is the suspicion of Lannin's great-grandson, Christopher Tunstall, who has carefully studied Lannin's life and duplicated his walk from Quebec to Boston in 2012. Tunstall, of Asheville, North Carolina, insists the family knew Lannin had been threatened for two years by members of a powerful family, to whom he refused to sell some properties. "He did not give in to their repeated requests and was killed because of that," Tunstall told *le Journal de Montréal* newspaper in 2016, when it chronicled the life of the famous Quebecker. He said Lannin was confronted by at least two men in the hotel room that morning, was struck over the head and then pushed out the window. Tunstall said the killers were acting on behalf of "a very rich and powerful family" that is still in business today.[35] Regardless of the nature of his untimely demise, Lannin had been a powerful influence in baseball and on the life of Babe Ruth. He had helped Dunn battle the Federal League Terrapins with a loan of $3,000, bought the Providence and then Buffalo franchises of the International League to keep them going and took the first step toward creating the farm team system. In 2004, Lannin's contributions to the game were recognized with his induction into the Canadian Baseball Hall of Fame.[36]

Sending Ruth to his new minor-league club for seasoning wasn't as easy as Lannin had anticipated. Baseball rules of the day required all other major-league teams to agree they did not want a player before he could be sent down to the minors. They had to formally waive their rights to the player. August Hermann, president of the Cincinnati Reds, refused to do so. He wanted to buy Ruth from the Red Sox. Hermann dug in his heels and Lannin turned to Ban Johnson, president of the American league, to intercede. Johnson did so, advising Hermann the Reds were the only club to block the transfer, that Lannin had spent a lot of money to acquire Ruth, would never sell him to another major-league club and planned to develop his potential. "He is unable to give him the work at Boston," Johnson told Hermann, "and by sending him to Providence he will have an opportunity to improve the team … and possibly make some money."[37] Hermann realized his effort was fruitless and he relented. On August 15, Ruth found himself on the Providence roster.

Babe was unhappy about being demoted to the minors—it seemed like a backward step. He retained his Red Sox salary, but Providence was minor league, like Baltimore. There was prestige in the majors; in Providence, not much. Even more troubling was being separated from the new love of his life. He was only 40 miles from Boston, but Providence seemed so much farther away. He visited Helen frequently, usually traveling by rail, but occasionally he dug into his pocket for a cab. When he got his driver's license, he drove to see her in his new car and, given his exuberant approach to motoring, the inevitable happened. On one trip, he had a terrible crash in Cambridge, wrecking the car and getting his new driver's license suspended.[38] More car crashes lay ahead for the man who was as undisciplined on the road as he was in life.

When Babe first donned a Grays uniform, Providence was in second place of the International League just behind Rochester. During his six weeks there, he helped the club reach first and take the league pennant. With the Grays he would not be idle, pitching every three or four days. This was just what he needed. The manager was Wild Bill Donovan, an outstanding pitcher when he was with Detroit. Babe would say he learned much about the art of throwing from Donovan.[39] Despite its size, Providence was once a major-league city, a member of the National League from 1877 to 1885 and had captured two pennants. That August, when Babe was reassigned, the world seemed on the brink of war. Austrian Archduke Franz Ferdinand, heir to the Austro-Hungarian throne, was assassinated in Sarajevo in late June and the major European powers were spoiling for a fight. Austria-Hungary declared war on Serbia, Russia mobilized, then Germany, declaring war on Russia and on France. Germany invaded Belgium, then Britain declared war on Germany on August 4. That same day, the United States, anxious to remain out of a distant European war, declared its neutrality. The newspapers of America were full of stories about the precarious political and military situation and the fighting that erupted. Closer to home, the "Miracle Braves" of Boston, who had been last in the National League on July 4, were putting together a sensational string of victories that would crown them League champions and then defeat the favored Philadelphia Athletics in the World Series.

On August 22, some 12,000 fans crowded Melrose Park to see Ruth's first start as a Gray in the first game of a doubleheader against Rochester. Spectators overflowed the stands and spilled onto the field, held back by ropes. According to ground rules, any ball hit into the crowd would be counted as a triple. Aside from pitching well for nine innings, Babe connected for two triples into the crowd, the crucial one coming in the ninth inning, when the Grays pulled off a three-run rally to defeat the visitors, 5–4. That timely hit prompted *Providence Journal* sportswriter Bill Perrin to get lyrical as he described Babe's clout of an offering from Rochester pitcher Bill Upham this way:

> The big stick tore through the air and met an Upham shoot with a crack that sounded above the roar of the fans. Higher and higher mounted the ball and then it descended in a beautiful spiral to land many feet over the heads of the crowd in center and in close proximity to the flag pole. A thousand straw hats were lost in the wild demonstration of joy that signalized the longest hit ever made at the ball park.[40]

It was a fine start to his stint in Providence for Babe, who showed excellent control pitching and timely hitting. In Buffalo, on August 26, Ruth had his second start, but was clobbered by the Bisons, surrendering 11 hits in an 8–2 defeat. In Rochester, he defeated the home team, 2–1, in the second game of a doubleheader, allowing only five hits. The next day the Grays, now in first place by a game, took an overnight steamer to Montreal for a three-game series to begin August 31.

The war in Europe was suddenly brought home to the Grays when they arrived in Canada. As a member nation of the British Empire, the Dominion automatically joined Britain in its August 4 declaration of war on Germany. Canada had mobilized quickly and uniformed men were posted everywhere, guarding key sites like railroad stations, bridges and other structures. The English- and French-language newspapers were full of stories about German troops crossing France in a bid to reach Paris and the first British Navy successes in the North Sea. With so much war news, coverage of baseball was skipped for evening editions and limited to morning papers only. The players found it difficult to keep abreast of baseball's pennant races, especially the exciting winning streak of the Boston Braves. Grays pitcher Wallace "Toots" Schultz, born in Pennsylvania, openly rooted for the Germans in the faraway conflict and picked up the name "Kaiser." His fellow players tormented him, sending news reports to his room about German losses on the battlefield, including one about 75,000 Germans being killed in France, turning the distant fighting into a locker room battle. They put papers highlighting German losses under his dinner plate, in his shoes and stockings and wrapped one around his bat.[41] The childish pranks masked their concern about men dying in far off battlefields while they played on ball fields closer to home. The tragedy unfolding in Europe was unprecedented and hard to grasp for men who made a living by playing a game.

After winning two games in Montreal and losing one, the Grays traveled 430 miles west by rail to Toronto, where Babe Ruth would make history during a three-game series set to begin September 3. The Ontario city, like Montreal, was on war footing and signs of it were abundant. The Union Jack—the flag Canada shared with Britain—flew everywhere. Soldiers drilled on the grounds of the University of Toronto, a recruiting office was set up outside city hall and men in uniform were stationed around sites considered strategic, like Union Station. Providence had slipped to third place behind Rochester and Buffalo by the time the Grays faced Toronto on September 3 at 18,000-seat Maple Leaf Park, located on Hanlan's Point, an island in the city harbor. The ballpark, one of the largest in the minor leagues, was alongside an amusement park featuring roller coasters and a dance pavilion. The park and the team were owned by the Toronto Ferry Company, whose boats provided access to the lakeside complex. The ballpark was a stout one, built of concrete and steel because fires had previously claimed two smaller frame structures on the site.[42]

The first game was called after four innings because of rain, with the score tied at 2–2. The next day, Toronto edged the visitors, 3–2, thanks to the heroics of right-hander Clint Rogge, who allowed three hits and struck out nine while leaving eight Grays on base. The game had been tied at two runs apiece when, with two out in the bottom of the ninth, Rogge singled to bring home the winning run. To make up for the rained-out game, a doubleheader was scheduled for September 5. That day, as *Toronto Star* headlines screamed that a German "Arrowhead" of troops was rushing past Paris and a massive clash was looming with French and British forces, Ruth was sent to the mound for the first game. He was a standout in his best game as a Gray. He allowed a single hit, walked three and struck out seven, shutting out the Leafs, 9–0, with what the *Toronto Daily News* described as his "masterly pitching."[43] Its reporter dubbed him "invincible." Meanwhile, Ellis Johnson, a six-foot right-hander who had played for Chicago and Philadelphia in the American League, saw his fastball "murdered" by Grays batters, according to the *Star*. He surrendered 15 hits. In the sixth inning, with Providence leading, 1–0, Johnson had two out when Paddy Bauman singled and Jack Onslow followed suit. Ruth came to the plate and crushed the first offering from the Toronto hurler. The ball sailed over the right field bleachers for three runs. Myth-makers said later it landed in Lake Ontario, but contemporaneous press accounts all agreed it simply cleared the bleachers and went no farther. The myth persists to this day, however. Bill Perrin, reporting for the *Providence Journal*, didn't bother to mention Ruth's blast until half-way through his story, calling it "a tremendous drive out of the park, over the right field fence." He focused instead on Ruth's work on the mound: "The big fellow had barrels of speed and some great curves that had the Leafs completely buffaloed."[44] The *Toronto Globe* noted Ruth's ability to "heave that old pill" and left mention of his hit until the fourth paragraph of their five-paragraph story.[45] Perrin and the *Globe*'s approach is understandable because this was still the "Deadball Era" in baseball, when hitting took a back seat to pitching and strong defensive play. With the arrival of Ruth, that era's days were numbered.

The slam in Toronto was Ruth's first official home run as a professional and it came almost exactly six months after his March 7 dinger into a Fayetteville cornfield during that spring training intrasquad game. The Toronto blast would be his only home run recorded in the minor leagues.

The Maple Leafs won the second game, 3–2, which was shortened to seven innings to let the Grays catch a train for home. Providence manager Wild Bill Donovan pitched and took the loss. A plaque marks Babe's first real home run on the Toronto waterfront, just as another salutes his exhibition game clout down in Fayetteville.

In his 1928 autobiography, Babe said he didn't recall when he hit his first home run. In the 1948 version of his life story, he and Considine reduced the historic achievement in Toronto to just one sentence: "During my stay in Providence I also hit my first home run in regular competition."[46]

Ruth won nine games and lost three while in Providence. He had plenty of work, pitching four games in eight days in one stretch, and won them all. At the plate he was 12-for-40, for a .300 batting average. Sportswriter Perrin observed the young hurler was "getting to the stage where he appears to be almost unbeatable." And his bat was coming around. On September 18, Ruth defeated Baltimore, 11–3, and "drove a tremendous wallop that almost hit the right field fence, counting for three bases. It was the longest hit ever sent to that part of the park."[47] He was finding his groove. By September 19, the Grays were back in first place, where they remained until the season ended a week later. Babe was making fans, prompting the *Providence Journal* to observe: "Babe Ruth seems to have gotten in on the ground floor with the fans as a result of his baffling southpaw pitching and his ability to give the horsehide punishment with the wagon tongue."[48] The creative pen of sportswriter Bill Perrin was again at work. The Grays captured the International League pennant, helped in large measure by the hurler lent them by J. J. Lannin.

The young man had done fine, just as Brother Matthias had predicted. But Boston's season was not yet over and a more seasoned Babe was summoned back to the big club.

11

A Real Major Leaguer

As he prepared to leave Providence, Babe pitched one last time for the Grays, taking the mound for an exhibition game against the National League Chicago Cubs. It was played on Sunday, September 26, in Rocky Point, about 12 miles south of Providence because of the city's ban on Sunday games. The park lay alongside Narragansett Bay and the game attracted a crowd of 2,400. Ruth allowed seven hits as he pitched the complete game and in the third inning launched a ball over the right field fence and into the bay. Cubs left fielder Wilbur Good managed the same feat, but the Grays won, 8–7.[1] It was Babe's first home run against a major-league club, but it wouldn't count because it was in exhibition play. This time, unlike the homer driven in Toronto earlier that month, the ball really did get wet.

Back in Boston, the Red Sox faced a four-game series against New York and three games with Washington before the season ended on October 7. Ruth took the mound October 2, winning 11–5 in a complete game, while allowing six hits and six walks. In the seventh inning, he doubled off Leonard "King" Cole, advanced to third on a sacrifice and scampered home on a long fly ball, thereby recording both his first major-league hit and first major-league run. Respected *Globe* sportswriter Tim Murnane said Ruth "pitched an excellent game."[2] In one Washington contest, Babe pinch-hit once and struck out, but in another he pitched three innings and hit a single.

An impressive rookie season had come to an end. Ruth, mere months out of St. Mary's Industrial Training School, had acquired a nickname, enjoyed his first train ride, stayed in his first hotel, gained experience with three teams in two leagues, recorded his first major-league wins as a pitcher and collected his first hits and runs. He had belted his first professional homer in the minors but had yet to put one out of a major-league park. He had newfound money and a girlfriend and was making a name for himself. It had been a great start. During his time in Baltimore and Providence, he won 23 games and lost 8, but his hitting was inconsistent. In Baltimore, his average was .200, but it rose to .300 with the Grays, for a combined average of .233. With Boston, he won two games, lost one and batted .200 as the Red Sox finished second in the American League.

That fall, however, the Red Sox were Boston's "other" team. The Braves of the National League had been dubbed the "Miracle Braves" for their stellar play. It was completely unexpected for a team that lost 18 of their first 22 games and found itself mired in last place on July 1. The Braves switched gears and put together a winning streak to claim the league pennant and then topple the heavily favored Philadelphia Athletics four games straight in the World Series.

For Babe, getting back to breakfast at Lander's and seeing Helen were highlights of returning to Beantown. He had planned to spend the winter in Baltimore, but couldn't leave Helen. One morning at breakfast, he said: "How about you and me getting married, hon'?"[3] She accepted. He was 19, she was 17 and they had known each other less than three months. Babe bought a new car and drove them to Maryland, where, on October 13, they acquired a marriage license in Ellicott City, a town just west of Baltimore. Four days later, they were married at St. Paul's Catholic Church in Ellicott City by Father Thomas Dolan. Ruth biographer Robert Creamer surmised that particular venue was chosen to keep the wedding a secret from the Xaverian Brothers at St. Mary's, who might not have approved because Ruth had not yet reached the age of majority. Babe sought permission to marry from his father, rather than from Brother Paul, or even Jack Dunn.[4] The newlyweds made their home in Baltimore for the off-season.

Jack Dunn moved the Orioles to Richmond for 1915 and when the Federal League died, moved them back to Baltimore for 1916. Until his death in 1927, Dunn continued to find and successfully develop talent, his Orioles taking seven consecutive International League pennants between 1918 and 1924. Meanwhile, in January of 1916, J. J. Lannin sold the Providence Grays to businessman William H. Draper of that city for $40,000.[5]

Babe's salary was boosted from $600 to $3,500 for 1915. The Red Sox roster included stars Tris Speaker and Harry Hooper (both future Hall of Famers), along with pitchers Ernie Shore, Carl Mays, Rube Foster, Dutch Leonard and Ray Collins. Midway through the season, lefty Herb Pennock, another future Hall of Famer, was acquired from Philadelphia. Boston had won the World Series in 1912, finished fourth in the American League in 1913, second in 1914 and was expected to be a strong contender for 1915. Speaker was an outstanding center fielder who batted .345 during his 22-year career that began in 1907 with Boston. He had a strong arm and led the league in putouts seven times and double plays six times, while chalking up 3,514 hits before retiring. Harry Hooper, the right fielder, had been with Boston since 1909. He wielded a good bat and on Memorial Day, 1913, became the only lead-off batter in history to hit home runs in both games of a doubleheader.[6] The pitching rotation was solid and Ruth knew he'd have to be good to see any time on the mound. Mays was an effective pitcher who had a submarine motion that dipped so low he scraped his knuckles on the ground. He was one of the most disliked players of his day, however, because of his surly disposition. Mays didn't help his reputation when, in August of 1920, at the Polo Grounds in New York City, he struck and killed Cleveland shortstop Ray Chapman with an inside fastball that hit Chapman's temple and fractured his skull. With his otherwise outstanding record, Mays is one of the best pitchers not inducted into the Hall of Fame.[7]

Spring training began in March in Hot Springs, Arkansas, and as manager Carrigan worked with the pitchers it was clear he considered Ruth second-tier

As he continued to lead successful Orioles teams in Baltimore, Jack Dunn stayed in touch with Babe Ruth. In this 1923 image, he is seen with two of his "graduates," Babe (left) and Jack Bentley, a pitcher and first baseman for the New York Giants acquired the previous year from Dunn's club (Library of Congress).

talent. Before opening day, the Red Sox played only one major-league team and struggled early in the season with erratic performances on the mound. The only exception was Mays, who pitched well but within the first few days of the season twisted his ankle, sidelining him for nearly three weeks. This created an opening for Ruth. Carrigan sent him to the mound for the third game of the season against Philadelphia, but he was ineffective and Carrigan pulled him in the fourth inning. Ruth won his second start 9–2 against Philadelphia on April 26, and Carrigan's confidence in him began to grow. On May 6 in New York, Babe faced the Yankees and carried a 3–2 lead into the ninth inning. In that stanza, he allowed a double that drove in the tying run, forcing the teams into extra innings. Boston eventually lost 4–3, but his complete-game performance in the 13-inning clash so impressed Carrigan that he made him a starter. The *Boston Globe* reported Ruth "pitched a wonderfully good game from the start, [but] weakened a bit in the 13th, yielding two successive singles" which, combined with a stolen base, gave the Yankees the win.[8] At the plate, Babe faced veteran right-hander Jack Warhop, who was nearing the end of his career. Ruth led off the third inning and sent Warhop's low fastball into the right field stands of the Polo Grounds. He had his first homer in the major leagues.

Home runs were not common in baseball at the time and they drew no special attention. The most ever recorded in the major leagues was 27, by Ned Williamson of the National League Chicago White Stockings, in 1884. The feat was an aberration in Williamson's 13-year career, during which his previous high was nine homers. He took full advantage of the shortest outfield fences in the major leagues at Lake Front Park, where Chicago was playing its last season. Ruth began his career in the Deadball Era, when the baseball was comparatively lifeless and hard to drive long distances. The ball remained in play long after it became soft and scuffed. And it was retrieved from fans when it left the field of play. As a result, short, hard and timely hits were preferred, as were sacrifice bunts and stealing bases, in what today is known as "small ball." Meanwhile, some ballparks were cavernous and pitchers were allowed to doctor the ball by scuffing it to make it dip and dive. Some pitchers relied on the spitball to deceive batters. Good pitching, strategy and strong defensive play were considered the keys to success.

Less than a month later, Ruth victimized New York's Warhop again. On June 2 at the Polo Grounds, with a man on first in the second inning, he clouted a Warhop offering into the second deck, 10 feet farther than his first blast at the park. Homer number two was in the books and Boston won this time, 7–1.[9] Warhop retired from baseball two months later, but will always be remembered for his role in igniting the Babe Ruth home run machine. Babe was pitching well but it was his ability to hit the ball harder and farther than other players that was attracting attention. His third round-tripper, at Fenway

Park in late June, was considered the second-longest drive seen there. In St. Louis, on July 21, he hit the longest home run ever in Sportsman's Park. Boston downed the Browns 4–2 that day as Ruth went 4-for-4 at the plate, with a single, two doubles and the homer. The blast off Browns starter Bill James in the third inning soared over the right field fence, bounced on Grand Avenue and smashed through a store window. On the mound, Babe allowed only five hits.[10]

"I learned early that I could hit a ball much harder and farther than the average player, and up in the press box some of the boys were writing that if I could play every day, instead of every fourth, I'd be right up with the home run leaders of the league," Ruth recalled in his 1948 autobiography. "That still was a time when a guy with 10 or 12 homers was called a home run king."[11]

Manager Carrigan handled Babe carefully, gradually building his self-confidence. Early in the 1915 season, Carrigan used him against weaker teams but started him against better clubs when the Red Sox began a pennant drive in which they won 19 of 21 games. Ruth won 18 games, lost 8 and struck out 112, with an earned run average of 2.44. He batted .315 with four home runs. The American League record that year was 7, while the National League leader had 19.

During a series in Washington, Babe and his teammates had a Sunday off and Carrigan granted him permission to slip over to Baltimore to see some people, reminding him to be back in Washington for Monday's game. Babe later recalled things didn't work out as planned:

> I guess everything would have been all right if my dad hadn't come over from Baltimore to see the Monday ball game. They gave him a box near the Red Sox bench and when he saw me he yelled, "You're a fine son, George, down in this neighborhood and didn't even come home to see me." There wasn't much for me to say, with Bill standing there eyeing me and rocking back and forth on his heels.[12]

Babe had begun drinking about the time he married Helen or shortly afterward, and he may have wanted to have a few with his pals back home. The Washington anecdote suggested some lingering friction between father and son. Perhaps the source of it was his father's new wife. Drinking certainly didn't help Babe's careless driving and his tendency to drive too fast. He collected several speeding tickets, struck pedestrians and had an accident every calendar year, starting with a collision with a hay wagon in 1915.[13]

After an exciting pennant race, Boston edged Detroit by a single game to become American League champions. A four-game series at Fenway Park beginning September 16 was pivotal. The Red Sox took three of those contests, with Babe winning one of them, 3–2—although he had been lifted in the eighth inning, leaving the bases loaded for Rube Foster. The World Series pitted Boston against the Philadelphia Phillies. To accommodate more spectators than Fenway Park could handle, the Red Sox moved to larger Braves

The Boston Red Sox of 1916 won the World Series for the second year in a row. Babe Ruth was becoming a standout pitcher and promising batter. He is seated fourth from left in the front row, not surprisingly beside the bat boy. Ruth always retained a place in his heart for youngsters, no matter how successful he became in baseball (Library of Congress).

Field. After losing the first game in Philadelphia, 3–1, Boston swept the next four, each by a single run, to claim their second World Series victory in four years. Foster, Shore and Leonard did all the pitching as Carrigan benched Babe, preferring to rely on his right-handers. Babe made a pinch-hit appearance in the first game when he drove an offering from all-star hurler Grover Cleveland Alexander to the first baseman for an easy out. Despite the disappointment of not seeing more action, Ruth received a full share of the winner's money, $3,780.80, more than doubling his pay for the entire year. He promptly spent $500 on a 2.5-carat diamond solitaire ring for himself.

Babe was poor at handling his money and freely indulged his whims. Carrigan tried to help him learn the value of money and attempted to ration it to the 19-year-old, but his efforts proved unsuccessful. "He had no idea whatsoever of money," Carrigan said later. "You have to remember his background."[14] Ruth's early financial affairs had been handled by the Xaverians at St. Mary's, so it was to them he turned for advice. He had an idea to help his father get a new bar and sought and received support for his plan from Brothers Paul and Matthias.[15] So Ruth father and son bought a saloon and billiard parlor at 38 South Eutaw Street, at the corner of Lombard Street just north of

Camden Yards. It was directly across South Eutaw from the landmark Emerson Tower, one of the tallest structures in Baltimore at 15 stories. Built in 1911 as an architectural feature of the Bromo Seltzer factory, it later became known as the Bromo Seltzer Tower, promoting the headache remedy and hangover cure developed by chemist Isaac Emerson. With the factory across the street and Camden Yards so close, Babe and his father hoped customers would be numerous. The location was also in the heart of Baltimore's wholesale and clothing manufacturing district. By October, George Ruth left his bar at 552 West Conway Street and was operating Ruth's Café on South Eutaw. Babe worked alongside his father when he couldn't find a baseball game to play. He and Helen settled into an upstairs apartment. A famous photograph shows Babe and George Sr. behind the bar, which is decorated for Christmas. The physical resemblance of father and son is striking and the place appears prosperous. Baltimore historian Fred B. Shoken has carefully studied a pro-

Babe Ruth (second from right) and his father, George (far right), behind the bar at Ruth's Café at 38 South Eutaw Street, Baltimore, around Christmas, possibly as early as 1916. Babe helped his father buy the bar with his newfound baseball money and sometimes worked alongside him. Note the calendar at the top right, on which the image resembles Babe's first wife, Helen (courtesy of the Babe Ruth Birthplace Foundation, Baltimore).

motional calendar that appears in the upper right corner of an uncropped version of that image. It features a young lady sitting on a ballpark fence and the claim that Ruth's Café is "Babe Ruth's Favorite." In smaller type, George H. Ruth Sr. is identified as proprietor and George H. "Babe" Ruth as manager. The young lady pictured closely resembles Helen Ruth, Shoken believes.[16]

Babe played ball in the Baltimore area that fall and arranged at least one game at St. Mary's Industrial Training School. He conscripted New York Yankee third baseman Fritz Maisel, a Baltimore-area native, to join him on the "St. Mary's All Stars" for an October 24 game against the Albrecht Athletic Club at St. Mary's. Maisel's brothers George and Charlie also joined the All Stars. George had just been drafted by Detroit and Charlie was also a solid ballplayer. About 8,000 spectators surrounded the diamond on the big field at St. Mary's that Sunday afternoon, the largest crowd ever to witness a game outside one of Baltimore's professional parks. The school's two bands played at the event and Ruth was cheered constantly by his young fans for whom he was a hero and inspiration. Spectators ringed the playing field 15 or 20 rows deep to see Baltimore's gift to the baseball world perform. For his first at-bat, the cheering of the boys was deafening. Babe didn't disappoint that day, allowing only 4 hits and fanning 14 Albrecht batters as his team coasted to a 12–2 win. He managed two base hits on the same field where he had belted his first homers as a boy, inspired by the towering blasts of Brother Matthias, who was no doubt in attendance. Also watching the game was Helen, with whom he had just celebrated their first anniversary. She followed the game closely "and seemed to enjoy greatly the ovation given her husband."[17] The *Baltimore Sun* said the Ruths would likely remain in Baltimore for the offseason because of Babe's investment in his father's business. It added that Babe had abandoned a plan to become an "automobile demonstrator" in Boston that winter. Good thing. Given his carefree approach to motoring and his crashes, that would have been a short-lived proposition.

Shortly before the game at St. Mary's, Babe removed his brand-new diamond ring and asked one of the Xaverian Brothers to hold it for safekeeping. The unidentified Brother did the same favor for another player and slipped both rings on his fingers. During crowd control duties, the rings either fell off his hand or were pilfered. The second ring was found hanging from a coat button of a spectator, but Ruth's was gone. The next day, he placed a classified advertisement in the *Sun*: "LOST—2½-carat DIAMOND RING, Belgian setting, at St. Mary's Industrial School Grounds. Liberal reward if returned to GEO ('BABE') RUTH, 38 South Eutaw street."[18] It's not known if the ring was ever returned.

Babe's first full season had been a success and both his pitching and hitting had drawn attention. The baseball landscape changed for 1916 when a peace treaty was signed between the Federal League and Major League Baseball. Chicago Whales owner Charles Weeghman was permitted to purchase the National League Cubs and move them into his Weeghman Park, later renamed Wrigley Field. St. Louis Terriers owner Phil Ball was allowed to buy the St. Louis Browns of the American League. Other Federal League owners were offered cash settlements and their players were sold to the highest bidders. The only holdouts were the Baltimore Terrapins, who desperately wanted to keep major-league baseball in their city. They launched a separate anti-trust lawsuit against the established major leagues and the Federal League owners who had caved in. Eventually, in a 1922 decision, the Supreme Court ruled against the Terrapins, finding that baseball did not constitute interstate trade and therefore wasn't subject to federal anti-trust laws.

The end of the Federal League prompted National and American league owners to trim salaries they had boosted to keep the rebel loop from tempting their players. In Boston, J. J. Lannin did the same and engaged in a prolonged salary dispute with team star Tris Speaker that led him to sell Speaker to the Cleveland Indians for $50,000, the largest amount ever paid for a player.[19] The sale came just before the start of the season and removed a key contributor to the team's success. Babe Ruth was largely unaffected, entering his second year of a three-year contract with Lannin. Other players were not so lucky.

The Red Sox regrouped and won four of their first six games. Babe pitched the opening game on April 12 against the Philadelphia Athletics and won, 2–1. He also twice defeated Washington's Walter Johnson, who was considered the best pitcher in the American League. On June 1, Ruth notched his seventh win by shutting out Johnson and the Senators, 1–0, allowing only three hits. On August 15, Ruth again faced the future Hall of Famer, coming away with another 1–0 shutout for his 16th win, but it took 13 innings to do so. The Red Sox stumbled during the early weeks of the season but climbed to flirt with first place, and by season end again claimed the American League pennant. The young lefty was a big part of that success, winning 23 games (9 of them shutouts), losing 12 and recording a league-leading earned run average of 1.75. At the plate, he was less successful than in 1915, batting .272 in only 132 appearances. He had 37 hits, 3 of which were homers.

Boston finished two games ahead of the Chicago White Sox and four up on the Detroit Tigers. In the World Series, they faced the Brooklyn Robins, also known as the Superbas, and again played their home games at cavernous Braves Field. Boston won the first clash and Ruth took the mound for the second. It was a gray, muggy October 9, and the field was slippery. Despite the weather outlook, 41,373 fans showed up. In the first inning, Brooklyn's Hy Myers scored an inside-the-park home run when a Boston fielder fell down and another slipped as they tried to track his fly ball. Syndicated columnist Grantland Rice, who had warned before the game that Ruth had "stuff that very few can hit," colorfully described Myers's drive deep into spacious center field as "beyond any human or inhuman reach—a drive that no man could stop who was not accompanied by a taxicab and a 60-foot net."[20] Ruth brought home a Boston run in the third on a hard-hit groundout, tying the game. In three more appearances at the plate Ruth struck out each time, but he held Brooklyn scoreless. In the eighth inning, in a run-down between third and home, Ruth tagged out Brooklyn base runner Mike Mowrey, who was determined to tie the score. Boston finally prevailed 2-1 in 14 innings as darkness fell and Babe collected his first World Series win, throwing 13 scoreless innings in a memorable outing. It was a stunning achievement and the longest World Series game played up to that point. Ruth walked only three Robins and struck out four while throwing 147 pitches. He had been very efficient: in each of six innings he needed only nine pitches to retire Brooklyn batters. "I told you a year ago I could take care of those National League bums," a jubilant Ruth told manager Carrigan after his grueling performance. "You never gave me a chance."[21] Major League Baseball historian John Thorn has said this about the young lefty's performance that day: "History credits this as one of his greatest pitching feats in one of the greatest seasons any pitcher ever had."[22]

Ruth did not appear again in the World Series, which Boston won, 4-1. This time, the winner's share was $3,910.26. Bad news soon followed for Babe and his teammates. Manager Carrigan announced he was retiring and planned to return to his hometown of Lewiston, Maine, where he was in the banking business. Carrigan had been important to Babe, acting almost as a surrogate father as he taught his rough-hewn student the intricacies of pitching.

Even more startling for the Red Sox players and fans was the November 1 bombshell that J. J. Lannin had sold the club to well-known New York theatrical producer Harry Frazee and two of his associates. Lannin had grown weary of being an owner after three years, clashing with players over their pay and with league officials about umpiring and other issues. Lannin said he'd been too much of a fan to be an owner, was having trouble with his heart and had planned to sell if the price was right. The team fetched $675,000.

Babe returned to Baltimore for the offseason, to again work at Ruth's Café. Brother Paul told the *Baltimore Sun* he was pleased his former student had done so well and predicted even better things for him in baseball. But Brother Paul worried Ruth might suffer a "lame arm" at any time and be forced from the game. So he suggested Babe consider getting into some form of business up in Boston, "such, for instance, as automobile selling." The *Sun* agreed: "Ruth's career cannot last always and his former mentor wants him to get ready to be as good a business man as he is a pitcher."[23]

Despite his good intentions and sage advice, Brother Paul may have been unaware that Babe and automobiles were a dangerous combination. Shortly before Christmas, Babe had a serious crash near Boston. The *Washington Post* reported: "He and his wife were trying out a new car that he had recently purchased and in some way the auto turned over, and while Ruth was badly cut and bruised, his wife was thrown heavily to the roadside. She was rushed to hospital, where she is now in a serious condition."[24] Helen recovered, but the incident did nothing to improve Babe's behavior behind the wheel.

Meanwhile, Babe's father's marriage to Martha Sipes, a woman 20 years his junior, on Christmas Day, 1915, was creating problems between father and son.[25] Babe and his new stepmother, who was only three years older than he, clashed often. "Babe and Martha, they fought like cats and dogs," his sister Mamie recalled many decades later. "All they had to do was to look at one another—they disliked each other so much."[26]

On April 6, 1917, the United States declared war on Germany and the next month all able-bodied men were required to register for the draft. As a married man, Babe was deferred from active service and, along with several of his teammates, joined a National Guard unit in Massachusetts.[27]

Ruth won 24 games in 1917 and lost 13 as he pitched a league-leading 35 games. His earned run average rose slightly to 2.01 and he had six shutouts. At the plate, he managed only two home runs but his batting average was .325, the highest on the team. He chafed at sitting on the bench between starts but his value to the team lay in his pitching. Success went to his head that season and he began arguing with umpires about the strike zone when he didn't get a call he wanted. In a June 23 game against the Washington Senators, he walked the first batter on four pitches. Enraged at umpire Brick Owens, Ruth charged at him and threw a punch that landed on the back of Owens's head. He was ejected and a police officer escorted him from the field. Ernie Shore replaced him and, on his first pitch, the runner he inherited was thrown out trying to steal second. Shore retired the next 26 batters. He was credited with a no-hitter. In 1991, however, a committee for statistical accuracy in baseball ruled the game was a "combined no-hitter" for Shore and Ruth. It would be Ruth's only no-hitter.[28] For his outburst, Ruth was fined $100 and suspended 10 games.[29]

Boston finished second in the pennant race, nine games behind the Chicago White Sox. Their season had been marked by sharp fielding and they had held their opponents to the fewest runs in the league. Babe had been the busiest pitcher that year and was second in games won. But the White Sox and their pitchers had been better. By September, all teams began losing unmarried players to local reserve units, or to war-related factory jobs to avoid being called up into the regular forces. The Red Sox lost a dozen players, including Jack Barry, the playing manager. In early November, Babe had yet another car crash in Boston. This time, he collided with an electric streetcar shortly after 6 a.m. on November 8, not far from Fenway Park. The force of the collision derailed the streetcar and Babe careered into another streetcar, wedging his vehicle between them. A passenger in the first streetcar was taken to the hospital. Babe's 28-year-old female companion, Harriet Crane, the owner of the automobile, suffered facial cuts and was also taken to the hospital.[30] Babe was unhurt but had some explaining to do to Helen when he got home. This had been no demonstration drive. He was womanizing.

Babe was the first Red Sox to sign up for the 1918 season, agreeing to play for $7,000 while other players held back because of salary cuts made by Frazee amidst uncertainty about the war and coming cutbacks.[31] Frazee hired Edward Grant Barrow as manager. Never a player, Barrow had worked the concession stands at the ballpark in Pittsburgh with pioneer hotdog vendor Harry Stevens and managed in the minor leagues and the Detroit Tigers, eventually becoming president of the Eastern League, which was renamed the International League. He had just left the latter post. At six-foot-two, Barrow was the same height as Babe Ruth, but they would never see eye to eye. He was a puritanical, pugilistic tyrant and disciplinarian with whom Ruth would clash. Barrow realized his limitations at baseball strategy and players, however, so he relied heavily on Red Sox outfielder and captain Harry Hooper. Barrow wanted to keep the league's best pitcher pitching and turned a deaf ear to Ruth's pleas that he occupy another position so he could play every day.

At one point, following a particularly heated exchange with Barrow, Ruth threatened to quit the team if he couldn't play more often. In early July, he gave press interviews at Ruth's Café in Baltimore saying he was leaving Boston to play for a shipbuilding firm.[32] He didn't, however, despite the threat, and returned to the Sox. It wasn't until Hooper appealed to Barrow's business instincts that Ruth began to appear more often at first base and in the outfield and his pitching duties were reduced. Barrow often spoke about the $50,000 he had invested in a team that needed more offense, especially left-handed hitting. Hooper wanted Barrow to understand that Ruth had become an attraction and fans were anxious to see him.[33] Hooper argued that bigger crowds drawn by Babe on a daily basis would mean more money for team coffers, especially when attendance was suffering because of the war. This finally caught Barrow's attention and he began to place Ruth in the field on days he didn't pitch. Babe was fine with the arrangement, tiring as it was. He told *Baseball Magazine*: "I like to pitch but my main objection has always been that pitching keeps you out of so many games. I like to be in there every day." He didn't think a man could pitch in a regular rotation and play other positions between appearances for very long. "I am young and strong and don't mind the work. But I wouldn't guarantee it for many seasons. If I had my choice, I would play first base."[34] Because Brother Matthias had insisted he learn every position, Babe was willing and able to play any position and acquit himself well anywhere on the field.

11. A Real Major Leaguer 145

A "work-or-fight" rule went into effect on July 1 and draft boards began to reclassify ballplayers as draft eligible, married or not. It appeared baseball would come to an end on July 21, but team owners went to Washington and reached an agreement that the season would continue until Labor Day, with two weeks after that for the World Series.

Babe was playing first base and outfielder more often as he continued to pitch. When he hit, he was effective and Barrow grudgingly came to acknowledge Ruth was a box-office draw and a big factor in helping the Red Sox again claim the American League pennant. In his 95 games that year, he clouted 11 home runs, tying him with Philadelphia's Tillie Walker for most in the league, and had a .300 batting average and slugging percentage of .555. During one memorable 10-day stretch at Fenway Park, Ruth belted four singles, six doubles and five triples, for a .469 average. With his reduced workload of 166 innings pitched in 20 games (both numbers about half of the previous year), he had 13 victories and 7 losses and his earned run average was a respectable 2.22. In his last 10 starts, he only once allowed more than two runs. Overall, he had handled his increased workload well.

On Saturday night, August 24, as Babe celebrated his 3–1 victory over St. Louis that afternoon, his father's skull was fractured in a bar fight at Ruth's Café and within hours he was dead at the age of 46. The dispute had its roots in an incident involving a family member, Ruth Sr.'s brother-in-law Oliver S. Beefelt. Beefelt was the husband of Nellie, the sister of George Ruth's wife, Martha. Beefelt, 34, had been charged the previous month with assaulting 16-year-old Emma Stopford and luring her from her home for immoral purposes. He had abducted her and taken her to Cleveland, scandalizing his family. That fateful August night, Benjamin Sipes, 29, visited Nellie, his sister, at Ruth's Café, where she was then staying. Downstairs in the café, Sipes and Beefelt had a heated argument, most likely about Beefelt's behavior and the shame it had produced for his wife and her family. In a bid to restore order, George Ruth intervened and the dispute spilled onto South Eutaw. There, the short-tempered Ruth struck Sipes hard, knocking him to the pavement where Ruth kicked him. Sipes got to his feet and hit Ruth, who lost his balance, fell backward and struck his head on the curb. He died early next morning.[35]

Sipes was charged with causing Ruth's death, but an inquest accepted his assertion that he acted in self defense and he was let go.[36] Some observers find it strange that Ruth went after Sipes, rather than Beefelt, but Baltimore historian Fred B. Shoken suggests an answer. Sipes, he discovered, was a blacksmith who moonlighted by tending bar at Ruth's Café. On January 10, 1918, Sipes was arrested while working there and charged with selling morphine to a soldier stationed at nearby Camp Meade, Private Leo Burns. The address of Ruth's Café appeared in the newspapers, but it wasn't named. Sipes had been caught in a sting operation by police who were acting on a complaint filed by officers at the base.³⁷ The charge was later dropped when it was discovered the powder supplied by Sipes was actually sugar and starch. Shoken believes Ruth was incensed at Sipes, his brother-in-law, for threatening his livelihood, fired him and likely banned him from the premises. Ruth had already lost his liquor license on West Conway for selling liquor on a Sunday, and he didn't want a repeat. When he found Sipes in his saloon that August night, he violently turned on him, with tragic results.

Babe wept openly at his father's funeral, prompting a relative to remark: "It was the first time I ever saw George cry."³⁸ His stepmother Martha inherited $4,000 from Ruth Sr.'s estate and the contents of the saloon. Two years later, she married George Strohmann, the former bartender from West Conway Street.³⁹ The building that housed Ruth's Café still stands today, mere steps from Camden Yards, occupied by the Goddess Gentleman's Club, a strip parlor.

Despite the death of his father, Babe had to keep playing ball. The World Series began September 5 in Chicago when Barrow chose Babe to open the

This is the building on South Eutaw Street that once housed Ruth's Café in Baltimore. Babe's father died on the street outside when he fell and struck his head during an altercation in the summer of 1918. The building still stands today, mere steps from Oriole Park at Camden Yards. It houses a strip club (David B. Stinson).

series against the Cubs, rather than 21-game winner Carl Mays. Ruth pitched nine scoreless innings and won 1-0, and hit a triple. He was thrilled about shutting out the National Leaguers, and in his 1948 autobiography Ruth admitted: "I didn't do it, but I was in a mood to send Brother Matthias a wire saying, 'Thanks again for convincing me that I wasn't a catcher.'"[40] Barrow chose Ruth to start game four, with the Red Sox up 2-1. The previous night, while horsing around on the train back to Boston, Ruth injured the middle finger on his pitching hand. Despite the swollen digit, Babe pitched effectively at Fenway, holding the Cubs scoreless for seven innings and winning 3-2. He had pitched 29⅔ consecutive innings in World Series play without allowing a run. It was a record that stood until 1962, when Yankee Whitey Ford threw 33⅔ scoreless innings. Babe helped himself during his second victory in the series with a two-run triple in the fourth inning.

Chicago took game five, 3-0, but Boston then won 2-1 to claim its fifth World Series title. The final game was played under a cloud. The players threatened to strike because of the small sums they'd receive as a result of small crowds and a decision to share proceeds with other teams and with charity. After a lengthy delay, they reluctantly agreed to play and each member of the Red Sox took home $1,102 and the Cubs, $671. The previous year, the winner's bonus was $3,669 and the loser's, $2,442. Babe batted only .200 in the series but his earned run average was a miserly 1.06.

When baseball concluded for 1918, Babe reported to Lebanon, Pennsylvania, for a job at Bethlehem Steel, an important contributor to the United States war effort. He and Helen rented an apartment nearby. Most ballplayers took similar work and it was generally assumed baseball might not return for 1919. Moving out of town was fortunate. In Boston, the Spanish Flu claimed hundreds of lives—202 on October 2 alone.[41] Babe told his friends he expected to be drafted soon, but an armistice was signed on November 11 to end hostilities. The war had claimed nearly eight million men in uniform, among them nearly 60,000 Americans killed and almost 190,000 wounded.

With the return of peace, Babe and Helen returned to the rural property near Sudbury, Massachusetts, where they had been living in since 1916, about 20 miles west of Boston. The small, furnished fishing camp on Willis Pond, known as Ihatetoquitit, had been provided them by its owner, Bill Joyce.[42] They would later buy a larger property in the same area.

Babe Ruth earned $7,000 in 1918 and was looking to double that in 1919. One of the brightest lights in the game of baseball was on a collision course with Red Sox management, however. He had avoided war, but battles of another kind lay ahead.

12

Making History

Babe Ruth could look ahead to the 1919 season with some sense of satisfaction, if not relief. So far, he had belted 20 home runs, many of them impressive drives that left tongues wagging. On the mound, he had won 80 games and lost 41. He was a threat with both his bat and his arm, although he still sought more playing time to showcase the former. He was in the spotlight and enjoying it.

He knew he had been a big part of the success of the Red Sox, winners of three World Series in his time with them. And he knew he had become an attraction for fans and the subject of countless stories in newspapers. Babe felt it was time to cash in. "I'm going to ask for a figure in my contract that may knock Mr. Frazee silly," he said, rather foolishly. "But nevertheless I think I am deserving of everything I ask."[1] He demanded a doubling of his salary to $15,000 in a two-year deal. But Harry Frazee, knocked silly or not, rejected that completely. Frazee had lost money during the 1918 season, the second in which Red Sox attendance had fallen sharply, despite the World Series success. And on the theatrical front, things were looking grim as well. Frazee began selling off players to get out of a financial hole. Pitchers Ernie Shore and Dutch Leonard and left fielder Duffy Lewis were sold to the New York Yankees in deals totaling $50,000. Meanwhile, Babe hired Johnny Igoe as his first business manager and was determined to make Frazee pay a premium for his services. If not, Babe said he'd retire to become a farmer in Sudbury, or perhaps a boxer. And he wanted to play left field so he could hit every day, saying: "I'll win more games playing every day in the outfield than I will pitching every fourth day."[2] Unimpressed, Frazee likened Ruth to the actors who were always trying to hit him up for more money. "They swear they are through with the show, they'll leave it flat," he said. "But it would take at least two squads of marines to keep them out of the theater and off the stage."[3] Frazee was a hard bargainer, but he realized his baseball show called the Red Sox desperately needed their star if he was going to attract fans back to Fenway.

Negotiations went back and forth for many weeks, continuing past March 18, when the Red Sox went south for spring training. Babe remained with Helen at the farm he'd purchased in Sudbury. Three days later, Frazee called him to New York and the two men agreed fairly quickly to $30,000 in a three-year deal (although it was reported as $27,000 at the time). Frazee told the press Babe would soon be on his way to Florida. Ruth was asked by reporters what position he'd play in the upcoming season. "I'm going to pitch, and I'm going to play in the outfield and in the infield, and any place else I can," he said, expansively. "Oh, yes, I expect to play every day."[4] It was unusual for a young player to agree to lock into a three-year deal, but it shielded him from salary cutbacks during a period of financial uncertainty and bought him some time to establish himself as a top hitter. His was among the top baseball salaries of the day.[5]

Ruth had been working out to shed some weight he had gained and when he reported for training camp he was in decent shape. He was single-mindedly determined to demonstrate to manager Barrow his value as a hitter. It didn't take him long. On April 4, in an exhibition game in Tampa against the New York Giants, he connected with a George Smith fastball and belted it to deep right center field. Observers gasped and said no ball had ever traveled so far. Reporters located some surveying equipment and found it landed 508 feet from home plate, then rolled another 71. Barrow was suitably impressed and placed Ruth in the outfield rather than on the mound. Barrow said years later that the towering drive in Tampa was a significant factor in his ultimate decision to convert his successful but reluctant pitcher to outfielder.[6] Giants manager John McGraw was among those who were impressed that day, even though he favored "small ball," in which hitting was less important than strong defense and effective pitching. "I believe that's the longest ball I ever saw," he marveled.[7] Thirteen days later, Babe hit four home runs in an exhibition game with the Orioles in Baltimore. The following day, again facing Orioles pitching, he drove two more. He was delighted to perform for old friends in the crowd, who included Xaverian Brothers and students from St. Mary's. "Today was my day to show them what I could do, and I did," he said later.[8] He was showing Barrow, too. He already had 18 homers in exhibition play.

The Red Sox appeared at the Polo Grounds for opening day, April 23, against the Yankees. The crowd of 30,000 was the largest opening crowd in New York baseball history. The war was over and returning troops helped boost attendance. Babe hit fourth in the order, and in his first at-bat connected for an inside-the-park homer as Boston blanked the Yankees 10–0. Ruth had set the tone for what would be a breakout season with his bat and he was becoming a box-office draw.

On April 24, fire destroyed the main building of St. Mary's Industrial Training School in Baltimore. All 850 boys and 30 Xaverian Brothers escaped safely, but two firemen were killed and fourteen others hurt in the blaze, which was traced to a hot rivet lost by a tinsmith during roof repairs. Damage was set at $750,000, a massive loss at the time. The main building, including its eastern and western wings, had been gutted, but the chapel was spared. Insurance was said to cover only $244,000. Directors decided almost immediately to launch a fundraising campaign to replace what had been lost.[9] A target of $500,000 was set by directors to allow for a modest expansion, and a public appeal for funds was launched. Meanwhile, about 550 of the boys were placed at the U.S. Army's Camp Holabird in southeast Baltimore, while the remainder were accepted by nearby institutions or returned to their parents.

News of the fire was devastating for Babe Ruth, its most famous alumnus, and he vowed to help. In early June, it was reported he sent a "large check" to Brother Paul "and said he wanted to do all he could to help the school."[10] A series of fundraising events was arranged in short order and the campaign was off to a good start. Even though they had lost their uniforms and instruments, the senior band scrambled to pitch in. They borrowed instruments from Camp Holabird and, despite initially lacking uniforms, embarked on

A fire started by a hot rivet lost by a roofer heavily damaged St. Mary's School in 1919. Two firefighters lost their lives but the boys and the Xaverian Brothers escaped. Babe Ruth donated money and helped raise funds to rebuild it. The school band joined Ruth and the New York Yankees for a road trip during which they raised more than $20,000 (Xaverian Brothers).

fundraising appearances throughout the area, producing "a handsome sum" for St. Mary's.[11] Movie nights and baseball games were arranged along with a "buy-a-brick" program, athletic carnivals, and boxing and wrestling matches. Response to the campaign was dramatic. By late June, donations climbed past the $300,000 mark, reflecting the goodwill St. Mary's had generated in the wider Baltimore area. The Xaverian Brothers and their board of directors were heartened by the response from the community and in early September awarded a contract to replace a dormitory building. Work on the main building, it was said, would be undertaken when more funds were available. On September 7, Babe Ruth brought his Red Sox to Oriole Park for a benefit game against the local Dry Docks, attracting an overflow crowd of 10,000. Among the spectators, no doubt, were Brother Paul and Brother Matthias and boys from St. Mary's and Mount St. Joseph. Baltimore's baseball prodigy delighted everyone by belting two home runs, the first in the opening inning that traveled so far it left the ballpark and bounced off the porch of a house on Greenmount Avenue.[12] Babe would hatch other ideas to help rebuild the school to which he owed so much, but for now he was busy hitting home runs at an unprecedented rate in the American League. In November, a Thanksgiving Ball was held at the Fifth Regiment Armory, which attracted 3,000 couples and produced $6,000 for the building fund. Such was the regard for the school and its work that the event attracted two senators, three congressmen, the Maryland governor and governor-elect, along with the mayor and former mayor of Baltimore.[13]

Early in the season, Babe and manager Ed Barrow clashed about Ruth's late-night carousing and Barrow assigned one of his coaches to keep an eye on him. But that did little to curb the prowling that kept his star player out until 4 a.m. or later on nights before games. At one point, Barrow confronted Ruth in front of the team, prompting Ruth to threaten Barrow with fisticuffs before backing off. Barrow suspended Ruth for a game, but the pair patched things up when a contrite Ruth attributed his behavior to an unsettled childhood and Barrow seemed willing to make peace. The pair agreed to a plan whereby Babe would leave a note in the hotel mailbox reporting when he had missed curfew and stating when he got in. It was far from ideal, but it allowed Babe to continue his party ways and Barrow to get his sleep.[14]

By May, Ruth became a permanent outfielder, although he would still be called upon to pitch from time to time. His regular appearances at the plate worked wonders. He was driving the baseball over outfield fences at a prodigious rate. On May 20, he hit the first grand slam home run of his career in a 6–4 victory in St. Louis. By July 29, in Boston, he tied the American League record of 16 home runs when the Red Sox lost 10–8 to Detroit. He did his best to win, playing left field and going to the plate five times, scoring three runs on three hits. With that performance, he'd hit homers in every American

League park. He didn't collect his record-setting 17th home run until August 14 in Chicago, but then he went on a tear, belting seven in 12 days, including his fourth grand slam. He was still far shy of the all-time record of 27 set by the National League's Ned Williamson in 1884. Ruth matched that mark on September 20 in Boston with a drive over the left field wall at Fenway Park. By now, the crowds were cheering for Babe to hit homers.[15] His timing was perfect. The day had been billed as Babe Ruth Day at Fenway and he delivered a memorable performance for the more than 30,000 fans, pitching six innings in the first game of a doubleheader against the league-leading Chicago White Sox. Four days later at the Polo Grounds in New York, Babe broke the all-time home run record in a manner that biographer Marshall Smelser said had "theatrical quality." His clout off Yankee pitcher Bob Shawkey came in the ninth inning, to tie the score at 1–1. The ball soared over the right field stands and landed in an adjacent park called Manhattan Field, making it the longest home run in Polo Grounds history.[16] The game went to 13 innings before Boston prevailed, 2–1. After his colossal blast, jeering from the hometown New York crowd turned to cheers each time Babe came to bat. On September 27, in Washington, he collected his 29th and final homer of the season. In celebration, he sent the bat to St. Mary's Industrial Training School, where it may have been used to assist fundraising efforts.

The season had been shortened to 140 games and the Red Sox played only 137. Babe went to bat in 130 of them, but the Red Sox finished sixth, far behind the pennant-winning Chicago White Sox. Ruth played 111 games in the outfield, made only two errors and had a fielding percentage of .996. Aside from his record 29 homers, he led the league in runs with 103, runs-batted-in with 113 and recorded a batting average of .322. He appeared in 17 games as a pitcher, 12 of them complete games, credited with winning 9 and losing 5. His earned run average was 2.97. Overall, his pitching record with Boston stood at an impressive 89 wins and 46 losses. Between 1915 and 1919, Babe's earned run average was 2.02 when American League pitchers collectively had averages ranging from 2.66 to 3.21.[17] His pitching was so good it was worthy of induction into a future hall of fame. But Babe Ruth preferred to play outfield so he could hit every day. His approach was working out well and he had become the talk of the game—as a batter.

The Chicago White Sox faced the Cincinnati Reds in the World Series that fall in what would become known as the Black Sox Scandal. Several members of the White Sox, initially favored to win, conspired with gamblers to "throw" the series for a reported $100,000, to be split among all participating players. Several of them had heard rumors the crosstown Chicago Cubs had received $10,000 to drop the 1918 World Series to the Boston Braves. Even though the Sox were well paid, they sought some of that kind of action as financial gravy. The Reds won the series, but not all the money promised to the

Sox players was paid. Rumors persisted they had thrown the series for gamblers, but it wasn't until October 29, 1920, that five indictments of conspiring to obtain money by false pretenses were returned by a grand jury. In all, eight White Sox were named along with several gamblers.[18] A judge dismissed the charges, but new indictments were filed and the trial began in June of 1921. In the end, the jury found all defendants not guilty. It was said the defense was able to get jurors to identify with the accused, especially the working-class jurors who may also have been fans. Meanwhile White Sox owner Charlie Comiskey was painted as wealthy and unsympathetic. The verdict was not the end of the woes for the Black Sox, however. Newly appointed commissioner of baseball, Judge Kenesaw Mountain Landis, banned the eight from ever again playing in organized baseball. Landis, a baseball fan and sometimes irascible jurist and moralist, had been hired to end discord among owners, especially about players which the three-member National Commission he replaced had failed to address adequately. Landis took it upon himself to forever rid the game of the scourge of gambling.[19] Those banned were ringleader Eddie Cicotte, Chick Gandil, Buck Weaver, "Shoeless" Joe Jackson, Happy Felsch, Swede Risberg, Lefty Williams and Fred McMullin. Four civil lawsuits filed by the banned players were later settled out of court for modest sums. The Black Sox Scandal cast a pall over the game and public confidence in it suffered. It was a low point for professional baseball.

As soon as the 1919 season ended for the Red Sox, Babe played in a series of exhibition games in the northeast and in late October left for Los Angeles for a series of games in California. Before leaving, he turned in his Red Sox uniforms at Fenway Park and declared he was done with the team "unless Frazee comes through good." He wanted to tear up his three-year contract for $30,000 (signed just a year earlier) and wanted $20,000 for 1920. He was being difficult again, saying he would quit baseball for the movies or switch to boxing if Frazee didn't see things his way.[20]

Frazee had grown tired of fighting with his star player and desperately needed money for his theatrical operation. The producer had overextended himself and was in a receptive mood to sell players. In addition to his theatrical woes, he owed former Red Sox owner J. J. Lannin $262,000 in a note that was due November 1, 1919. It was the balance of the purchase price for the club.[21] During the 1919 season, Frazee sold pitcher Carl Mays, who had quit the Red Sox, complaining he wasn't supported by his teammates on the field. Disliked by the other players, Mays was about to be suspended by manager Ed Barrow but Frazee had him delay doing so and sold Mays to the Yankees. At the end of the previous season, the Yankees paid $25,000 for three Red Sox players who had returned from the war—Frazee knew how deep the pockets were of Yankee owners Col. Jacob Ruppert and Col. Tillinghast L'Hommedieu Huston. Ruppert and Huston had purchased the Yankees, formerly known as the Highlanders, in 1914. The team, well behind the Giants in fan support in New York, had finished the 1919 season in third place. They played their games at the Polo Grounds, which they rented from the Giants. The two sometimes-feuding colonels, Ruppert a brewer, Huston an engineer, were planning an assault on the American League pennant. The pair asked manager Miller Huggins what he needed to make champions of the team. He suggested obtaining Ruth and the colonels promptly dispatched the diminutive Huggins to talk to Frazee. The Yankee owners learned Frazee wanted $125,000 for Ruth, the greatest sum ever demanded for a player (the deal for Mays and two other players had fetched $75,000). Frazee felt Ruth had been too difficult to deal with, his salary demands were excessive and his off-field behavior was bad for team morale. Frazee thought the proceeds would let him buy quality players who were more committed to team than to personal pleasure. And the funds would address his financial issues in the theater. When Ruppert agreed to lend Frazee $300,000 in a personal loan, in effect secured by Fenway Park, the blockbuster deal was signed on December 26.[22] The Yankees sweetened Babe's existing contract, agreeing to pay him $41,000 in total for the 1920 and 1921 seasons. Of that, $1,000 was an immediate bonus. He would receive from Ruppert the $20,000 salary he had demanded from Frazee.[23] Ruppert and Huston were willing to pay a premium, gambling that Ruth would draw new fans and significantly improve their team and its finances.

Shortly after the deal was struck, Prohibition began in the United States on January 17, 1920, when the Volstead Act went into effect. Despite that development, it was a good time for Babe to land in New York City, a city that would never abandon fun and where alcohol could always be found. Ruth biographer Jane Leavy eloquently described the fortuitous timing of Ruth's arrival in the American metropolis:

> It was his good fortune to become famous at the precise moment in history when mass media was redefining and amplifying what it meant to be public, and when societal upheaval was creating a new cast system for celebrity. Among the casualties of the Great War were old money and the old aristocracy; out of the ashes rose consumerism and marketing and a new, more equitable American star system featuring rags-to-riches heroes: Babe Ruth, Jack Dempsey, Clara Bow, and Rudolph Valentino. Their ascendance from lower stations, palpable need for public approbation, personal tragedies, and failings—and, critically their triumphs over those tragedies and failings—affirmed the animating principle of the American dream.[24]

Babe was ready for New York and the city was ready for him. New York was the epicenter of mass media, with 18 daily newspapers when Ruth signed with the Yankees. Circulation wars were underway in the city of 5.6 million, and sports coverage accounted for 10 to 15 percent of the space in newspapers. "New York was the most glamorous, most vibrant city in the postwar world," Ruth biographer Leigh Montville noted, and newspapers sought to capture and reflect that. Before long, radio began broadcasting baseball games, with breathless accounts of the play making the stars come alive for listeners.[25] Babe Ruth's accomplishments with a bat made him a character larger than life. The media merely amplified that further and he became their

For 1920, Babe was focused on his hitting with the New York Yankees. Note his beautiful handwriting. Brother Matthias made the natural lefty switch to his right hand to write. Ruth's flowing script adorned baseballs and contracts he signed over the years, as well as photographs such as this one. Brother Matthias never tampered with Ruth's throwing or batting from the left side (Library of Congress).

darling. The Roaring Twenties, with their rampant hedonism, were underway. Pursuit of pleasure was key, with newfound individual freedoms and progressive sexual and social attitudes. It was the Jazz Age, an entirely new era. Prohibition be damned. Babe was far from the cloistered deprivations of St. Mary's Industrial Training School. And he ate it up.

In his new playpen of the Polo Grounds, Babe would benefit from the livelier, cork-centered baseball that had been introduced. And pitchers were no longer allowed to doctor balls by scuffing them or by other means. They had done so to alter the flight of the ball, making it more deceptive. The spitball was banned, and 17 pitchers who had come to rely on it were grandfathered. As a pitcher, Babe had never needed to doctor the ball. Another rule change allowed scorekeepers to record home runs that drove in winning runs to end a game. Previously, they were considered hits. Ruth and others had been denied home runs under the old rule.[26] Things were breaking Babe Ruth's way as he joined his second major-league team. And he would exploit every break.

Many fans in Boston were upset at the blockbuster deal. How could Frazee sell off such a talented player? Some, however, including former players, realized Ruth was largely a one-man show and a cohesive team was more likely to find success. Johnny Keenan, leader of the Royal Rooters fan club, was blunt in his assessment from the fan's perspective. "Ruth was 90 per cent of our club last summer. It will be impossible to replace the strength Ruth gave the Red Sox.... The Red Sox management will have an awful time filling the gap caused by his going. Surely gate receipts will suffer."[27] Frazee tried to explain. "There is no getting away from the fact that despite his 29 home runs, the Red Sox finished sixth last year," he said. "What the Boston fans want, I take it, and what I want because they want it, is a winning team, rather than a one-man team that finishes in sixth place." And Frazee dismissed Ruth's home run hitting as "more spectacular than useful."[28] Ruppert and Huston would exploit the spectacle that was Babe Ruth. And for decades Boston fans would lament the "Curse of the Bambino" that befell the Red Sox after Frazee sold the Babe.

After a slow start for 1920, Ruth set a major-league record of 11 homers in the month of May, then again with 13 in June. By July 16, he tied his 29 homers from 1919. Three days later, he drove two offerings from Chicago lefthander Dick Kerr into the right field bleachers at the Polo Grounds to break his own record, delighting the 26,000 fans. He doffed his cap to the crowd as he trotted around the base paths on the second round-tripper.[29] His hometown Baltimore and St. Mary's Industrial Training School also celebrated his achievement. Mayor William F. Broening sent a telegram of congratulations, saying: "We are proud that the home-run king is one of our boys." At St. Mary's, Brother Matthias took to the grandstand at the ballfield where Babe had played to announce with pride his latest accomplishment. Brother Matthias read the entire account of the game from the *Baltimore Sun* to the cheers of the boys and Xaverian Brothers present. Brother Matthias then sent Babe a note about how well the news had been received at the school, wished him well for the rest of the season and added he was hoping for 40 homers.[30]

Babe far exceeded the hopes of the students and staff at St. Mary's. He recorded a startling 54 home runs, putting more blasts out of the park than the 14 other major-league teams. Ruth was fourth in batting average with .375, but first in runs with 158, first in runs-batted-in with 135 and first in slugging average with .847, the latter mark standing for more than 80 years. Ruppert and Huston smiled at the production of their new acquisition, although the Yankees again finished third. Attendance was on the upswing, however, as fans flocked to see their new slugging sensation. The Yankees became the first team in baseball history to draw one million fans in a season. At 1,289,422 paid admissions, attendance was nearly twice that of 1919. They even outdrew the Giants, their in-town National League rivals, by 100,000 fans. The senior team noted the sudden popularity of the upstart Yankees and owner Charles A. Stoneham suggested they find a new home because the welcome mat at the Polo Grounds was being withdrawn.[31] After the season, Ed Barrow was hired as general manager of the Yankees, reuniting him with Ruth.

Babe's exploits were celebrated by the press and despite the fact he already had a nickname, the writers tripped over themselves to come up with other catchy monikers. He'd been called "Colossus" by the Boston press, but in New York that became the Colossus of Clout. Some of the new names verged on silly. He was the Wizard of Wham, the Sultan of Swat, the Prince of Pounders, Maharajah of Mash, Wali of Wallop, Caliph of Clout and Behemoth of Bash, among many others, such as the Bambino and Big Fella. His teammates simply called him Jidge, a variation of George.[32]

Midway through the season, he purchased a bright red Packard touring car with his newfound wealth and was allowed to travel separately on some team road trips. He liked cars but his driving remained terrible and far too fast. In fact, he cheated death at one point. He and the Yankees whitewashed the Washington Senators 17–0 on July 6 in Washington and Babe and Helen opted to stay behind and drive home the next day. They offered a ride home to three players in the large luxury machine: Frank Gleich, a substitute outfielder, Fred Hofman, third string catcher, and Charley O'Leary, an assistant Yankees coach and former second baseman for Detroit. At about 3 a.m. on July 8, Ruth was at the wheel near Wawa, Pennsylvania, just west of Philadelphia, when he left the road while traveling too quickly through a sharp bend and the Packard flipped upside down. One report said it occurred when he tried to pass another car, while another said he had swerved to avoid an oncoming vehicle. Regardless, Babe and Helen and the three others were trapped underneath the big car but all managed to crawl out. Babe had a badly bruised knee and Helen received a cut to her leg. All were shaken up and it was a miracle no one was killed. The *Baltimore Sun* said it was lucky that "the [convertible] top was up" and the car came to rest in a clay bank beside the road.[33]

When Ruth got free of the wreckage he readily found Helen, Gleich and Hofman. But O'Leary was lying on his back in the middle of the road. Ruth feared he was dead. He went to O'Leary, fell to his knees and, wracked by guilt, cried out: "Oh, my God! Oh, God, bring Charley back! Don't take him. I didn't mean it."

As he lifted O'Leary's head, his eyes fluttered open. Ruth begged him: "Speak to me, Charley, speak to me."

Dazed and confused, O'Leary looked around, came to his senses and croaked: "What the hell happened? Where's my hat?"

O'Leary suffered nothing more than a headache.[34]

The fivesome made it to a nearby farmhouse where Helen's cut was bandaged, and soon afterward the party caught a train in Wawa for Philadelphia and then on to New York.[35] Ruth told a local mechanic to sell the wreck for whatever it would fetch, explaining: "I am in a hurry. I'll get a new one in New York."[36] In his 1948 autobiography penned by Bob Considine, Babe admitted he had been driving too fast for the curve. He marveled at the outcome. "For some reason which I can never understand if I live to be a hundred, none of us was hurt."[37]

Despite a noticeable limp, Babe played later that day at the Polo Grounds, delivering a triple in a 4–3 loss to Detroit. By now, stories about Ruth's poor driving were well known. In September, some Wall Street bookmakers anxious to improve the odds of Cleveland beating the Yankees spread a false story to the newspapers that New York's Bob Meusel and Del Pratt had been killed in a car crash near Cleveland in which Babe broke a leg and shoulder and crushed three ribs, while another player, Duffy Lewis was badly bruised.[38] The story was exposed for the lie it was, but the Indians won the game anyway, 10–4, on September 9. It had gained an instant aura of believability because of Ruth's reputation behind the wheel.

Late in the 1920 season, Yankees management agreed to help with the ongoing fundraising efforts at St. Mary's. The school was still short of its $500,000 goal. So the school band was allowed to join the team for a western road trip, accompanied by several Xaverians, including Brothers Paul, Matthias, Gilbert and music director, Brother Simon.[39] Fifty excited musicians, aged 9 to 17, left Baltimore with their chaperones on September 8 and joined the Yankees in Cleveland, Detroit, Chicago, St. Louis, Indianapolis, Pittsburgh, New York, Boston and Philadelphia, ending with an exhibition game in Baltimore. On the day they left town, band members marched past the *Baltimore Sun* offices on their way to the train station. They sang in unison a newly composed song, "Batterin' Babe," whose lyrics celebrated their hero's record-breaking home runs. In every city, the band paraded from their hotel to the ballpark where they played until game time. Band members often went through the stands seeking donations, carrying a sign that read: "Babe Ruth's Boys Band. Do Your Bit to Help Rebuild the School That Made Babe Ruth Famous." The band played evening concerts and afternoons wherever crowds gathered, such as racetracks. Babe would appear with the band and mug with it for the local press to encourage donations. The tour opened in Cleveland with that 10–4 Yankees loss on September 9 that bookies had tried to influence. Babe hit a homer and the young musicians cheered so hard he bought 50 bags of peanuts for them. After traveling by steamer from Cleveland to Detroit, the band pulled in $1,200 at a concert staged by the Knights of Columbus. Babe arranged a special concert at the encampment of the Grand Army of the Republic (a fraternal organization of Union Army veterans from the Civil War) in Indianapolis and a giant ice cream party in Pittsburgh when the Yankees played special exhibition games in those two cities.[40] The tour ended September 23 with a benefit game back home in Baltimore between the Yankees and Jack Dunn's Orioles, who had just won another International League pennant. When Babe took the field to play first base, he had already belted 49 home runs in league play and the crowd was his. About 15,000 fans packed the ballpark and saw the Orioles win, 1–0.

The tour had been a smashing success. In all, the band traveled 2,500 miles, played before 400,000 people and turned a profit of $13,387 on a total income of $25,488, once expenses were deducted. Babe himself contributed $4,100. "Those kids really could play," Ruth said of the band in his 1948 autobiography. "The fans were most liberal, and those good-will offerings were a big factor in erecting the new and better buildings now at St. Mary's."[41]

In August, the first telling of the Babe Ruth story was published to meet public demand for tales about baseball's new hero. The United News Service retained young sportswriter Westbrook Pegler to ghostwrite an 80,000-word (book-length) newspaper serial as though it came from the pen of Ruth. It ran to 12 installments in newspapers. Pegler was hobbled by Ruth's unwillingness to sit still to be interviewed.[42] In all, he had about 15 minutes with the star and was forced to cobble together much of his life story from newspaper accounts and other sources, some of which included Pegler's imagination. (In 2011, William Cobb edited the columns into the book *Babe Ruth: Playing the Game. My Early Years in Baseball.*) Over the years, other ghostwriters were hired to tell the story of Ruth, with mixed success.

In 1921, Ruth hit 59 home runs and led the league in runs scored with 177, runs-batted-in with 168 and a slugging average of .846. On July 18, Ruth recorded his 139th homer, to break the career home run record set by longtime Giant Roger Connor. The Yankees took the American League pennant for the first time in their history but fell to the Giants in the World Series. Ruth was injured during the series, cutting his left arm while sliding in game two and it became infected. In the fifth game, he wrenched a knee. After the season, despite a new ban on barnstorming by pennant-winning teams, Babe did just that with his Babe Ruth All Stars, visiting upstate New York and Pennsylvania. In previous years, he had doubled his income with such post-season tours, but Major League Baseball now felt the practice detracted from the prestige of the World Series. Babe and fellow Yankee Bob Meusel drew the ire of Kenesaw Mountain Landis, the commissioner of baseball, who fined each $3,362 and suspended them for the first six weeks of the 1922 season.[43]

Because of his suspension, Ruth saw action in only 110 games in 1922, with an associated loss of production at the plate. He managed 35 homers, but led the league in slugging percentage at .672. The Yankees again won the American League pennant and again fell to the Giants in the World Series. It was the last year the club would play at the Polo Grounds from which they were being evicted. In 1923, the team moved to Yankee Stadium, built for $2.3 million, across the Harlem River in the Bronx. Babe's drawing power was credited with making the new home possible and it quickly became known as "The House That Ruth Built." With its short right field fence, some observers suggested it was instead "The House Built for Ruth" because that was the fence over which most of his drives soared. All 62,000 seats were occupied, and thousands more stood, for opening day on April 18 as the Yankees downed the Red Sox, 4–1. Rising to the occasion, as he so often did, Babe drove a Howard Ehmke offering over the fence into the right field bleachers in the third inning. It was a fitting way to christen the new ballpark. In all, he belted 41 homers that season and recorded a batting average of .393. Yet again, the Yankees faced the Giants in the World Series, but this time the American Leaguers prevailed, as Ruth went 7-for-19 at the plate and had three homers. Among the fans on hand was Brother Matthias, who Babe invited to every World Series game as his guest.[44] Ruth was named the American League's Most Valuable Player, the only time he won the honor.

In 1924, Babe won his only batting title, with a .378 batting average and slugging percentage of .739, while collecting 46 home runs. But the Yankees finished the season in second place, behind the Washington Senators. The following season was a bad one for Ruth and for the team, which dropped to seventh place. He showed up at training camp weighing 256 pounds and had the worst season of his career. He fell ill during April with a mysterious ailment originally attributed to consuming too many hot dogs. It was dubbed the "Bellyache Heard 'Round the World." Ruth required surgery for what doctors called an "intestinal abscess." Upon recovery, he went back to partying all night, chasing women and good times, and by the end of the season he was in poor condition. Yankee manager Miller Huggins battled with Babe about his off-field antics and in August hired a private detective to trail him when the team played in Chicago and St. Louis. Ruth was with six different women one night in the Windy City and had patronized the most famous whorehouse in St. Louis, the detective reported. At the end of August, Huggins fined Ruth $5,000 and said he was suspended for the balance of the season. On Labor Day, however, Huggins relented and let a chastened Ruth return to the lineup.[45] During his suspension, Brother Matthias and Brother Paul defended the wayward son of St. Mary's. "He is just a kid," Brother Paul told the *Baltimore Evening Sun*. "Illness and bad influences are responsible." The school principal, newly promoted to the post of "Provincial," or leader of the Xaverian Order in the United States, said he had "utmost faith in Ruth and believes that with proper handling he will continue to be one of the brilliant figures in baseball."[46] Brother Paul noted that Brother Matthias met with Ruth in New York before the western road trip. "At that time it appeared that his physical condition was improving…. He had dinner with Babe and his family and found him apparently in the best of spirits." Babe could always rely on Brothers Paul and Matthias to vouch for him. Overall, the 1925 season had been dismal for the slugger with his illness, suspension and extracurricular activities, all of which affected his performance. He managed only 25 home runs, while seeing action in only 98 games.

Babe realized he had to shape up for the 1926 season as fans began wondering if his best years were behind him. Working in the gym in the off-season and going on a diet, he reported for spring training having shed 44 pounds. Aside from weight, he had lost even more because of his constant womanizing. He and Helen had separated and she had moved to Boston from the farm in Sudbury. Babe considered divorce, but Brother Matthias talked him out of it.[47]

For 1926, the 31-year-old Babe Ruth was reborn, rising from the ashes of 1925. From 1926 until the end of 1931, he was an impressive and reliable hitter, averaging more than 50 home runs during each of those six seasons. "Ruth put on the finest sustained display of hitting that baseball had ever seen," biographer Robert W. Creamer declared.[48]

In 1926, he played 152 games and launched 47 home runs while batting .372. Ruth continued to be a headache for general manager Ed Barrow and his diminutive on-field manager Miller Huggins, with whom he clashed about his behavior on and off the field. The Yankees continued to hire private detectives to keep an eye on their star. And from time to time, Brother Matthias was called upon to provide fatherly advice to which Babe seemed to respond positively. In June, on their first trip to Chicago, a city whose delights invariably led Babe astray, the Yankees stayed at the Del Prado Hotel and decided once again to call upon Brother Matthias. Their four-game series began June 17 and the city was hopping. The XXVIII (28th) International Eucharistic

Congress was being held from June 20 to 24 and Brother Matthias was invited to attend the event and counsel his former student while in town. The Congress, a sort of spiritual Olympics for Catholics, was expected to attract nearly a million attendees for its first time held in the United States. One of the featured events was a Pontifical High Mass at Soldiers' Field, celebrated on June 21, by Giovanni Cardinal Bonzano, a papal delegate, that attracted half a million adherents of the faith.[49]

One evening, Brother Matthias came to the Del Prado and occupied a chair in the lobby from which he could see the hotel elevator. Ruth soon appeared, with plans for another night on the town. When he spotted Brother Matthias the two greeted each other warmly. Brother Matthias explained he happened to be in the Windy City for the Congress, but also wanted to see Ruth play. So he found where the Yankees were staying and wanted to take his former pupil out to dinner. Ruth altered his plans for the night and stayed out with Brother Matthias until nearly 11 p.m. During their meal, Brother Matthias delivered strong advice to Ruth about his need to clean up his act. It can be easily surmised he told Ruth he was disappointed in his off-field activities. Brother Matthias hadn't encouraged young Ruth to live a God-centered life only to see him pursue a lifestyle filled with women and booze. The boys at St. Mary's looked up to him and they deserved a hero whose behavior they could model. Babe, he said, was letting them down. Brother Matthias also suggested Ruth should try to rebuild his relationship with Helen. The papers had been full of stories about his marital woes, but Brother Matthias said divorce remained out of the question. The prodigal son listened intently and promised to do better. As Ruth biographer Marshall Smelser put it, "this was the turning point in Ruth's behavior. Certainly he no longer after that time had the reputation for hell-raising that he had before."[50] There would still be lapses. After all, he was Babe Ruth.

Brother Matthias, Ruth's surrogate father, always brought him back to earth and the superstar mended his ways, if only for a time. His deep and abiding respect for Brother Matthias saw him purchase his mentor a shiny new Cadillac as a thank you after one of their "Come to Jesus" sessions. This was in 1922, 1925 or 1926, depending on the source. Biographer Marshall Smelser said the gift came after Babe received one of his first big pay checks from the Yankees in 1922.[51] That date seems to be confirmed by a report in the *Baltimore Sun* from early 1923 about Brother Matthias driving some visiting theatrical performers to St. Joseph's Monastery in the Baltimore suburb of Irvington "in an automobile given the latter by 'Babe' Ruth, the baseball player."[52]

Biographer Kal Wagenheim said the extravagant gift was bestowed on Brother Matthias during Babe's dismal 1925 season, when he seemed to hit rock bottom as an overweight, ill and sometimes suspended troublemaker.

12. Making History

Babe had invited Brother Matthias to New York and the two talked as they strolled along the streets of the city. Babe loved shiny new cars and when he spotted a Cadillac in a Manhattan showroom he was distracted, and asked his towering mentor: "Do you think I ought to buy that car?" Brother Matthias replied: "If you can afford it, George." Brother Matthias couldn't believe his eyes the next day when the Cadillac was delivered to his hotel, with a note thanking him "for what you and St. Mary's have done for me."[53] The gift put Brother Matthias in a quandary. When he became an Xaverian, he made a vow of poverty and couldn't own worldly possessions. So the vehicle was registered to the school but he retained priority use of it to ferry students around to various destinations. In return, they helped him clean and maintain it, learning the basics of auto mechanics. Ever a teacher, Brother Matthias turned his gift into a teaching tool. Ruth Biographer Jane Leavy said Ruth bought Brother Matthias a second Cadillac in 1926, shortly after the Chicago visit, but doesn't indicate when the first was given.[54]

With a recharged and refocused Ruth in their lineup for 1926 and some talented new players, the Yankees claimed the American League pennant. They faced the St. Louis Cardinals in the World Series and in the fourth game Babe connected for three home runs, a first for him in a single game. But the Yankees lost the seventh and deciding game when Babe was thrown out trying to steal second.

Babe and his bat were back. But the greatest season for the Yankees and their slugger lay just ahead.

13

The Peak and Past It

Babe spent the first couple of months of 1927 in California where he starred in a movie called *The Babe Comes Home*. The silent film, shot in 22 days, was about a character named Babe Duggan, a hard-hitting slugger for the Los Angeles Angels who falls for a woman assigned the job of cleaning his uniforms that were stained by chewing tobacco. They fall in love and plan to marry, but the woman insists he quit his tobacco habit. He does so, but his hitting suffers. In a climactic moment in a crucial game he is struggling at the plate and sees his love sitting in the stands. She takes pity on him, tosses him a plug of chewing tobacco and he does the predictable by hitting a homer. And in Hollywood fashion, they marry and live happily ever after. The film opened May 22 and was quickly forgotten. Less than five months later, another St. Mary's alumnus, Al Jolson, starred in *The Jazz Singer*, a feature-length film using the new sound system known as Vitaphone. In the musical, Jolson delivered one of the most famous lines in movie history when he said: "Wait a minute. Wait a minute. You ain't heard nothin' yet." It marked the beginning of "talkies," and the era of short silent films such as *The Babe Comes Home* soon went the way of the dinosaur.[1]

For the new season, Ruth told Colonel Jacob Ruppert he wanted $100,000 a year in a two-year contract. He'd heard that an aging Ty Cobb was offered $75,000 a year by the Philadelphia Athletics, so he was determined to exceed that. As it turned out, Cobb actually received $50,000 with bonuses that added another $25,000.[2] The Yankees replied with an offer of $52,000 a year, the same deal they had had with Babe since 1922. Eventually, both sides settled on $70,000 in a three-year pact. The newspapers had a field day with the size of his new pay packet. They calculated Babe would be earning $457.79 a day, enough money for a trip to Europe. His $11,666 every month would buy a new home and they estimated his annual salary could support 20 families for a year. Meanwhile, the median pay for Yankee players that year stood at $7,000, about two weeks in Babe money.

Many observers regard the 1927 Yankees team as the greatest of all time. The powerhouse assembled by Ed Barrow and Colonel Ruppert included not only Ruth, but second baseman Tony Lazzeri, outfielder Bob Meusel, first baseman Lou Gehrig and pitchers Waite Hoyt, Herb Pennock, Urban Shocker and a new addition, Wilcy Moore. Pitching was much improved, with Hoyt and Shocker recording the best and second-best earned run averages in the American League. Waite won 22 games, Pennock and Moore, 19 each, and Shocker, 18. Everything came together for the Yankees, who seemed nearly invincible. New York batted .307 as a team, won 110 games and lost only 44, a winning record that endured until 1954 when the Cleveland Indians won 111. In all, Yankee batters hit 158 home runs, to set a major-league record. Gehrig clouted 47 homers and Lazzeri, 18, but it was Babe's year for glory. As the season wore on, he and Gehrig matched each other for homers day in and day out. But Ruth continued to launch balls out of the park at a faster clip than Gehrig. With four games left to play, Babe had collected 56 dingers and the baseball world held its breath. In the first of those four final games, he belted a grand slam for number 57. On September 29 at Yankee Stadium, he homered twice against the Senators in a 15–4 win to tie his 1921 record of 59. The following day, in the second-to-last game of the season, he again faced the Senators. With the score tied 2–2 in the eighth inning and one out, Babe came to the plate to face left-hander Tom Zachary. Yankee Mark Koenig was at third, having tripled. The Senators hurler could have walked Ruth in a bid for a double play to end the inning and keep Koenig from scoring. But Zachary decided to pitch. Babe looked at a called strike and then laid off a high ball. Observers think Zachary then went with a screwball that broke inside, about ankle high. Ruth reached down and connected with a mighty whack to send the offering halfway up the right field bleachers.[3] He had his 60th. Babe's record performance wasn't eclipsed until 1961 by Yankee Roger Maris. His blast won the game and the Yankees took the pennant by 19 games.

Babe had been obsessed with exceeding the 59 homers he hit in 1921. He'd been challenged by 24-year-old Gehrig and Ruth, now 32, was determined to assert himself as the unquestioned home-run king. In the clubhouse afterward, he was like a kid again. "Sixty, count 'em, sixty!" he crowed. "Let some other son of a bitch match that!"[4] Later that night, still excited, he telephoned St. Mary's to share the news with his mentor and father figure. "I got my sixtieth today, Brother," he told Brother Matthias. Several years later, the gentle Xaverian fondly recalled that night. He said the boy-turned-man he knew as George was "just as proud and as happy as when he was a kiddo at the school."[5] Babe had a right to be proud. He made history, and did so after some scribes began hinting his decline had begun. In the *New York Times*, columnist John Kieran described his feat this way: "It will be a long time before anyone else betters that home-run mark, and a still longer time before any aging athlete makes such a gallant and glorious charge over the come-back trail."[6]

Despite his record-setting clip that summer, Babe was distracted by an incident that could have claimed the life of his mentor. It came on August 14 as he and Gehrig were engaged in their battle of bats. Gehrig stood at 38 homers and Ruth had 36 when the Yankees met Washington at Griffith Stadium to conclude a four-game series. Neither slugger added to his tally that day and both delivered rather lackluster performances; Gehrig had a single in four at-bats, while Ruth went 1-for-5, singling in the fourth inning. By now, newspapers such as the *New York Daily News* were providing daily updates on the "stickwork" of the two Yankee sluggers.[7] Ruth's bad day that Sunday was nothing compared to that of Brother Matthias, however. That evening, Brother Matthias and his nephew were returning from a visit with friends in Dorsey, just southwest of Baltimore. He was driving the big Cadillac Babe had given him through a rainstorm, when the vehicle stalled while crossing the tracks of the main line of the Baltimore and Ohio Railroad. The *Baltimore Sun* described what happened next:

> Unable to move it, Brother Matthias summoned help. He was told the express was due in a few minutes. As a small group pulled, pushed and tugged at the machine a man ran down the tracks and attempted to flag the train.
>
> The engineer presumably did not see the distress signal and the train continued on its way. Hearing its approach, Brother Matthias and his helpers stood nearby as the engine crashed into the automobile.
>
> When the train had passed all that remained of "Babe's" gift was two spare tires.[8]

Babe learned of the mishap soon afterward and no doubt called Brother Matthias to express relief no one had been hurt. It had been a close call.

The Yankees faced the Pittsburgh Pirates in the World Series that fall and yet again Babe invited Brother Matthias to the games in New York, this time providing him with four tickets. Joining Brother Matthias were Brother Benjamin, the new superintendent of St. Mary's, who had replaced Brother Paul the previous year, Catholic priest Louis C. Vaeth and Vincent DeP. Fitzpatrick, managing editor of the *Baltimore Catholic Review*. The tickets were for box seats directly behind the Yankees dugout. The series began October 5 in Pittsburgh. The Pirates were a good team, but no match for the Yankees, who won the first game 5–4 despite being outhit. Neither Ruth nor Gehrig homered. In game two, the big bats of Ruth and Gehrig again failed to connect for any round-trippers, but the Yankees won again, 6–2. Without a day off, the series moved to New York. Gehrig connected for a triple early in the first inning of the opening game in Yankee Stadium, but was thrown out at home when he tried to stretch his drive into an inside-the-park home run. Ruth parked one in the right field bleachers in the seventh inning and the Yankees cruised to an 8–1 win. In the fourth game, Babe blasted his second homer of the series deep into center field in the fifth inning, and the Yankees won 4–3, to sweep the series. More than 201,000 attended the games, but doubtless none enjoyed Babe's heroics more than his four guests who enjoyed a close-up view.

Before Brother Matthias left town, Babe gave him another Cadillac to replace the car destroyed two months earlier on the train tracks. The date is hard to pin down, but a photograph of Babe and Brother Matthias with the latest automotive gift includes Brother Benjamin, the new superintendent of St. Mary's, so it must have been later than mid–1926. Evidence suggests it was 1927 because we know Benjamin, Brother Matthias, Vaeth and Fitzpatrick were in New York for the World Series that year. Benjamin appears in the photo. Ruth and teammate Bob Meusel are wearing sweaters and the woman is wearing a fur coat, consistent with clothing required in October. The stylish woman may be Claire Hodgson, whom Babe had been seeing by then. Helen's last World Series appearance with Babe was in 1926. The venue is not clear, but it resembles an exterior wall at St. Mary's and the image may have been taken in Baltimore when the car was delivered. One photo shows Brother Matthias towering over Babe as they stand beside the vehicle, while another shows him behind the wheel. In his 1948 autobiography, Babe described his shiny gifts to Brother Matthias this way:

> Once, in a burst of gratitude, when I got sentimental about what he had done for me as a kid, I presented Brother Matthias with a Cadillac. He stalled it on some train tracks near St. Mary's not long after that, and a freight came along and smacked it lopsided. So I gave him another one. I'd have bought him one every week, if he hadn't put a stop to it.[9]

The winning share for players in the series was $5,782, almost the same amount as the retail cost of a top-of-the-line Cadillac, although several years later Brother Matthias recalled the car cost $8,000.[10] The Xaverian could be excused for getting the figure incorrect because his vow of poverty precluded him from having the sort of consumer savviness of someone familiar with luxury cars.

The Yankees of 1928 again took the American League pennant, winning 13 fewer games than during their memorable 1927 season. Babe hit 54 home runs and led the major leagues in slugging with a .709 average. The Yankees swept the St. Louis Cardinals in the World Series, with Babe batting .625 and hitting three homers.

With the help of sportswriter Ford Frick of the *New York Evening World*, Babe "wrote" his first autobiography in book form. *Babe Ruth's Own Book of Baseball* was released early in 1928 and Frick found the same practical problem faced by Westbrook Pegler eight years earlier in the newspaper series he produced: Babe refused to sit down for the lengthy interviews required to chronicle his life story accurately. The book was generally well received, however. The public couldn't get enough of Babe Ruth, now at the peak of his success. The book's focus was on how Babe played the game, the men he played against and his observations about them. And it included plenty of tips for kids. Ruth likely never found the time to read the book, which the publisher attributed to one George Herman Ruth. Had Babe done so, he might have demanded a correction on one important aspect. Frick credited Brother Gilbert as the discoverer, nurturer, coach and mentor of Babe. Brother Matthias was mentioned in only two sentences, described as one of the "fine men" at St. Mary's.[11] And his name was misspelled as "Mathias." In Frick's telling of Babe's story, Brother Gilbert met Ruth during his early days at St. Mary's, where Brother Gilbert was teaching. Babe said he wasn't happy at St. Mary's initially. "But Brother Gilbert stuck with me. I owe him a lot. More than I'll ever be able to repay.... He used to coach our baseball team, and he liked the way I did things." He said Brother Gilbert's letter suggesting him to Jack Dunn of the Orioles led to his signing his first baseball contract. At least the latter assertion was partly true. Because Frick credited Brother Gilbert with giving Ruth to the world, and barely mentioned Brother Matthias, the sportswriting fraternity assigned Brother Gilbert more credit than he deserved.

Later that same year, the *Boston Globe* asked Brother Gilbert to write a series of articles about Ruth's career. By then, Brother Gilbert was a member of the faculty of St. John's Preparatory School in Danvers, Massachusetts, another Xaverian-operated school. Brother Gilbert was also head of the boys' department of Mission Church High School in Boston. His seven-part series ran once a week from October 14 to November 25. In an editorial introduction, the newspaper said the author had guided Babe to "high places in baseball," adding, "No other man, except the Babe himself, knows more about his life than does Brother Gilbert."[12] Brother Gilbert described first seeing Babe pitch during the fall of 1913 at St. Mary's, which he visited at the insistence of one of his players from Mount St. Joseph's in Baltimore. Brother Gilbert wrote that he was impressed with Babe, both as a pitcher and a hitter. Brother Gilbert mentioned Brother Matthias briefly and how he had assured Brother Gilbert and Orioles owner Jack Dunn that "Ruth can hit." Brother Gilbert recounted Babe's early career, his affection for youngsters and his greatest homers. In the series, Brother Gilbert neither claimed to have coached Babe nor to have taught him at St. Mary's. But newspaper stories continued to say he did so until 1948, when Babe and Bob Considine collaborated on *The Babe Ruth Story*.

In January of 1929, tragedy struck when Babe's estranged wife Helen perished in a house fire in Watertown, Massachusetts. She had been living with dentist Edward Kinder, to whom neighbors thought she was married, but she and Babe had never divorced. At her funeral, Babe wept uncontrollably. Then, on April 17, he married Claire Hodgson, the attractive dark-haired widow from Georgia he had been seeing since 1923, after meeting her at a ballgame in Washington. She was visiting that city as a member of a touring theatrical production, but lived in New York, where she modeled and appeared on stage. The day after their wedding, performed by the Rev. William F. Hughes in New York, Claire attended the Yankees season opener in which they defeated Boston 7–3. In the first inning, Babe drove a home run to left field and doffed his cap to Claire as he trotted around the bases and blew her a kiss on his way to the dugout.[13] Claire had a daughter, Julia; Babe also had a daughter, Dorothy, from his marriage to Helen. (Decades later, Dorothy wrote that it wasn't until 1980 she learned Helen was not her biological mother.) The couple adopted each other's child to create a blended family. Ordinarily, Yankee wives were not allowed to travel with the team, but Col. Ruppert made an exception for Babe, thinking Claire would ensure he behaved. She traveled with the team that season and Ruppert's hunch she'd be a good influence paid off.[14]

The Yankees began 1929 strongly, winning 13 of their first 17 games, but the Philadelphia Athletics of Connie Mack were even better, claiming first place by May 13 and never relinquishing it. Babe developed a severe chest cold in June and missed 17 days, but still managed to launch 46 homers by season end. On August 11, in Cleveland, he recorded his 500th career homer, his sixth round-tripper in six games. He had now amassed more than twice as many home runs as any major leaguer in baseball history.[15] The team was shaken in late September when manager Miller Huggins died suddenly from a skin disease at the age of 50. "It is one of the keenest losses I have ever felt," Babe said of the man with whom he feuded initially but had grown to respect.[16] Powerhouse Philadelphia went on to win the American League pennant and then defeat the Chicago Cubs in the World Series. The Athletics featured the bats of Jimmie Foxx and Al Simmons and the effective pitching of Lefty Grove. They would go on to be World Series champions again in 1930 and 1931.

After protracted negotiations for 1930, Babe signed with Ruppert for $80,000 a year in a two-year contract, despite the onset of the Great Depression, when simply having a job would be appreciated by most Americans. Babe sought $100,000 a year and Huggins's job as manager, but received neither. "You can't manage yourself, so how are you going to manage the Yankees?" Ruppert said in dismissing Babe's bid to replace Huggins.[17] Undaunted, Babe led the American League in home runs in 1930 with 49 and tied Gehrig for the lead in 1931 with 46. Time was passing and even though Babe was becoming injury-prone, he continued to post impressive numbers.

Still following his career closely back at St. Mary's was mentor and friend Brother Matthias, who turned 59 in 1931. He had been at the school for more than three decades and had seen thousands of students pass through its doors, but none quite like "George." He was quietly proud of Babe's accomplishments and, unlike the garrulous Brother Gilbert who was receiving press attention, did not tout his own contribution to creating the baseball sensation.

The aging disciplinarian had marveled at the scrapes involving his former charge but always stood by, ready to provide advice or counsel for Babe when his excesses got the better of him. But as 1931 dawned, Brother Matthias was involved in his own questionable conduct that nearly had him ousted from the Xaverians. He was seeing a young woman of 23 on a regular basis and her neighbors recognized Brother Matthias and reported him to the Catholic Archdiocese of Baltimore and to the Xaverian Brothers at Mount St. Joseph College. Matthias's motivations will never be known. Perhaps he wanted to see what he had been missing because of his vow of celibacy, or possibly he was somehow inspired by the skirt-chasing of his surrogate son, Ruth. Then again, it may simply have been love, despite a 35-year age gap.

In June, Brother Matthias was interviewed by lawyer William L. Galvin, who had been retained by Archbishop Michael J. Curley to investigate the allegation of misbehavior.[18] Also present for the interview was Monsignor William E. Mackessy, chancellor of the archdiocese, who dealt with administrative and personnel matters. Archbishop Curley was taking the matter seriously and had directed that if Brother Matthias admitted to an inappropriate relationship with the woman, Helen Bowness, he was to be dealt with promptly by the Xaverians. For his part, Brother Matthias steadfastly denied he had any improper relations with the young woman, who lived in a row house with her mother and other family members on Amberley Avenue, just a few blocks north of Mount St. Joseph College.

After first denying an allegation he'd been seen with Miss Bowness within the past week, Brother Matthias conceded he had been at her place the previous day, June 20. He said he joined her to go swimming, returned to her home for supper and left at 7 p.m. Brother Matthias admitted he attended a party there one night and hadn't departed until 3 a.m. He also conceded that on occasion he had lent Miss Bowness his Cadillac, the gift from Babe. Neighbors had seen the car and provided a description and license plate number to church officials. Nearby residents Charles and Louise Wallace produced detailed accounts of the comings and goings of Brother Matthias from their vantage point on the street and shared them with the lawyer for the church. The couple said Matthias's behavior was well known by various members of nearby St. Joseph's Monastery Parish, who lived in the area and recognized him from church activities. The visits had been ongoing for six months, the Wallaces reported, during which time Brother Matthias often appeared in the morning to take Miss Bowness to her job (as a stenographer at a trucking firm). The big man, they said, drove other vehicles aside from the Cadillac, sometimes cruising through the neighborhood as late as 1 a.m.[19] And they noted that license plates were switched among the cars. Brother Matthias stoutly defended himself, denying a relationship with Bowness. He had everything at stake and so much to lose. He could have been expelled from the Xaverians, a man approaching 60 without any worldly possessions forced to start his life over again.

In the end, the Xaverians opted to relocate Brother Matthias rather than summarily dismiss him. The Brothers answer to the Pope rather than to the

In his later years, Brother Matthias taught at schools in Massachusetts, where he had been transferred by the Xaverian Brothers (National Baseball Hall of Fame and Museum, Cooperstown, New York).

head of the diocese, but Archbishop Curley endorsed the solution that saw Brother Matthias banned from Baltimore. The wayward Brother was transferred to the Xaverian-operated St. John's Preparatory School in Danvers, Massachusetts, where Brother Gilbert had been posted. Brother Matthias was ordered never to return to Baltimore, his home for the past 38 years. But the big man couldn't stay away and he was seen back in Baltimore at various times between July 9 and 27. He was confronted by Xaverian officials on October 11 in a disciplinary hearing held at St. Joseph's Juniorate, an Xaverian school in Peabody, Massachusetts. Brother Matthias readily conceded he had returned to Baltimore, but insisted it was only to "close up" some matters of personal business. He denied a new and damning report saying he had been there for a stretch of 8 to 10 days and was seen driving an automobile with Miss Bowness (who celebrated her 24th birthday on July 13, two days after Brother Matthias turned 59). But when confronted with proof of the allegation, he admitted it was true. With this confession, Brother Osmund, the Xaverian official in charge, said it was clear Brother Matthias could no longer be trusted to tell the truth. The seriousness of "keeping company early and late with the Bowness woman" was explained to him and how he had violated his vow of poverty by giving her the Cadillac, which was legally registered to St. Mary's. He was reminded he had been given a break by the Xaverians despite his scandalous behavior.

Brother Matthias was given one last chance: he must obey to the letter all orders of his superiors or withdraw from the Xaverians. He agreed to comply and to obtain written permission if he wanted to leave his new posting at any point. Brother Matthias was lectured that his shameful behavior had humiliated the entire Xaverian community. The superior in charge of the hearing concluded matters by noting "if Brother Matthias had been more amenable to discipline over a period of years, his scandalous actions might have been avoided."[20] There was no mention or record of what those breaches of discipline had been. With that scolding, however, the matter was concluded.

The irony of Brother Matthias's troubles was that the head disciplinarian for so many years at St. Mary's had now been disciplined by his own religious community. He renewed his pledge of obedience and his file with the Xaverian Brothers contained no subsequent reports of misdeeds. Brother Matthias continued to serve God and to educate and help shape young minds for the rest of his days, without further incident. Meanwhile, Bowness married a man named Alexander Hyland and lived until 1963.

In 1932, the Yankees again took the American League pennant and faced the Chicago Cubs in the World Series. Babe managed 41 home runs and his batting average slipped to .341. For the first time since 1925, he was not the home-run king. Philadelphia's Jimmie Foxx took that honor with 58, as he did the following year with 48. In his tenth and last trip to the World Series, however, Ruth helped the Yankees sweep the Cubs. In so doing, he attracted attention during the third game, in Chicago, when he gestured toward the bleachers before he hit one of the longest home runs ever seen at Wrigley Field. It was his second homer of the game. Sportswriters began calling this Babe's "called shot" and eventually even Babe accepted their story that the gesture warned Cubs pitcher Charlie Root about the ultimate destination of his next pitch. Ford Frick, who penned Babe's 1928 autobiography, hadn't witnessed the game and some time later asked the slugger point-blank if he had really pointed to the bleachers where he planned to park the ball. Ruth replied, "It's in the papers, isn't it?," in apparent confirmation.[21] He wasn't inclined to ruin a good story about one of the most famous homers of all time.

By 1933, the Depression had deepened and the Yankees began to trim salaries. Babe, his best years now behind him, was offered $50,000, a cut of $30,000 from the previous year. He and Ruppert again engaged in prolonged dickering before they settled on a figure of $52,000. In his 20th year in the majors, Babe managed to belt 34 home runs and his batting average slipped to .301. His decline was becoming apparent. One bright spot came in the first-ever All-Star Game held at Comiskey Park in Chicago, when he hit the game's first run and the American League triumphed 4–2. The Yankees finished seven games behind the Washington Senators in the pennant race and, in a gimmick to attract fans for the final home game, the Yankees asked the 39-year-old Ruth to pitch against the Red Sox. He held Boston hitless for five innings before weakening in the sixth. He earned a 6–5 complete-game win, but paid the price with a sore pitching arm for a week afterward.

Babe faced another pay cut in 1934, this one to $35,000. There was no back-and-forth this time. He understood his playing career was near its end and his bargaining position had weakened. Although this was his smallest pay packet since 1921, it remained the highest in baseball at the time. In Detroit on July 13, he belted his 700th career home run in a 4–2 Yankees win. The hit, off the Tigers' Tommy Bridges, came in the third inning and sailed over the right field wall at Navin Field. The ball was retrieved from 16-year-old Lennie Bielski, who had pulled the history-making ball from under a car parked on nearby Plum Avenue.[22] Ruth ended the 1934 season with 22 home runs in all and a batting average of .288 while the Yankees finished seven games behind Detroit. Gehrig led the home run parade with 49. On September 24, a sunny and pleasant day that sportswriters suggested would be Babe's last appearance in Yankee Stadium, only 2,000 fans showed up. He started in right field where he made an easy catch and was walked in the first inning. He limped to first base and was replaced by a pinch-runner. He was done. Only a thin smattering of applause acknowledged his departure.

Babe's last game of the season came on September 30 in Washington, and it was in stark contrast to his Yankee Stadium appearance. A crowd of

15,000 was on hand and entertainment was provided by the band brought in from St. Mary's Industrial Training School. Babe was presented with a large scroll saluting him, signed by President Franklin Roosevelt, members of his cabinet and thousands of fans. Babe took to the public-address system to deliver his thanks and say he'd like to remain in baseball "as long as I can do anybody any good."[23] At the plate, he was held hitless in three appearances but drew a walk and went on to score a run. The Senators won, 5–3.

Col. Ruppert could see the sharp decline in the man who had helped him build Yankee Stadium and didn't want him back for 1935. Ruppert sold Babe to Boston Braves owner Emil Fuchs, who offered him a contract of $35,000 for the season. The clincher for Babe was the titles being offered him as assistant manager and vice-president with the National League organization. He believed he was realizing his dream of becoming a manager. But Fuchs wanted Ruth for his drawing power at the gate and had no intention of granting him any real managerial responsibilities. Babe played only 28 games with the Braves, batting .181. On May 25, in Pittsburgh, he placed an exclamation point on his remarkable career. He homered three times and drove in six runs, with his final homer, number 714, clearing the roof over the double-decked right field stands at Forbes Field, for the longest home run ever seen there. Despite his heroics, the Braves lost the game, 11–7. His final appearance came on May 30 in Philadelphia in the first half of a Memorial Day doubleheader. He struck out in the first inning and hurt his knee while chasing a fly ball in the bottom of the same inning, forcing him out of the game. Not long afterward, he and Fuchs had a bitter fight and Ruth, realizing the managing position he so coveted would never materialize, retired from the game he loved. He was 39.

A call offering Babe a major-league job as manager never came. He tried his best to fill the sudden void in his life with public appearances, golf, bowling, fishing and hunting. He was an avid golfer with a three handicap, and he bowled for hours on end but remained only fair on the hardwood lanes, with a 177 average.[24] He enjoyed fishing and hunting in the company of friends and loved showing off evidence of his success in both pursuits. Once, in 1937, he returned to New York from a hunting trip to Nova Scotia with three deer tied to the front fenders of his Stutz Bearcat car and a large dead bear sitting in the rumble seat. Needless to say, the sight turned heads, just as he intended. His favorite place to fish and hunt, however, was Greenwood Lake, about 50 miles northwest of New York City.

On the Fourth of July, 1939, members of the 1927 Yankees team returned to Yankee Stadium to honor Lou Gehrig, who was dying of amyotrophic lateral sclerosis (ALS). Despite a falling out and not having spoken to Gehrig in five years, Babe attended the sad event and did his best to make amends. That same year, he was among the first class of inductees into the new Baseball Hall of Fame in Cooperstown, New York. In 1942, he appeared in a movie about Lou Gehrig, *The Pride of the Yankees*. To improve his appearance for the film, Babe shed 40 pounds from his bulk that had grown to nearly 270 pounds. During the Second World War, he helped the Red Cross, bought $100,000 in War Bonds and appeared frequently at events and benefit baseball games to boost America's war effort.[25] In April 1947, Major League Baseball celebrated Babe Ruth Day in every major-league ballpark and Ruth, frail and shrunken from his battle with throat cancer, was saluted in Yankee Stadium by 58,339 fans. In June of 1948, with mere weeks to live because the cancer had spread to his liver, lungs and kidneys, he rallied to attend the 25th-anniversary celebration of Yankee Stadium. His number 3 jersey was retired that day. It was his last public appearance. He passed away on August 16 at the age of 53.

Babe Ruth was buried beneath an elaborate headstone featuring an image of Jesus blessing a young boy wearing a baseball uniform in Gate of Heaven Cemetery in Hawthorne, New York. An epitaph from Francis Cardinal Spellman, who conducted his funeral mass, reads as follows: "May the Divine Spirit that Animated Babe Ruth to Win the Crucial Game of Life Inspire the Youth of America!" Had he lived to see it, Brother Matthias, who himself inspired at least one youth to great things, would have smiled.

Even in death, America couldn't get enough of Babe Ruth. In the ensuing decades, more than 30 books were written about him and his impact on America, sport and pop culture. Many of them were acclaimed, including Robert W. Creamer's 1974 *Babe: The Legend Comes to Life*, Leigh Montville's 2006 *The Big Bam: The Life and Times of Babe Ruth* and Jane Leavy's 2018 *The Big Fella: Babe Ruth and the World He Created*.

Late in 2018, United States President Donald Trump posthumously awarded Ruth the Presidential Medal of Freedom, the country's highest honor for a civilian. It is bestowed for "meritorious" achievements in a variety of fields, including cultural, or other significant endeavors. Babe became the 14th baseball personality so honored. Some of Ruth's family members attended the ceremony at the White House, but his daughter, Julia Ruth Stevens, age 102, was unable to travel from her home in Nevada. Her son, Tom Stevens, spoke for the family and expressed delight at the recognition for his grandfather.

"It's wonderful that he's finally been recognized," Stevens said, noting the medal highlighted Babe Ruth as a humanitarian.[26] Then he posed a question that was likely on everyone's mind: "But what the heck took so long?"

Epilogue

With his move to St. John's Preparatory School in Danvers, Brother Matthias dropped out of sight. Not so for Brother Gilbert. After his seven-part newspaper series about the Babe in the *Boston Globe*, Brother Gilbert continued to be in demand to talk about the Bambino, dining out on his connection to the star. One of his speeches was a 90-minute presentation to the Knights of Columbus of North Adams, Massachusetts, in April of 1929. It was one of more than 1,000 he delivered in his career, many about Babe.[1] Brother Gilbert told the crowd that anyone could have spotted the natural talent of young George Ruth, but that he, Brother Gilbert, had the "privilege of being the first to aid George Herman in the development of his talents." That was a stretch. Brother Matthias had already helped shape the boy into a baseball player by the time Brother Gilbert first laid eyes on him. Brother Gilbert told the crowd he was working on a biographical sketch titled "The Million Dollar Babe," which he hoped would soon appear in newspapers. The report of his appearance said he taught Babe "in an orphan home at Baltimore," although it's unclear if that information was attributable to Brother Gilbert or was an assumption by the reporter. Brother Gilbert was no stranger to this North Adams crowd, which ate up his colorful recollections, this being the second year in a row he had addressed their annual father-and-son event.[2]

Two years later, Brother Gilbert was a guest of the Baltimore Old-Timers, who played the Orioles in a fun game. In yet another after-dinner speech, he recounted his role in signing Babe Ruth to the professional ranks. "It was a case of self-defense," he admitted. "I had a great left-hander at Mount St. Joseph's College named Meadows, and [Jack] Dunn wanted him for the Orioles. I did not want to part with him at that time, and recommended a stockily built youth who had all the earmarks of a great pitcher.... Dunnie signed him and what he has done is history."[3] Lowell Thomas, a prominent writer and broadcaster, took liberties with the truth when he told his readers about Brother Gilbert's role in the early days of the Babe. In a lengthy feature published in the *Baltimore Sun* and elsewhere soon after Ruth signed with the Boston Braves for 1935, Thomas wrote that Brother Gilbert had not only taught Babe at St. Mary's, but also coached him there.[4]

Brother Gilbert retained his connections to Baltimore despite his subsequent postings to several schools in Massachusetts. In 1936, he took his Malden Catholic High School baseball team to Baltimore for a game against Mount St. Joseph College.[5] Rain canceled the game, so, forced to remain indoors at Mount St. Joseph, Brother Gilbert regaled reporters and anyone within earshot with stories about players he had coached over the years. He didn't overlook Babe. Listeners were struck by the obvious fondness Brother Gilbert retained for Ruth. "His voice warms when he talks of him as a great, big grown-up boy whose place in the sport he rebuilt after its near-wrecking should be a lot more secure than it is today," the *Sun* reported, referring to Babe's then-uncertain future.[6] Brother Gilbert was a popular coach and teacher in Malden, where in 1938 the stadium at the school was named in his honor. When Malden Catholic High School relocated across town in 1968, the new stadium was called Brother Gilbert Field.[7]

In 1939, Brother Gilbert appeared at the annual dinner of the New York Chapter of the Baseball Writers of America. The invitation reflected his continued connection to sportswriters who had always found him an entertaining and colorful character willing to talk about his role in the saga of Babe Ruth. In an Associated Press report of the affair, Brother Gilbert was incorrectly referred to as a faculty member of the "orphan home" where Babe was sent. Brother Gilbert recounted his early days with the boy who became a legend and described him as a "big, long-legged kid." His speech, one sportswriter noted, attracted some special attention. "As he spoke, a large, fat, middle-aged man, with wide spread nose and a mop of black hair sat at a table down front and listened intently. The Babe, in the flesh."[8]

By 1942, Brother Gilbert was reportedly trying to persuade Babe to attend a Red Cross benefit golf tournament in Baltimore.[9] It's not known if his attempt was successful, given Babe's busy golf schedule at the time, but it's noteworthy Brother Gilbert felt close enough to Ruth to seek the favor.

Brother Gilbert died in October of 1947, at the age of 62, having served the Xaverians for 46 years. At the time of his passing, he was headmaster at Keith Academy in Lowell, Massachusetts, where he suffered a cerebral hemorrhage and died in prayer. It was said he'd been writing his memoirs at the time of his death and had already completed about 15,000 words.[10] Babe Ruth, fighting his throat cancer, was too ill to attend the funeral in Danvers. "His death comes as a great shock," he said in a statement he issued to the press. "It deprives America and the young kids of a great man."[11]

Out of the blue, a freckle-faced, 10-year-old Babe Ruth fan living in Danvers stepped forward. A few weeks earlier, young Frank Haggerty had sent his hero a letter wishing him a speedy recovery and saying he was praying for him. In response, Babe sent the boy an autographed baseball, along with his thanks. Haggerty felt a strong connection to Ruth and wanted to help when he learned Babe had lost Brother Gilbert. "I'm sorry your friend died," the boy wrote in a follow-up note. "If you wish, and the brothers will let children go to the Mass, I will for you as I live in Danvers," adding: "I will behave." Babe, it was said, had tears in his eyes upon reading the scrawled note from Haggerty. The boy was a godsend for Ruth. He replied by wire: "I will be most grateful to you … but will feel I am there in spirit through your gracious gesture to go in my place."[12] The truth is Ruth hadn't been inclined to attend because he had grown to dislike Brother Gilbert in recent years and Haggerty gave him a convenient way to avoid the funeral.[13] And so, Babe Ruth found a pinch-hitter to honor Brother Gilbert at St. Peter's Church alongside the grieving Xaverian Brothers. The press had yet another field day with a story about Babe Ruth and his touching relationship with a young fan.

The falling out between Brother Gilbert and Ruth was confirmed by the Babe's daughter, many years later. Early in 2017, as she approached the age of 101, Julia Ruth Stevens was still sharp and willing to share her memories about the man she revered and those who were close to him. She was asked if her father had ever compared Brother Gilbert to Brother Matthias in any way. "The Babe, for whatever reasons, was not fond of Brother Gilbert," she replied. But she didn't know why. "Brother Matthias was a different story," Julia said. "Babe thought the world of Brother Matthias, who became essentially a father figure to him."[14]

Death did not mark the end of the story of Brother Gilbert. His memoirs were uncovered in about 1996 in the Xaverian Archives kept at their St. Xavier High School in Kentucky. The school was established in 1864 and had a reputation for excellence that attracted local boy Harry Rothgerber as a student in the 1960s. "I happened to find the original, dog-eared, yellowing manuscript of Brother Gilbert's memories about Babe Ruth—the one that he himself had typed—which was filled with his handwritten notes and edits," Rothgerber said. "Holding them in my hand, I immediately knew that my project would consist of the 'gentle' editing and publishing of these interesting memoirs about one of the most interesting personalities in American sports history."[15] Rothgerber, a lawyer, who has maintained a long attachment to the Xaverians and deeply appreciates their work, said his discovery came as a revelation and he wanted to do justice to Brother Gilbert's memoirs. "I was energized by the thought of publishing a book that would more adequately explain the role of the Xaverians in 'saving' Ruth by nurturing his baseball skills and instilling in him a sense of service and duty to others, especially youngsters." His book, *Young Babe Ruth: His Early Life and Baseball Career, From the Memoirs of a Xaverian Brother*, was published in 1999 by McFarland Publishers, with Rothgerber's role identified as editor. He skillfully combined key aspects of Babe's career and accomplishments with Brother Gilbert's first- and second-hand accounts about young George Ruth and his rise to fame. Out of his admiration and respect for the Xaverians, Rothgerber donated half his royalties to them.

For his part, Brother Matthias remained in the shadows during his final years, whether by design or requirement of the Xaverian community. Brother Gilbert had attracted the attention of the press and kept it, even after his death. But Brother Matthias was not an outgoing personality like Brother Gilbert. He was painfully shy and uncomfortable speaking about himself. One exception came in 1935, when he granted his only interview to the press that has been found to date. Tom Shehan had been a student at St. John's Preparatory School in Danvers during the early 1930s and learned Brother Matthias was nearby. Shehan was an apprentice sportswriter at the *Boston Evening Transcript* when Babe was traded to the Boston Braves. Shehan's editor learned his young scribe might have an inside track with the player's old coach through his connection with the Xaverians, so he asked him to interview Brother Matthias as part of the paper's coverage of Babe's return to Beantown. In 1996, Shehan recalled the assignment from 61 years earlier in a Catholic publication called *The Church World*. Brother Matthias was not an easy interview subject and Shehan learned why the press usually went to Brother Gilbert. The personalities of the two men were dramatically different, he noted in the Catholic journal:

> Brother Matthias and Brother Gilbert were as different as a boiled potato and pizza. Brother Gilbert was an extrovert, bubbling with personality and wit, with a wide circle of friends among the important, and an amazing command of the English language, thanks to his hobby of digesting a page of the dictionary every day.[16]

Shehan's 1935 story ran to 15 paragraphs, full of direct quotes from Brother Matthias, whom he described as "a quiet and diffident man." He said the big Xaverian had "managed to avoid the publicity that comes with reflected glory." (The entire article can be found in Appendix One.) For Shehan, Brother Matthias recounted how he made Ruth take the mound when he found the pitching by another boy to be a laughing matter. Shehan observed that when Brother Matthias spoke, with his "modulated throaty voice he invokes a warm feeling of friendliness in return. His favorite subject is 'George.'"[17]

"I'm glad he's coming back to Boston," Brother Matthias told Shehan. "The fans here like him and he'll awaken new interest in the Braves. There never was a better boy at St. Mary's School in Baltimore than 'George.' I was stationed there thirty-eight years and there were better ball players, but never a better boy. Why, he was so loyal, always thinking of the school, the Xaverian brothers and the boys that went to school with him." Brother Matthias

Babe often found excuses to return to St. Mary's once he became successful; here, in a photograph from the early 1920s. From left: Yankees catcher Benny Bengough, left fielder Bob Meusel, Brother Paul, Ruth, Brother Matthias, third baseman Joe Dugan, infielder Mike Gonzalez and Brother Sebastian (Xaverian Brothers).

spoke of Babe's continued interest in children and how they idolized him in return. "He seems to have some magic touch with them," he marveled. Brother Matthias insisted Babe never forgot what the school did for him and had helped the band raise $20,000 "for something or other" (to rebuild the school after the fire). Brother Matthias recalled the $8,000 Cadillac Ruth gave him and how generous he was. "I used to speak to him about giving so much away to the hangers-on and he would say, 'Brother, you don't know what it is to be down and out. God has been good to me.'" Brother Matthias extended best wishes to his former student upon returning to Boston. The historic and enlightening interview was abruptly terminated when the school chapel bell rung, summoning Brother Matthias to prayer.

In recalling his journalistic coup for *The Church World* so many decades later, Shehan said Bob Considine told him that until he saw the *Evening Transcript* article he had never heard of Brother Matthias. Likely as a consequence, Considine assigned Brother Matthias an important role in the 1948 version of Ruth's life story. Until then, the gentle giant had successfully avoided the bright lights that had been trained on Ruth and occasionally spilled onto

Epilogue 181

Brother Gilbert. The 1935 article by Shehan generated some long-overdue recognition.

In 1938, Brother Amandus, Brother Matthias's older brother, passed away at Mount St. Joseph College in Baltimore. He had spent nearly his entire career at the school in an administrative capacity. Thomas Boutilier was 74. Upon his death, only four of his siblings in the large Boutilier clan remained: Brother Matthias; Sister Eunice (Mrs. John Kelly, of New York); Henry, a detective in Boston; and Francis, chief engineer of the Massachusetts State House in Boston.[18]

In 1942, Brother Matthias celebrated 50 years with the Xaverians at St. Joseph's Juniorate in Peabody, Massachusetts, where he had been living in retirement. Now 70, he was fêted with a dinner marking his jubilee and students presented him a "beautiful spiritual bouquet." In all, 51 Xaverians joined him, with an Xaverian reporter noting there was "one for each year and one for good measure, for Brother Matthias is a man of generous measure, as well as heart, himself."[19] Brother Benjamin brought congratulations and greetings from the Xaverian headquarters in Baltimore. Several Brothers praised Matthias's contribution to boys at St. Mary's School, where he was still remembered fondly. Never much for words, and uncomfortable with all the attention, Brother Matthias read his heartfelt response to the tribute.[20]

Two years later, on the morning of October 16, 1944, it was noticed Brother Matthias was absent from his usual place in the chapel and Brother Godfrey went in search of him. Brother Matthias was found dead in his room at St. Joseph's. At the age of 72, Brother Matthias had been in failing health for several years. He was buried in the Xaverian Brothers cemetery on the grounds of St. John's Preparatory School, four miles away in Danvers. On his headstone, his surname is spelled the Xaverian way, missing the first "i" in Boutilier. The simple marker noted his 52 years of religious life. There was no story about his passing in the newspapers, which later gave prominent coverage to the death of Brother Gilbert, who

Brother Matthias lived quietly in retirement in Massachusetts, where he died in 1944 at age 72 (Xaverian Brothers).

was interred a few feet away. The newspapers were preoccupied with war news and perhaps the Xaverians simply forgot to the notify them—or chose not to, for reasons of their own. It's doubtful that Babe Ruth, or any designate, attended Brother Matthias's funeral, a rather odd fact given how much Babe had done to salute his friend and mentor in life. Perhaps, given his outpouring of emotion and display of tears at the funerals of his father and first wife, Babe couldn't cope with the loss of the human being who had been closest to him and preferred to grieve alone, rather than in front of the press. It's also ironic, given all the attention later given to the passing of Brother Gilbert, a man from whom he had become estranged for reasons unknown. Perhaps Brother Gilbert's penchant for self-promotion and seeking the limelight irritated Babe and created some distance between the two men. When it came to Xaverians, the extrovert Babe apparently preferred boiled potato to pizza.

Brother Matthias, of course, didn't live to read Ruth's 1948 autobiography penned by Considine or see the movie based on it. In *The Babe Ruth Story*, he belatedly received credit as the true discoverer, nurturer and mentor of the baseball star. Shehan's article was likely responsible for the recognition by Considine and the filmmakers. Charles Bickford gave a strong performance

Brother Matthias, whose surname is missing an "i" from his birth name Boutilier on his headstone, is buried in the Xaverian Brothers cemetery at St. John's Preparatory School in Danvers, Massachusetts. A few feet away lies Brother Gilbert, who died four years later in 1948 (Jean Mor).

as a kind and caring Brother Matthias in an otherwise forgettable movie. The quiet brother from the tiny mining outpost on Canada's East Coast finally received some attention. Given his abiding shyness, Brother Matthias would have blushed at the turn of events.

After viewing the movie, one Xaverian Brother, pleased at the depiction of his religious community, and of Brother Matthias, was moved to opine:

> Though many [boys] … failed to benefit from the care of the Brothers at St. Mary's, a countless number have gone forth to live better Catholic lives. None made such a spectacular showing before the public as Babe Ruth … there has been only one Babe Ruth and one Brother Matthias; but the good work of a religious teacher emphasized in the story has been performed over and over again.[21]

Upon the death of Babe, little was said in the press about Brother Matthias and his role in helping shape a troubled boy into a great baseball player and pop culture hero. Baltimore and St. Mary's did not forget. In an editorial, *The Baltimore Sun* noted Ruth had become a national figure and his millions of followers likely didn't associate him with any particular place. "Yet Baltimore cannot forget that he was born here, and that it was Brother Matthias, of St. Mary's Industrial School, who discovered his talent and developed it."[22] The newspaper also credited Orioles owner Jack Dunn with signing Babe to his first professional contract. Brother Gilbert was not mentioned.

The telling of the story of Brother Matthias, the gentle giant of St. Mary's, is long overdue. During his long life, Brother Matthias was outshone by a gregarious and colorful confrere, but the quiet Brother accepted his situation without complaint.

He and Babe Ruth knew the real story—and that was all that was important to them.

Appendix I: Brother Matthias Speaks

From the Boston Evening Transcript, February 28, 1935, page 6.

Brother Matthias Talks of George
The "Boss" Recalls Ruth's Early Days at St. Mary's School in Baltimore
By Thomas Shehan

Danvers, Feb. 28

Baseball's No. 1 artillery piece, Babe Ruth, comes back this evening on his old proving grounds—Boston. Here, where he saw the first flush of the light of greatness that was to be his, he is to spend the twilight of his career in the game.

What could be more appropriate than that he should write finis to the final chapter of his career with the man who gave him his start in the national pastime at his side. Brother Matthias, C.F.X., has been at once the idol, father, counselor, coach and "big brother" of Ruth. Yet through all these twenty-odd years that Babe has been under the "big tent" the good brother has managed to avoid the publicity that comes with reflected glory.

Brother Matthias, originally an East Boston boy and product of the old Adams School, is spending his final years in the quiet cloisters of a monk's retreat at St. John's Prep in Danvers just twenty miles down the 'pike. In his late sixties, Brother Matthias still has the remarkable framework of a real athlete. It's only two years ago that he stopped playing ball, and confined his exercises to good long walks and the chores that are part of a holy monk's life.

He's the "Boss" to the Babe and even now he has the bearing of a kindly martinet. Broad shouldered, with a shuffling gait that makes one realize where the "Sultan of Swat" got his peculiar stride, he still is a fine looking man. Well over six feet in height and with the broad shoulders and frame of an athlete he is a pleasant faced old gentleman with steel gray hair receding just a bit at the temples into a "widow's peak." When he talks in his modulated throaty voice he invokes a warm feeling of friendliness in return. His favorite subject is "George."

"I'm glad he's coming back to Boston. The fans here like him and he'll awaken new interest in the Braves. There never was a better boy at St. Mary's School in Baltimore than 'George.' I was stationed there thirty-eight years and there were better ball players, but never a better boy. Why, he was so loyal, always thinking of school, the Xaverian brothers and the boys that went to the school with him. I can't believe some of this talk I have heard about him. He couldn't do a mean thing if he had to. He was above all that. And did he like the young kiddoes! They idolized him when he was just a boy himself. He seems to have some magic touch with them."

With "Red Sox" at School

"He came under me when he was eight years old and played ball for me until he signed with the Baltimore team. We used to have a league of teams named after the big leagues out there. Funny thing, Babe played with the 'Red Sox' in that league. Afterward, when he played with the real Red Sox he used to remark to me about playing on the school 'Red Sox' without dreaming that he was going to sign with the real team.

"Brother Paul, now stationed in the Mother House, Bruges, Belgium, was in charge of St. Mary's while Babe was there. Many of the things that have been written about Babe are just myths. He never ran away from the school. He loved the place and for years after, always came back and visited. He never forgot what the school did for him.

"Once the school needed money for something or other and Babe made arrangements for the fifty-piece school band to travel the circuit. Why we came back with $20,000, all donated by fans who took an interest in the Babe's alma mater.

"He gave me an $8,000 Cadillac car to ride around in when I was at Baltimore. In addition he took me to the World Series every year but last year since he has been in the majors. Oh, he's a generous boy. I used to speak to him about giving so much to the hangers-on and he would say, 'Brother, you don't know what it is to be down and out. God has been good to me.'

"He never forgets and he's always the same. The time he made his sixtieth home run, he called me up that night and shouted over the phone, 'I got my sixtieth today Brother,' just as proud and as happy as when he was a kiddo at the school."

A "Pied Piper" of Baseball

"I think that eventually George will be the game's chief ambassador. It is my opinion that he could sell the game back to the youth of today better than any other individual in the world. Despite the fact that he is the game's greatest, the boys and girls don't feel awe stricken when with him. He warms them up with his smile and they would move the world for him.

"On a trip around the world instructing boys and girls everywhere in the fine points, he would be the 'Pied Piper' of baseball, and the youngsters would flock to him. He's the right man for that job, for while the baseball writers say they never saw him pull a 'boner' since he has been in the majors. I never saw him make a mistake as a lad. The first time he went after a ball he fielded it like a 'leaguer' and that was when he was eight years old.

"Ruth was never a trouble maker. He could take a jest with anyone. He did have the 'fight' in him, however, and were he convinced that somebody wasn't straight with him he would take pretty good care of them. He could handle his fists pretty well too.

"There's a funny story connected with how I happened to make a pitcher out of him. He always used to catch and one day he was standing on the side lines during a game among the younger boys. One of the lads was trying to pitch and only succeeded in making himself ridiculous. George thought it very funny and laughed and laughed. Just to show him up a little bit I ordered him to go in and pitch. He mowed everything down and I concentrated on his pitching from that day on. Yes, yes, I think he'll do well in Boston and wish him every luck for me."

With that the good brother was gone for the Chapel bell was ringing.

Appendix I: Brother Matthias Speaks

As far as can be determined, this is the only press interview Brother Matthias ever granted. The writer, Tom Shehan, had been a student at an Xaverian high school and knew Brother Matthias lived in the area. Shehan was asked by the sports editor at the Boston Evening Transcript *to interview Brother Matthias on the eve of Babe Ruth's return to Boston in 1935, when he joined the Boston Braves. Shehan wrote that Brother Matthias had been living the life of a monk in Danvers. But Xaverians are not monks and do not live the cloistered lives of monks.*

Brother Matthias was 62 at the time and some of the details he shared were a bit off. The most expensive Cadillac Babe could have purchased for him was less than $6,000, even his second one, in 1927. And Brother Matthias managed to forget the St. Mary's School band toured with the star to help raise funds to rebuild the school after the 1919 fire that destroyed so much of it.

It is noteworthy that Brother Matthias made no claim here about identifying Babe's talent and then nurturing it, or to preparing him for a career in baseball, which he could have easily done. It was classic Brother Matthias, a selfless man who had nothing but praise for a boy he once taught.

Appendix II: Statistics—Batting

Year	Team	Games	Runs	Hits	Home Runs	Average	OPS*	WAR*	Salary
1914	Boston AL	5	1	2	0	.200	0.5	0	$350
1915	Boston AL	42	16	29	4	.315	0.952	1.7	$2,500
1916	Boston AL	67	18	37	3	.272	0.741	1.6	$3,500
1917	Boston AL	52	14	40	2	.325	0.857	2.1	$3,500
1918	Boston AL	95	50	95	11	.300	0.966	4.7	$5,000
1919	Boston AL	130	103	139	29	.322	1.114	9.1	$10,000
1920	NY AL	142	158	172	54	.376	0.376	11.9	$20,000
1921	NY AL	152	177	204	59	.378	1.359	12.9	$20,000
1922	NY AL	110	94	128	35	.315	1.106	6.3	$52,000
1923	NY AL	152	151	205	41	.393	1.309	14.1	$52,000
1924	NY AL	153	143	200	46	.378	1.252	11.7	$52,000
1925	NY AL	98	61	104	25	.290	0.936	3.5	$52,000
1926	NY AL	152	139	184	47	.372	1.253	11.5	$52,000
1927	NY AL	151	158	192	60	.356	1.258	12.4	$70,000
1928	NY AL	154	163	173	54	.323	1.172	10.1	$70,000
1929	NY AL	135	121	172	46	.345	1.128	8	$70,000
1930	NY AL	145	150	186	49	.359	1.225	10.3	$80,000
1931	NY AL	145	149	199	46	.373	1.195	10.3	$80,000
1932	NY AL	133	120	156	41	.341	1.15	8.3	$75,000
1933	NY AL	137	97	138	34	.301	1.023	6.3	$52,000
1934	NY AL	125	78	105	22	.288	0.985	5.1	$35,000
1935	Boston AL	28	13	13	6	.181	0.789	0.2	
Totals		**2503**	**2174**	**2873**	**714**	**.342**	**1.164**	**162**	**$856,850**

*OPS: On-Base Plus Slugging, sum of on-base percentage and slugging percentage, measuring a player's ability to both get on base and hit for power. WAR: Wins Above Replacement, measuring a player's overall value versus a replacement-level player in the same position.

Appendix III: Statistics—Pitching

Year	Team	Games	Won	Lost	W-L %	ERA*	Games	WAR	Innings
1914	Boston AL	4	2	1	0.667	3.91	4	-0.3	23
1915	Boston AL	32	18	8	0.692	2.44	32	2.4	217.2
1916	Boston AL	44	23	12	0.657	1.75	44	8.8	323.2
1917	Boston AL	41	24	13	0.649	2.01	41	6.5	326.1
1918	Boston AL	20	13	7	0.65	2.22	20	2.3	166.1
1919	Boston AL	17	9	5	0.643	2.97	17	0.8	133.1
1920	NY AL	1	1	0	1000	4.50	1	-0.1	4
1921	NY AL	2	2	0	1000	9.00	2	-0.3	9
1930	NY AL	1	1	0	1000	3.00	1	0.2	9
1933	NY AL	1	1	0	1000	5.00	1	0	9
Totals		163	94	46	0.671	2.28	163	20.3	1221

*ERA: Earned Run Average: not including defensive errors, the average of runs given up by a pitcher per nine innings pitched.

Chapter Notes

Chapter 1

1. Babe Ruth, as told to Bob Considine, *The Babe Ruth Story* (New York: E.P. Dutton, 1948), 242.
2. James P. Moore Jr., *Prayer in America: A Spiritual History of Our Nation* (New York: Image Books, 2005), 294.
3. Bosley Crowther, "'The Babe Ruth Story,' Starring William Bendix as Baseball Hero Opens at Astor," *New York Times*, July 27, 1948, and Marshall Smelser, *The Life That Ruth Built: A Biography* (Lincoln: University of Nebraska Press, 1975), 542.
4. Lew Sheaffer, "Astor's 'Babe Ruth Story' Swings Too Wide and Misses," *Brooklyn Eagle*, July 27, 1948, 4.
5. Marshall Smelser, *The Life That Ruth Built*, 540, 542.
6. Robert W. Creamer, *Babe: The Legend Comes to Life* (New York: Simon & Schuster, 1974), 418.
7. Kal Wagenheim, *Babe Ruth: His Life and Legend* (Chicago: Olmstead Press, 2001), 262.
8. Wagenheim, 264.
9. Leigh Montville, *The Big Bam: The Life and Times of Babe Ruth* (New York: Anchor Books, 2006), 359.
10. Creamer, 419.
11. Montville, 361.
12. Wagenheim, 264.
13. Babe to Considine, 235.
14. Smelser, 537.
15. *Ibid.*, 538.
16. Wagenheim, 268.
17. Creamer, 423.
18. Montville, 366.
19. "Chandler Expresses Shock," *Baltimore Sun*, August 17, 1948, 16.
20. "George Herman Ruth, Jr.," *Baltimore Sun*, August 18, 1948, 12.
21. Wagenheim, 271.
22. Babe to Considine, 237–238.
23. Babe Ruth, "The Kids Can't Take It If We Don't Give It!," *Guideposts Magazine*, October 1948, 1–2, 23–24, accessed February 10, 2018, http://www.baberuthcentral.com/remembering-the-babe-/babe-ruths-public-statement.

Chapter 2

1. "Nova Scotia," The Canadian Encyclopedia, accessed February 13, 2018, http://www.thecanadianencyclopedia.ca/en/article/nova-scotia/.
2. Glossems on Historical Events, Conditions and Movements: Immigrant Ships: Halifax, in support of Blupete's History of Nova Scotia: 1600–1763, accessed November 26, 2018, http://www.blupete.com/Hist/Gloss/ImmigrantShips1750-52.htm#Sally.
3. Source of much of this family history is Xavier McGillivary, a descendant of the Boutiliers (fourth cousin, once removed, of Martin Leo Boutilier) who visited their ancestral home in Montbéliard and has reviewed census, shipping and other records.
4. "The Foreign Protestants," Nova Scotia Archives, accessed November 21, 2018, https://archives.novascotia.ca/genealogy/foreign-protestants.
5. Margaret R. Conrad and James K. Hiller, *Atlantic Canada: A Concise History* (Don Mills, ON: Oxford University Press, 2006), 70.
6. Ted Boutilier, "The Mines of New Waterford and District," New Waterford Historical Society, accessed February 13, 2018, https://cbushare.cbu.ca/sites/library/brasdor-collection/Lists/Bras%20dOr%20

Collection/Attachments/9332/2544_bdc_0.pdf. The late Ted Boutilier is not related to Martin Leo Boutilier.

7. The story about Joseph Boutilier working on a schooner that sailed to Boston in about 1847 is from Xavier McGillivary, previously referred to. His research uncovered an 1857 trip Joseph made to Boston to visit his brother Henry and his wife, who had already settled there.

8. This story was shared with the author by Jean Mor, of Stoughton, Massachusetts, who is descended from Martin Leo Boutilier's brother, Henry, making Martin her great grandfather's brother. It is based on stories handed down in the family. Mor recalled Henry was an avid bowler and two of his brothers competed in wrestling and boxing.

9. A move of the Boutilier family to Halifax was recorded by Cape Breton researcher Virginia MacDonald, of Sydney, in the November 24, 2007, edition of the *Cape Breton Post*. Her grandfather was born in Lingan in 1873 and her father, Bernard, was a machinist/engineer. The 1881 Census of Canada recorded them still in Lingan. Descendants of the Cape Breton Boutiliers, Jean Mor and Xavier McGillivary confirm the move to Halifax was about this time in email exchanges with the author.

10. Conrad and Hiller, 135.

11. Muise/Brookes, 44.

12. One Ruth biographer said that while still in Lingan, Martin Boutilier and his brothers may have played a crude bat-and-ball game. Xavier McGillivary, of Ottawa, Ontario, told the author that his grandfather, Francis McGillivary, who lived next door to the Boutiliers, played with Martin as a child. Francis never mentioned any such game to his grandson, Xavier said.

13. William Humber, *Cheering For The Home Team: The Story of Baseball in Canada* (Erin, ON: Boston Mills Press, 1983), 87.

14. David Block, *Baseball Before We Knew It: A Search For the Roots of the Game* (Lincoln: University of Nebraska Press, 2005), 157.

15. John Thorn, *Baseball in the Garden of Eden: The Secret History of the Early Game* (New York: Simon & Schuster, 2011), 46–48.

16. William J. Ryczek, *Blackguards and Red Stockings: A History of Baseball's National Association, 1871–1875* (Jefferson, NC: McFarland, 2016), 142–171.

17. Stephen Hardy, *How Boston Played: Sport, Recreation and Community, 1865–1915* (Knoxville: University of Tennessee Press, 2003), 185.

18. *Boston Globe*, August 19, 1883, cited in Hardy, *How Boston Played*, 187.

19. Dr. Regina Marchi, *East Boston, Massachusetts* (Charleston, SC: Legendary Locals, 2015), 91.

20. "Congregation of the Brothers of Charity," Catholic Online, accessed February 21, 2017, http://www.catholic.org/encyclopedia/view.php?id=2818.

21. Peter C. Halloran, *Boston's Wayward Children: Social Services for Homeless Children, 1830–1930* (Cranbury, NJ: Associated University Presses, 1989), 91.

22. "A Silver Jubilee: The Brothers of Charity and Their Quarter of a Century of Work in Boston," *The Sacred Heart Review* (Boston), February 11, 1899, 18.

23. Letter from Rev. Hugh Roe O'Donnell, of St. Mary Star of the Sea Church, East Boston, dated October 18, 1891, to "Brother Superior" at the Xaverian Brothers, in which he recommended Thomas Boutilier and explained his failure to remain in Montreal was because "he did not know French." Letter contained in the Brother Amandus Dossier CCFX, 6/03 #318, of the Xaverian Brothers, University of Notre Dame Archives, South Bend, IN.

24. Letter from Father Candide, dated October 14, 1891, Brother Amandus Dossier CCFX, 6/03 #318.

25. Brother Gilbert, C.F.X., *Young Babe Ruth: His Early Life and Baseball Career, from the Memoirs of a Xaverian Brother*, edited by Harry Rothgerber (Jefferson, NC: McFarland, 1999), 5.

26. Brother Julian, C.F.X., *Men and Deeds: The Xaverian Brothers in America* (New York: Macmillan, 1930), 140–156.

27. Brother Julian, 101.

28. "Form of Questions to be Answered by Applicants for Admission into the Novitiate of the Xaverian Brothers," Brother Matthias Dossier, CCFX 6/04 #329, of the Xaverian Brothers, University of Notre Dame Archives, South Bend, IN.

29. "Xaverian Brothers's Novitiate, Mount St. Joseph, Appendix to the Ceremonial," July 13, 1892, Xaverian Brothers, University of Notre Dame Archives, South Bend, IN.

30. Various official documents contained in Brother Matthias Dossier, CCFX 6/04 #329.

31. "Form of Questions to be Answered by Applicants for Admission into the Novitiate of the Xaverian Brothers," Brother Amandus Dossier, CCFX 6/03 #318.
32. "Visitors From Boston," *Baltimore Sun*, June 9, 1899, 10.
33. "Two Xaverians Laid to Rest," *Xaverian Brothers Auxiliary Bulletin*, December 1944, 19–21.
34. Brother Gilbert, 15–18.

Chapter 3

1. "The History of Baltimore," Baltimore City Department of Planning, 25, accessed March 3, 2018, https://planning.baltimorecity.gov/sites/default/files/History%20of%20Baltimore_1.pdf.
2. "The History of Baltimore," 29.
3. "History of the System," Baltimore City Department of Public Works, accessed October 29, 2018, https://publicworks.baltimorecity.gov/pw-bureaus/water-wastewater/surface/history.
4. H.L. Mencken, *Happy Days: Mencken's Autobiography 1880–1892* (Baltimore: Johns Hopkins University Press, 1996), 70.
5. Ken Mars, *Baltimore Baseball: First Pitch to First Pennant* (Parkville, MD: Old Frog Publishing, 2017), 5–7.
6. James H. Bready, *Baseball in Baltimore: The First 100 Years* (Baltimore: Johns Hopkins University Press, 1998), 15–17.
7. "The Base Ball Season," *Baltimore Sun*, April 23, 1872, 1.
8. "The Championship Professionals. Mutual vs. Baltimore," *New York Clipper*, May 4, 1872, 37.
9. "An Exciting Contest in Baltimore," *New York Clipper*, May 4, 1872, 73.
10. William J. Ryczek, *Blackguards and Red Stockings (revised edition)* (Jefferson, NC: McFarland, 2016), 184.
11. Mars, 140–142.
12. David Nemec, *The Beer and Whisky League* (New York: Lyons & Burford, 1994), 16.
13. Mars, 275–276.
14. Bready, 108–111.
15. "Major and Minor League Baseball in Baltimore," Teaching American History in Maryland, accessed March 3, 2018, http://teaching.msa.maryland.gov/000001/000000/000176/html/t176.html.
16. "Ned Hanlon," SABR BioProject, accessed February, 12, 2018, www.sabr.org/bioproj/person/1e360183.
17. "Jack Dunn," SABR BioProject, accessed February 12, 2018, www.sabr.org/bioproj/person/e1addacb.
18. Linda Gordon, Ph.D., "Child Welfare: A Brief History," VCU Libraries Social Welfare History Project, accessed March 5, 2018, https://socialwelfare.library.vcu.edu/programs/child-welfare-overview/.
19. Patricia A. Schene, "Past, Present, and Future Roles of Child Protective Services," *Protecting Children From Abuse and Neglect, Volume 8, Number 1* (Spring 1998), accessed March 5, 2018, http://thesociologycenter.com/GeneralBibliography/vol8no1ART2.pdf.
20. "The New York Society for the Prevention of Cruelty to Children: 125th Anniversary, 1875–2000," accessed March 4, 2018, www.nyspecc.org/wp-content/uploads/booklet.pdf.
21. Herbert. G. Goldman, *Jolson: The Legend Comes to Life* (New York: Oxford University Press, 1988), 20.
22. John Kenrick, "Al Jolson: A Biography," Musical101.com, accessed February 12, 2018, https://www.musicals101.com/jolsonbio.htm.
23. Neil A. Grauer, "Al of Two Cities," *The Washington Post*, August 17, 1997, accessed March 8, 2018, https://www.washingtonpost.com/archive/lifestyle/style/1997/08/17/al-of-two-cities/67497830-61d5-4695-96d1-6fac22a4cb5a/?utm_term=.0f2637bda24e.
24. Goldman, *Jolson*, 288.
25. *Ibid.*, 21.
26. "St. Mary's Industrial School Boys Hear Jolson Sing Again," *Baltimore Sun*, September 27, 1949, 34.
27. "Jolson Story Features Stop in Baltimore. Entertainer: The Son of an Orthodox Rabbi, the Musical Star Spent Time as a Youth at St. Mary's Industrial School for Boys," *Baltimore Sun*, November 22, 1998, 40.
28. "St. Mary's Industrial Home: A Grateful Look at the Past," Living the Charism: Exploring the Xaverian Way, March 27, 2015, accessed March 9, 2018, http://livingthecharism.com/saint-marys-industrial-home-a-grateful-look-at-the-past/.
29. Brother Gilbert, C.F.X., *Young Babe Ruth: His Early Life and Baseball Career, from the Memoirs of a Xaverian Brother*, edited by Harry Rothgerber (Jefferson, NC: McFarland, 1999), 8–9.

30. "1885–1929: Segregation and the Fourteenth Amendment," Baltimore's Civil Rights Heritage, accessed March 14, 2018, https://baltimoreheritage.github.io/civil-rights-heritage/overview/1885-1929/.
31. "Brother Dominic Honored. He is Appointed Provincial of the Xaverian Order," *Baltimore Sun*, March 23, 1900, 10.
32. Brother Julian, C.F.X., *Men and Deeds: The Xaverian Brothers in America* (New York: Macmillan, 1930), 255.
33. Marshall Smelser, *The Life That Babe Ruth Built: A Biography* (Lincoln: University of Nebraska Press, 1975), 12.
34. Brother Gilbert, *Young Babe Ruth*, ix–x.
35. Marie O'Dea, "They Reared Babe Ruth," *Catholic Digest*, September 1938, 29–30.
36. Smelser, 20.
37. Robert W. Creamer, *Babe: The Legend Comes to Life* (New York: Simon & Schuster, 1974), 43.
38. "Musical Notes: St. Mary's 'Little Band,'" *Concordia*, Volume 9, Number 3, November 1994, 2.
39. "Joliet Honors School Band As It Again Wins," *Chicago Tribune*, May 28, 1928, 16.
40. "Band Goes to Ball Game," *Baltimore Sun*, May 28, 1928, 24.
41. "Sousa Leads St. Mary's Band," *Baltimore Sun*, December 9, 1927, 6.
42. Brother Julian, *Men and Deeds*, 61.

Chapter 4

1. Robert W. Creamer, *Babe: The Legend Comes to Life* (New York: Simon & Schuster, 1974), 24.
2. "Cold Day in Baltimore," *Baltimore Sun*, February 7, 1895, 1.
3. Kal Wagenheim, *Babe Ruth: His Life and Legend* (Chicago: Olmstead Press, 2001), 11–12.
4. Leigh Montville, *The Big Bam: The Life and Times of Babe Ruth* (New York: Anchor Books, 2006), 10.
5. Druscilla J. Null, "'My Father Was of German Extraction': Babe Ruth's Ruth/Rudt Ancestors," *Maryland Genealogical Society Journal* 58 (2017), 377, accessed October 1, 2018, https://mdgensoc.org/upload/files/allowindex/MGS_Babe_Ruth_Article_2017.pdf.
6. Baltimore historian Fred B. Shoken, in his blog "Babe Ruth 100," accessed July 31, 2018, http://baberuth100.blogspot.com/2013/12/introduction.html.
7. "A Lofty Performance," *Baltimore Sun*, July 1, 1873, 4.
8. "Baltimore City's Jubilee," *Baltimore Sun*, October 12, 1880, 5.
9. Her birthdate is from the United States Census of 1900. Her headstone says 1873, but the headstone also gives her first name as Catherine.
10. U.S. Census Records, 1880; Baltimore (Independent City), Maryland; Roll 503; Page 200B; Enumeration District 153; Sheet 10.
11. Father Rob Carbonneau, "Batter Up! Baseball, Baptism, Babe Ruth, and Baltimore," Passionist Historical Archives, March 30, 2000, accessed March 22, 2018, http://www.cpprovince.org/archives/sesqui/sesqui3.php.
12. Shoken, accessed July 31, 2018.
13. Classfied advertisement, *Baltimore Sun*, March 20, 1897, 3.
14. Shoken, quoting U.S. Census Records, 1900; Baltimore (Independent City), Maryland; Roll 617; Page 15A; Enumeration District 262; Sheet 15.
15. Shoken, accessed July 31, 2018, http://baberuth100.blogspot.com/2013/12/chapter-2.html.
16. "License Applications," *Baltimore Sun*, April 13, 1901, 11.
17. "Local Briefs," *Baltimore Sun*, April 24, 1901, 6.
18. James H.N. Waring, *The Work of the Colored Law and Order League: Baltimore, Md.* (Cheyney, PA: Committee of Twelve for the Advancement of the Negro Race, 1908), 6.
19. Katie Ruth deposition in divorce court in 1906, from Maryland State Archives, Baltimore City Circuit Court No. 2 (Equity Papers B), #8962 B, George H. Ruth v. Katie Ruth, 5/14/1906 (MSA T-57-202, 3/18/10/017).
20. Marshall Smelser, *The Life That Ruth Built: A Biography* (Lincoln: University of Nebraska Press, 1975), 7.
21. Wagenheim, 13.
22. Babe Ruth, as told to Bob Considine, *The Babe Ruth Story* (New York: E.P. Dutton: 1948), 12–13.
23. A clear portion of the larger photograph can be found opposite page 180 in Leigh Montville's *The Big Bam: The Life*

and Times of Babe Ruth (New York: Anchor Books, 2006).

24. George Ruth deposition in divorce court in 1906, from Maryland State Archives, Baltimore City Circuit Court No. 2 (Equity Papers B), #8962 B, George H. Ruth v. Katie Ruth, 5/14/1906 (MSA T-57-202, 3/18/10/017).

25. "Jolly Brothers Give a Ball," *Baltimore Sun*, November 12, 1901, 7.

26. Wilborn Hampton, *Up Close: Babe Ruth* (New York: Viking, 2009), 27–28.

27. George Herman Ruth, *Babe Ruth's Own Book of Baseball* (Reprint, Lincoln: University of Nebraska Press, 1992), 3–4.

28. Wagenheim, 13.

29. Smelser, 10.

30. Montville, 16.

31. Babe Ruth, *Playing the Game: My Early Years in Baseball*, edited by William R. Cobb (Mineola, NY: Dover Publications, 2011), 1–2. This book contains all 12 installments of the United News syndicated autobiography of 1920, for which Ruth's ghostwriter was Westbrook Pegler.

32. Rodger H. Pippen, "80-Year-Old Ex-Cop Remembers Babe Ruth As Boy." This undated clipping appears on the Ridgely's Delight website, accessed October 18, 2018, http://www.ridgelysdelight.org/PDFs/CopStory.pdf. Ruth biographer Jane Leavy says it was published in 1947. That would make sense, because in the preamble Pippen referred to "the papers full of Babe Ruth's gallant fight for life...."

33. Smelser, 11.

34. "Five Fall From Heat," *Baltimore Sun*, June 14, 1902, 12.

35. "Man Who Escorted Babe Ruth Dies," *Baltimore Sun*, December 31, 1917, 11.

36. Wagenheim, 14.

37. Smelser, 11.

38. Creamer, 31.

39. Ruth, *Playing the Game*, 4.

40. Montville, 21.

41. Lou Leisman, *I Was With Babe Ruth at St. Mary's* (Aberdeen, MD: self-published, 1956), 15.

42. Creamer, 31–32.

43. Wagenheim, 14.

44. Creamer, 30.

45. Montville, 20–21.

46. Smelser, 12–13.

47. Creamer, 38.

48. George Herman Ruth, *Babe Ruth's Own Book of Baseball*, 7. "But to the Brothers down at St. Mary's I'm George, and always will be," he said in his 1928 autobiography.

49. Montville, 22.

50. From an email exchange with the author, April 2, 2018. At the time, Stevens's mother, Julia Ruth Stevens, was still quite lucid as she approached the age of 102.

51. Brother Gilbert, C.F.X., *Young Babe Ruth: His Early Life and Baseball Career, from the Memoirs of a Xaverian Brother*, edited by Harry Rothgerber (Jefferson, NC: McFarland, 1999), 41.

52. Wagenheim, 15.

53. Smelser, 15–16.

54. Creamer, 38.

55. Smelser, 14.

Chapter 5

1. Babe Ruth, *Playing the Game: My Early Years in Baseball* (Mineola, NY: Dover Publications, 2011), 2–3. This is a compilation of the United News Service syndicate series of 12 installments published in daily newspapers over the course of three months during Ruth's first season with the New York Yankees. It was edited by William R. Cobb.

2. Brother Gilbert, C.F.X., *Young Babe Ruth: His Early Life and Baseball Career, from the Memoirs of a Xaverian Brother*, edited by Harry Rothgerber (Jefferson, NC: McFarland, 1999), 17.

3. George Herman Ruth, *Babe Ruth's Own Book of Baseball* (Reprint, Lincoln: University of Nebraska Press, 1992), 5.

4. Babe Ruth, as told to Bob Considine, *The Babe Ruth Story* (New York: E.P. Dutton, 1948), 13–14.

5. Babe Ruth, *Playing the Game*, 5.

6. Marshall Smelser, *The Life That Ruth Built: A Biography* (Lincoln: University of Nebraska Press, 1975), 20.

7. Brother Thomas More Page, "Profiles of Brotherhood," *Concordia*, Volume 10, Number 3, November 1995, 7.

8. Lou Leisman, *I Was With Babe Ruth at St. Mary's* (Aberdeen, MD: self-published, 1956).

9. *Idid.*, 9.

10. Babe Ruth, *Playing the Game*, 1.

11. "Ruth 20 Years Ago Left St. Mary's for Orioles," *Baltimore Sun*, February 28, 1934, 13.

12. "Twenty-Four Blocks Burned in Heart of Baltimore. City's Most Valuable

Buildings in Ruins," *Baltimore Sun*, February 8, 1904, 1.
13. "February 07, 1904: The Great Baltimore Fire Begins," accessed April 17, 2018, https://www.history.com/this-day-in-history/the-great-baltimore-fire-begins.
14. "One Life Lost in Fire," *Baltimore Sun*, February 20, 1904, 12.
15. Bruce Hensler, *Crucible of Fire: Nineteenth-Century Urban Fires and the Making of the Modern Fire Service* (Dulles, VA: Potomac Books, 2011), 7, citing Momar D. Seck and David D. Evans, "Major U.S. Cities Using National Standard Fire Hydrants, One Century After the Great Baltimore Fire," National Institute of Standards and Technology, August 2004, 12.
16. Babe Ruth, *The Babe Ruth Story*, 14.
17. Smelser, 27.
18. Leisman, 21.
19. "Ruth Supernormal, So He Hits Homers," *New York Times*, September 11, 1921, 25.
20. Gerry Everding, "St. Louis Cardinals slugger Pujols gets Babe Ruth Test at Washington University," *The Source*, Washington University, August 22, 2006, accessed April 29, 2018, https://source.wustl.edu/2006/08/st-louis-cardinals-slugger-pujols-gets-babe-ruth-test-at-washington-university/.
21. Fr. Charles Grondin, "Was Being Left-Handed Ever a Sin?," Catholic Answers, accessed April 29, 2018, https://www.catholic.com/qa/was-being-left-handed-ever-a-sin.
22. "Brother Paul Recalls Early Days of 'Babe,'" *Daily News* (Newport News, VA), August 18, 1948, 10.
23. Babe Ruth, *The Babe Ruth Story*, 14.
24. Babe Ruth, *Playing the Game*, 6.
25. Babe Ruth, *The Babe Ruth Story*, 16.
26. Smelser, 28.
27. Leisman, 13.
28. Babe Ruth, *The Babe Ruth Story*, 14.
29. Mrs. Babe (Claire) Ruth, with Bill Slocum, *The Babe and I* (Englewood Cliffs, NJ: Prentice-Hall, 1959), 44.
30. Babe Ruth, *Playing the Game*, 6.
31. Smelser, 26.
32. Babe Ruth, *The Babe Ruth Story*, 14–15.
33. Mrs. Babe Ruth, *The Babe and I*, 45.
34. Babe Ruth, *The Babe Ruth Story*, 15.
35. Bozeman Bulger, "Babe Ruth's Beginnings," *Saturday Evening Post*, originally published in November–December edition, 1931, as part of a four-part series titled "And Along Came Ruth," republished April 10, 2017, and accessed April 9, 2018, http://www.saturdayeveningpost.com/2017/04/10/archives/historical-retrospectives/babe-ruths-beginnings.html.
36. Babe Ruth, *The Babe Ruth Story*, 15.

Chapter 6

1. Brother Thomas More Page, "Profiles of Brotherhood," *Concordia*, Volume 10, Number 3, November 1995, 3.
2. Lou Lesiman, *I Was With Babe Ruth at St. Mary's* (Aberdeen, MD: self-published, 1956), 19.
3. As quoted in Brother Gilbert, C.F.X., *Young Babe Ruth: His Early Life and Baseball Career, from the Memoirs of a Xaverian Brother*, edited by Harry Rothgerber (Jefferson, NC: McFarland, 1999), 24.
4. Brother Gilbert, *Young Babe Ruth*, 23.
5. Smelser, 15 (footnote).
6. "Minstrels at St. Mary's School," *Baltimore Sun*, November 27, 1908, 9.
7. Babe Ruth, *Playing the Game: My Early Years in Baseball*, 9.
8. Smelser, 17.
9. Creamer, 39.
10. Leisman, 14–15.
11. Leisman, 34–35.
12. Babe Ruth, *The Babe Ruth Story*, 13.
13. Leisman, 18–19.
14. "License Applications," *Baltimore Sun*, April 15, 1903, 5.
15. Baltimore historian Fred B. Shoken, based on Baltimore City Land Records, accessed July 31, 2018, http://baberuth100.blogspot.com/2013/12/chapter-5.html.
16. From George Ruth deposition in 1906 divorce court file from Maryland State Archives, Baltimore City Circuit Court No. 2 (Equity Papers B) #8962 B, George H. Ruth v. Katie Ruth, 5/14/1906 (MSA T-57–202, 3/18/10/017).
17. Confession note signed by Sowers in Ruth v. Ruth divorce file.
18. From deposition of Police Magistrate Daniel J. Loden in Ruth v. Ruth divorce file.
19. "Personal," *Baltimore Sun*, March 17, 1906, 3.
20. "In Divorce Court," *Baltimore American*, May 15, 1906, 15.
21. Jane Leavy, *The Big Fella: Babe Ruth and the World He Created* (New York: HarperCollins, 2018), 53.

22. Shoken, accessed August 3, 2108, http://baberuth100.blogspot.com/2013/12/chapter-6.html.
23. Smelser, 18.
24. Leisman, 17.
25. Wagenheim, 16.
26. Mrs. Babe (Claire) Ruth, will Bill Slocum, *The Babe and I* (Prentice-Hall: Englewood Cliffs, NJ, 1959), 45.
27. Leisman, 21.
28. Babe Ruth, *The Babe Ruth Story*, 16-17.
29. Thomas Shehan, "The 'Boss' Recalls Ruth's Early Days at St. Mary's School in Baltimore," *Boston Evening Transcript*, February 28, 1935, 6.
30. Interview in *Baseball Magazine*, February 1918, as quoted in Creamer, 44.
31. F. C. Lane, "The Season's Sensation," *Baseball Magazine*, October 1918, 471-472.
32. Creamer, 43-44.
33. Death Certificate C56458, Health Department, City of Baltimore, August 13, 1912.
34. Katie Ruth obituary, *Baltimore Sun*, August 13, 1912, 6.
35. Rick Maese, "A Buried Past," *Baltimore Sun*, February 6, 2008, accessed January 16, 2018, http://articles.baltimoresun.com/2008-02-06/sports/0802060363_1_babe-ruth-katie-grave.
36. Montville, 27.
37. Al Kermisch, "The Babe Ruth Beginning," Society for American Baseball Research Journals Archive, accessed June 5, 2018, research.sabr.org/journals/babe-ruth-beginning.
38. Smelser, 31.
39. Creamer, 45.
40. Montville, 27.
41. Quoted in Smelser, 31.
42. Smelser, 31.

Chapter 7

1. For instance, "Lightning Rods," *Baltimore Sun*, June 25, 1911, 5.
2. "Board Dismisses McCotter," *Baltimore Sun*, January 28, 1908, 12.
3. "Married at City Hall," *Baltimore Sun*, January 30, 1908, 7.
4. "Grind of the Divorce Mill," *Baltimore Sun*, September 11, 1908, 8.
5. From ancestry.com profile of George Ruth, accessed August 13, 2018, https://www.ancestry.com/family-tree/person/tree/27255928/person/420196646343/facts.
6. "Men Flee Over Roofs," *Baltimore Sun*, March 18, 1912, 14.
7. "Patrolman as Life Net," *Baltimore Sun*, July 11, 1912, 8.
8. "Six Saloons Raided," *Baltimore Sun*, November 6, 1912, 16.
9. "Thieves Get Jewelry," *Baltimore Sun*, November 1, 1912, 11.
10. "Lightning Rods," *Baltimore Sun*, July 17, 1914, 11.
11. Brother Gilbert, C.F.X., *Young Babe Ruth: His Early Life and Baseball Career, from the Memoirs of a Xaverian Brother*, edited by Harry Rothgerber (Jefferson, NC: McFarland, 1999), 12-15.
12. "White Sox Pick Roth," *Baltimore Sun*, September 16, 1913, 8.
13. "Gossip of Baltimore's Amateur Balltossers," *Baltimore Sun*, March 17, 1914, 10.
14. "Bits of Baseball Gossip From Many Diamonds," *Baltimore Sun*, May 15, 1913, 8.
15. "Morrisette is to Sign With Dunn Tomorrow," *Baltimore Sun*, May 25, 1913, 16.
16. "Indians Use Tomahawk," *Baltimore Sun*, May 28, 1913, 8.
17. Jimmy Keenan, "Jack Dunn," SABR Bioproject, accessed March 3, 2018, https://sabr.org/bioproj/person/e1addacb.
18. Babe Ruth, *The Babe Ruth Story* (New York: E.P. Dutton, 1948), 18.
19. Babe Ruth, *Playing the Game: My Early Years in Baseball* (Mineola, NY: Dover Publications, 2011), 9-11.
20. George Herman Ruth, *Babe Ruth's Own Book of Baseball* (Lincoln: University of Nebraska Press, 1992), 8-11.
21. Ruth, *The Babe Ruth Story*, 20.
22. Jack Dunn, "Ten Times with Pennant Winners," *Baltimore Sun*, March 10, 1923, 10.
23. Brother Gilbert, C.F.X., "Babe Ruth's First Great Home Run—Brother Gilbert Discovers Him," *Boston Sunday Globe*, October 14, 1928, 20.
24. Lou Leisman, *I Was With Babe Ruth at St. Mary's* (Aberdeen, MD: self-published, 1956), 23.
25. Robert W. Creamer, *Babe: The Legend Comes to Life* (New York: Simon & Schuster, 1974), 48.
26. Ruth, *The Babe Ruth Story*, 18.
27. "Dunn Now Trying to Bolster Club," *Baltimore Sun*, February 15, 1914, 15.

Chapter 8

1. Babe Ruth, *The Babe Ruth Story* (New York: E.P. Dutton, 1948), 21.
2. "Brother Gilbert Dies at Lowell; Started Babe Ruth to Fame," *Boston Globe*, October 20, 1947, 1.
3. Brother Gilbert, C.F.X., *Young Babe Ruth: His Early Life and Baseball Career, from the Memoirs of a Xaverian Brother*, edited by Harry Rothgerber (Jefferson, NC: McFarland, 1999), 44.
4. Ruth, *The Babe Ruth Story*, 21.
5. "Storm Wreckage Strewn Over City and the East" and "City's Loss $600,000," *Baltimore Sun*, March 3, 1914, 1.
6. Ruth, *The Babe Ruth Story*, 21.
7. *Ibid.*, 22.
8. "Orioles Play Basketball," *Baltimore Sun*, March 7, 1914, 7.
9. As quoted in Wilborn Hampton, *Up Close: Babe Ruth, A Twentieth-Century Life* (New York: Viking, 2009), 57.
10. "Homer By Ruth Feature of Game," *Baltimore Sun*, March 8, 1914, 13.
11. Marshall Smelser, *The Life That Ruth Built: A Biography* (Lincoln: University of Nebraska Press, 1975), 42.
12. "Orioles Become Hikers," *Baltimore Sun*, March 9, 1914, 9.
13. Robert W. Creamer, *Babe: The Legend Comes to Life* (New York: Simon & Schuster, 1974), 62.
14. "Cree and Ruth on Job," *Baltimore Sun*, March 11, 1914, 5.
15. "Yanigans Show Class," *Baltimore Sun*, March 14, 1914, 7.
16. "Dunn Picks Men He Will Retain," *Baltimore Sun*, March 15, 1914, 13.
17. Dan O'Brien, "Rube Waddell," SABR BioProject, accessed August 17, 2018, https://sabr.org/bioproj/person/a5b2c2b4.
18. Quoted in Kurt Wagenheim, *Babe Ruth: His Life and Legend* (Chicago: Olmstead Press, 2001), 21.
19. Smelser, 39.
20. Babe Ruth, *The Babe Ruth Story* (New York: E.P. Dutton, 1948), 25–26.
21. *Ibid.*
22. Leigh Montville, *The Big Bam: The Life and Times of Babe Ruth* (New York: Anchor Books, 2006), 36.
23. Wagenheim, 22.
24. "Babe Ruth 'A Natural' Even as Oriole Rookie," *Baltimore Sun*, August 17, 1948, 15.
25. Creamer, 65–66.
26. Brother Gilbert, 74.
27. "Orioles Yans are Busy; Regulars are Idle," *Baltimore Sun*, March 22, 1914, 13.
28. "Dunn Praises Ruth," *Baltimore Sun*, March 16, 1914, 8.
29. "Orioles Beat Phillies," *Baltimore Sun*, March 17, 1914, 10.
30. Creamer, 66.
31. "Orioles Make it Two," *Baltimore Sun*, March 19, 1914, 8.
32. "Phillies Lose One, Two, Three To The Orioles," *Wilmington Morning Star*, March 20, 1914, 2.
33. "Ruth Saves The Day," *Baltimore Sun*, March 20, 1914, 9.
34. "Regulars Beat Yans," *Baltimore Sun*, March 25, 1914, 8.
35. "Orioles Start Home And Dunn Reaches Here Today," *Baltimore Sun*, March 26, 1914, 5.
36. Creamer, 67–68.
37. "Birds Beat Athletics," *Baltimore Sun*, March 26, 1914, 5.
38. "Baltimore Birds Defeated Mack's World Champions," *Wilmington Morning Star*, March 26, 1914, 2.
39. Babe Ruth, *The Babe Ruth Story*, 28.
40. Brother Gilbert, 86.
41. Babe Ruth, *Babe Ruth Story*, 31–32.
42. "Orioles Pile Up Runs," *Baltimore Sun*, March 27, 1914, 8.
43. "Mackies Make Merry Music Meeting Ruth," *Philadelphia Inquirer*, March 29, 1914, 53.
44. "Baker's Batting Helps To Defeat Jack Dunn's Club," *Baltimore Sun*, March 29, 1914, 13.
45. "Ruth Beats Dodgers," *Baltimore Sun*, April 6, 1914, 8.
46. Creamer, 69–70.
47. "Orioles are Blanked," *Baltimore Sun*, April 11, 1914, 10.
48. Brother Gilbert, C.F.X., "His Training Trip With Orioles Brings Ruth His First Fame—and a Nickname," *Boston Sunday Globe*, October 21, 1928, 65.

Chapter 9

1. "Glorious Inaugural for the Terrapins: Quinn Hero of Day," *Baltimore Sun*, April 14, 1914, 1.
2. G. Edward White, *Creating the National Pastime: Baseball Transforms Itself,*

Notes—Chapter 10

1903–1953 (Princeton: Princeton University Press, 1996), 65.

3. Zack Triscuit, "Ned Hanlon," SABR BioProject, accessed August 27, 2018, https://sabr.org/bioproj/person/1e360183.

4. David Pietrusza, *Major Leagues: 18 Professional Baseball Organizations, 1871 to Present* (Jefferson, NC: McFarland, 1991), 209–212.

5. "Terrapin Park is Ready to Welcome Baltimore Fans," *Baltimore Sun*, April 12, 1914, 14.

6. "Birds Blank Bisons," *Baltimore Sun*, April 22, 1914, 8.

7. "Bisons Drop First Game," *Buffalo Commercial*, April 22, 1914, 6.

8. "Quinn the Hero of Great Game," *Baltimore Sun*, April 22, 1914, 8.

9. "Ruth Scores Shutout," *Baltimore Sun*, April 23, 1914, 11.

10. "Terrapins are Game," *Baltimore Sun*, April 23, 1914, 11.

11. "Parent's Muff Costly," *Baltimore Sun*, April 24, 1914, 11.

12. "Senators Play Orioles Today: 2 Games Monday," *Baltimore Sun*, April 26, 1914, 13.

13. "Double-Header Today," *Baltimore Sun*, April 27, 1914, 9.

14. Babe Ruth, *The Babe Ruth Story* (New York: E.P. Dutton, 1948), 31.

15. Brother Gilbert, C.F.X., *Young Babe Ruth: His Early Life and Baseball Career, from the Memoirs of a Xaverian Brother*, edited by Harry Rothgerber (Jefferson, NC: McFarland, 1999), 97.

16. "The Out-of-door Life! Indian Motocycles for 1914," advertisement in *Popular Mechanics Advertising Section*, April 1914, 104.

17. "Bicycles and Motorcycles," advertisement in *Baltimore Sun*, April 25, 1914, 13.

18. "The Rise of Babe Ruth," *Baltimore Sun*, July 10, 1914, 5.

19. "Ruth Wins for Orioles," *Baltimore Sun*, May 2, 1914, 10.

20. "Orioles Divide Double-Header With The Leafs," *Baltimore Sun*, May 3, 1914, 26.

21. Robert W. Creamer, *Babe: The Legend Comes to Life* (New York: Simon & Schuster, 1974), 75–76.

22. "Orioles Home Today," *Baltimore Sun*, June 4, 1914, 9.

23. "Dunn Makes Final Statement," *Richmond* (Virginia) *Times Dispatch*, June 19, 1914, 8.

24. "Dunn Not Given Encouragement," *Richmond* (Virginia) *Times Dispatch*, June 21, 1914, 7.

25. "Orioles Celebrate Major League Debut," *Baltimore Sun*, June 21, 1914, 13.

26. "Nothing in Baltimore Shift," *Sporting News*, June 25, 1914, 1.

27. Pietrusza, 213.

28. Ibid., 231–232.

29. Leigh Montville, *The Big Bam: The Life and Times of Babe Ruth* (New York: Anchor Books, 2006), 40.

30. "Ruth Blanks Leafs," *Baltimore Sun*, June 24, 1914, 5.

31. Marshall Smelser, *The Life that Ruth Built: A Biography* (Lincoln: University of Nebraska Press, 1975), 47

32. "International Notes," *Baltimore Sun*, June 27, 1914, 8.

33. Creamer, 74.

34. Ibid., 77.

35. Smelser, 47.

36. Montville, 41.

37. Smelser, 46.

38. Ibid., 47.

39. "Brooklyn Brief," *Sporting Life*, July 4, 1914, 13.

40. Montville, 40.

41. David Quentin Voigt, *American Baseball: From the Commissioners to Continental Expansion, Volume Two* (University Park: Pennsylvania State University Press, 1983), 21.

42. "The Rise of Babe Ruth," *Baltimore Sun*, July 10, 1914, 5

43. "Stephens, of Reds, Here," *Baltimore Sun*, July 7, 1914, 5.

44. "Cree Sold to Yankees," *Baltimore Sun*, July 8, 1914, 5.

45. "All Orioles for Sale," *Baltimore Sun*, July 9, 1914, 5.

46. "Indians Make it Two," *Baltimore Sun*, July 10, 1914, 5.

Chapter 10

1. Leigh Montville, *The Big Bam: The Life and Times of Babe Ruth* (New York: Anchor Books, 2006), 41.

2. "Union Scale of Wages and Hours of Labor, May 1, 1915 [and May 1, 1914]: Bulletin of the United States Bureau of Labor Statistics, No. 194," Fraser, accessed September 9, 2018, https://fraser.stlouisfed.org/title/3912/item/476868?start_page=22.

3. Brother Gilbert, C.F.X., *Young Babe Ruth: His Early Life and Baseball Career, from the Memoirs of a Xaverian Brother*, edited by Harry Rothgerber (Jefferson, NC: McFarland, 1999), 117.

4. On her later marriage certificate, Helen indicated she was from Galveston, Texas, and in his 1948 autobiography Babe said she was from Nova Scotia, but he also said her last name was Woodring, betraying his notoriously poor memory. Accurate family details can be found in the 1910 United States Federal Census, enumeration district 1443, sheet 13B, for the City of Boston, and marriage and birth information from Massachusetts Marriage Records, 1840–1915, for the City of Boston, 1893.

5. Robert W. Creamer, *Babe: The Legend Comes to Life* (New York: Simon & Schuster, 1974), 84.

6. Babe Ruth, *The Babe Ruth Story* (New York: E.P. Dutton, 1948), 32.

7. George Herman Ruth, *Babe Ruth's Own Book of Baseball* (Lincoln; University of Nebraska Press, 1992), 14.

8. Creamer, 85.

9. "Ruth Leads Red Sox to Victory," *Boston Globe*, July 12, 1914, 11.

10. Quoted in Montville, 42.

11. Creamer, 89.

12. Marshall Smelser, *The Life That Ruth Built: A Biography* (Lincoln: University of Nebraska Press, 1975), 53.

13. Babe Ruth, *The Babe Ruth Story*, 55.

14. Wilborn Hampton, *Up Close: Babe Ruth* (New York: Viking, 2009), 77.

15. Brother Gilbert, 117–118.

16. Babe Ruth, *The Babe Ruth Story*, 32.

17. *Ibid.*, 32.

18. Lawrence S. Ritter, *The Glory of Their Times* (New York: Perennial, 2002), 145.

19. Kal Wagenheim, *Babe Ruth: His Life and His Legend* (Chicago: Olmstead Press, 2001), 29.

20. Babe Ruth, *The Babe Ruth Story*, 39–40.

21. Creamer, 19.

22. Creamer, 222, and Ralph Berger, "Ping Bodie," SABR BioProject, accessed September 23, 2018, https://sabr.org/bioproj/person/712236b9.

23. Montville, 53.

24. Ritter, 145.

25. Creamer, 90–91.

26. Jim Reisler, *Babe Ruth: Launching the Legend* (New York: McGraw-Hill, 2006), 21.

27. "Red Sox Pitchers Doing Great Work," *Boston Globe*, August 3, 1914, 7.

28. "Joseph Lannin," Baseball Reference, accessed September 16, 2018, https://www.baseball-reference.com/bullpen/Joseph_Lannin.

29. "Joseph Lannin, Canadian 'Bell Hop,' Who Became Baseball Magnate," *Chicago Tribune*, January 11, 1914, 21.

30. "Joe Lannin, Former Red Sox Owner, is Dead," *Boston Globe*, May 15, 1928, 1.

31. *Ibid.*

32. "Comment in Sport Topics," *Buffalo Evening News*, October 25, 1920, 16.

33. "Buys Providence Club," *Baltimore Sun*, January 25, 1916, 9.

34. "J. J. Lannin Plunges to Death at Granada," *Brooklyn Daily Eagle*, May 15, 1928, 1.

35. "From Lac Beauport to Fenway Park," Jonathan Guay, *le Journal de Montreal*, March 31, 2016, translated from French, accessed September 17, 2018, https://www.journaldemontreal.com/2016/03/31/de-lac-beauport-a-fenway-park.

36. "Andre Dawson Leads Canadian Baseball Hall of Fame, Class of '04, James McKean, N.E. Peter Hardy & Joseph John Lannin Also Named," *Canadian Baseball News*, February 19, 2004, accessed September 18, 2018, http://www.canadianbaseballnews.com/StMarys/04Inductees.html.

37. Quoted in Marshall Smelser, *The Life That Ruth Built: A Biography* (Lincoln: University of Nebraska Press, 1975), 54.

38. Wagenheim, 29.

39. Creamer, 94.

40. Leonard Levin, "Baseball. Arrival of Ruth turned Grays' Skies to Blue 81 years Ago, the Bambino Led Providence to the International League Pennant," *Providence (Rhode Island) Journal*, August 14, 1995, B4.

41. Creamer, 97.

42. "Hanlan's Point Park," Closed Canadian Parks, accessed September 19, 2018, http://cec.chebucto.org/ClosPark/HanPoint.html.

43. "Leafs Failed to Hit Ruth," *Toronto Daily News*, September 5, 1914, 2.

44. Levin, "Baseball...," B4.

45. "Leafs Couldn't Get Runner Past First," *Toronto Globe*, September 7, 1914, 10.

46. Babe Ruth, *The Babe Ruth Story*, 34.

47. Levin, "Baseball...," B4.

48. Quoted in Creamer, 98.

Chapter 11

1. "Minor Leaguers Beat Cubs, 8 to 7," *Chicago Tribune*, September 28, 1914, 13.
2. "Highlanders Out of Running From Start," *Boston Globe*, October 3, 1914, 7.
3. Babe Ruth, *The Babe Ruth Story* (New York: E.P. Dutton, 1948), 44.
4. Robert W. Creamer, *Babe: The Legend Comes to Life* (New York: Simon & Schuster, 1974), 101.
5. "Buys Providence Club," *Baltimore Sun*, January 25, 1916, 9.
6. Paul Zingg and E. A. (Betsy) Reed, "Harry Hooper," SABR BioProject, https://sabr.org/bioproj/person/4f4206c6.
7. Allan Wood, "Carl Mays," SABR BioProject, https://sabr.org/bioproj/person/99ca7c89.
8. "Red Sox Lose to Yanks in 13th," *Boston Globe*, May 7, 1915, 9.
9. Smelser, 74.
10. "Red Sox March On In Triumph," *Boston Globe*, July 22, 1915, 1.
11. Babe Ruth, *The Babe Ruth Story*, 37.
12. Ibid., 40.
13. Leigh Montville, *The Big Bam: The Life and Times of Babe Ruth* (New York: Anchor Books, 2006), 54.
14. Montville, 55.
15. Brother Gilbert, C.F.X., *Young Babe Ruth: His Early Life and Baseball Career, from the Memoirs of a Xaverian Brother*, edited by Harry Rothgerber (Jefferson, NC: McFarland, 1999), 141.
16. Baltimore historian Fred B. Shoken, in his blog Babe Ruth 100, accessed July 31, 2018, http://baberuth100.blogspot.com/2013/12/introduction.html.
17. "Big Crowd Sees Game," *Baltimore Sun*, October 25, 1915, 5.
18. "Lost and Found," *Baltimore Sun*, October 25, 1915, 9.
19. Creamer, 120.
20. Quoted by John Thorn in "When the Babe Played Second Fiddle," in his blog Our Game, October 26, 2018, accessed October 26, 2018, https://ourgame.mlblogs.com/when-the-babe-played-second-fiddle-9f472a4b94c7.
21. Montville, 58.
22. John Thorn, "When the Babe Played Second Fiddle," Our Game, October 26, 2018, accessed October 26, 2018, op. cit.
23. "Has Plans for Babe," *Baltimore Sun*, October 15, 1916, 4.
24. "Ruth's Wife Badly Hurt," *Washington Post*, December 21, 1916, 8.
25. Marriage date is from marriage records in Baltimore Court of Common Pleas, quoted in Druscilla J. Null, "'My Father Was of German Extraction': Babe Ruth's Ruth/Rudt Ancestors," *Maryland Genealogical Society Journal* 58 (2017), 377.
26. Jane Leavy, *The Big Fella: Babe Ruth and the World He Created* (New York: HarperCollins, 2018), 157, quoting a Mamie Ruth Moberly interview with Mike Gibbons, director emeritus of the Babe Ruth Birthplace and Museum, Baltimore.
27. Kal Wagenheim, *Babe Ruth: His Life and Legend* (Chicago: Olmstead Press, 2001), 38.
28. Montville, 59.
29. Allan Wood, "Babe Ruth," SABR BioProject, accessed December 31, 2016, https://sabr.org/bioproj/person/9dcdd01c.
30. "'Babe' Ruth in Bad Automobile Crash," *Boston Globe*, November 8, 1917, 2.
31. Creamer, 148.
32. "Ruth Jumps Red Sox," *Baltimore Sun*, July 4, 1918, 7.
33. Montville, 68–69.
34. F. C. Lane, "The Season's Sensation," *Baseball Magazine*, October 1918, 472.
35. "Fight Ends in Death," *Baltimore Sun*, August 26, 1918, 12.
36. "Killed Man in Self-Defense," *Baltimore Sun*, August 27, 1918, 4.
37. "Sold Soldier Dope Is Charge," *Baltimore Sun*, January 11, 1918, 12.
38. Wagenheim, 43.
39. Shoken, accessed July 31, 2018, http://baberuth100.blogspot.com/2013/12/introduction.html.
40. Babe Ruth, *The Babe Ruth Story*, 63.
41. Montville, 79.
42. Leavy, 243.

Chapter 12

1. Leigh Montville, *The Big Bam: The Life and Times of Babe Ruth* (New York: Anchor Books, 2006), 82.
2. Robert W. Creamer, *Babe: The Legend Comes to Life* (New York: Simon & Schuster, 1974), 187.
3. Montville, 82–83.
4. "Ruth Gets $27,000," *Boston Globe*, March 22, 1919, 1.
5. Creamer, 189.
6. Marshall Smelser, *The Life That Ruth Built* (Lincoln: University of Nebraska Press, 1975), 110.

7. Montville, 85.
8. *Ibid.*, 86.
9. "St. Mary's to be Bigger," *Baltimore Sun*, April 29, 1919, 8.
10. "Babe Ruth Aids St. Mary's," *Baltimore Sun*, June 5, 1919, 7.
11. "School Band Out To Aid Campaign For St. Mary's," *Baltimore Sun*, June 21, 1919, 16.
12. "Babe Ruth Shows Off," *Baltimore Sun*, September 8, 1919, 7.
13. "Dancers Aid St. Mary's," *Baltimore Sun*, November 28, 1919, 5.
14. Montville, 87–88.
15. Smelser, 110–111.
16. Montville, 90.
17. Smelser, 119.
18. William F. Lamb, "The Black Sox Scandal," Society for American Baseball Research, accessed November 7, 2018, https://sabr.org/research/black-sox-scandal-bill-lamb.
19. G. Edward White, *Creating the National Pastime: Baseball Transforms Itself, 1903–1953* (Princeton: Princeton University Press, 1996), 105.
20. Montville, 92.
21. "Seeks Settlement by Red Sox Owners," *Boston Globe*, February 11, 1920, 7.
22. Kal Wagenheim, *Babe Ruth: His Life and Legend* (Chicago: Olmstead Press, 2001), 59–60.
23. Creamer, 209–210.
24. Jane Leavy, *The Big Fella: Babe Ruth and the World He Created* (New York: HarperCollins, 2018), 101–102.
25. Montville, 159–160.
26. Smelser, 115.
27. Montville, 100.
28. Allan Wood, "Babe Ruth," SABR BioProject, accessed December 31, 2016, https://sabr.org/bioproj/person/9dcdd01c.
29. "Ruth Breaks Record for Home Runs," *Baltimore Sun*, July 20, 1920, 1.
30. "Ruth, Prince of Sluggers, Hears From Home City," *Baltimore Sun*, July 21, 1920, 5.
31. Wagenheim, 79.
32. Wood, "Babe Ruth," SABR BioProject.
33. "Ruth Escapes Injury When His Auto Upsets," *Baltimore Sun*, July 8, 1920, 12.
34. Creamer, 231.
35. "Babe Ruth Hurt When Auto Upset," *Philadelphia Inquirer*, July 8, 1920, 16.
36. "Ruth Escapes Injury When His Auto Upsets," *Baltimore Sun*, July 8, 1920, 12.
37. Babe Ruth, *The Babe Ruth Story* (New York: E.P. Dutton, 1948), 107.

38. "Yankees Lose; So Do Bookies," *New York Daily News*, September 10, 1920, 16.
39. Smelser, 159–162.
40. Brother Gilbert, C.F.X., *Young Babe Ruth: His Early Life and Baseball Career, from the Memoirs of a Xaverian Brother*, edited by Harry Rothgerber (Jefferson, NC: McFarland, 1999), 141.
41. Babe Ruth, *The Babe Ruth Story*, 132.
42. Leavy, 46.
43. Wood, "Babe Ruth," SABR BioProject.
44. "Brother Matthias talks of 'George,'" *Boston Evening Transcript*, February 28, 1935, 6.
45. Montville, 207–212.
46. "Boyhood Teacher Defends Babe Ruth," *Baltimore Evening Sun*, August 31, 1925, 1.
47. Brother Gilbert, C.F.X., 168.
48. Creamer, 301.
49. "Program of the Congress," *Chicago Tribune*, June 14, 1926, 17.
50. Smelser, 333.
51. Smelser, 239.
52. "White House Talk Explained by Lang," *Baltimore Sun*, March 17, 1924, 4.
53. Wagenheim, 147. This account is derived from a report in *The Sporting News*, November 5, 1925, 2.
54. Leavy, 162.

Chapter 13

1. Leigh Montville, *The Big Bam: The Life and Times of Babe Ruth* (New York: Anchor Books, 2006), 241, 251.
2. Kal Wagenheim, *Babe Ruth: His Life and Legend* (Chicago: Olmstead Press, 2001), 162.
3. Marshall Smelser, *The Life That Ruth Built: A Biography* (Lincoln: University of Nebraska Press, 1975), 355.
4. Robert W. Creamer, *Babe: The Legend Comes to Life* (New York: Simon & Schuster, 1974), 309.
5. Thomas Shehan, "Brother Matthias Talks of 'George,'" *Boston Evening Transcript*, February 28, 1935, 6.
6. Wagenheim, 168.
7. "Stickwork of Ruth and Gehrig," *New York Daily News*, August 15, 1927, 30.
8. "Auto presented by Babe Ruth To St. Mary's Smashed by Train," *Baltimore Sun*, August 17, 1927, 22.
9. Babe Ruth, *The Babe Ruth Story* (New York: E.P. Dutton, 1948), 107.

10. Shehan, "Brother Matthias Talks of 'George.'"
11. George Herman Ruth, *Babe Ruth's Own Book of Baseball* (Reprint, Lincoln: University of Nebraska Press, 1992), 6.
12. "Babe Ruth's First Great Home Run— Brother Gilbert Discovers Him," *Boston Sunday Globe*, October 14, 1928, 20.
13. Creamer, 344.
14. Gary A. Sarnoff, *The First Yankees Dynasty: Babe Ruth, Miller Huggins and the Bronx Bombers of the 1920s* (Jefferson, NC: McFarland, 2014), 206.
15. Montville, 292.
16. Montville, 294.
17. Sarnoff, 221.
18. Much of the information about Matthias's troubles of 1931 is gleaned from the Brother Matthias Dossier, CCFX 6/04 #329, of the Xaverian Brothers, University of Notre Dame Archives, South Bend, Indiana.
19. Letter from law offices of Galvin and McCourt, dated June 21, 1931, found in Brother Matthias Dossier, CCFX 6/04 #329, of the Xaverian Brothers, University of Notre Dame Archives, South Bend, Indiana.
20. Report of disciplinary hearing into the official warning of Brother Matthias, conducted October 11, 1931, at St. Joseph Juniorate, Peabody, Massachusetts, found in Brother Matthias Dossier, CCFX 6/04 #329, of the Xaverian Brothers, University of Notre Dame Archives, South Bend, Indiana.
21. Creamer, 368.
22. Montville, 326.
23. Smelser, 473.
24. Montville, 350, 351.
25. Creamer, 416.
26. Jacob Bogage, "Babe Ruth is Finally Awarded Medal of Freedom. Family and Fans Wonder, 'What the Heck Took So Long?,'" *Washington Post*, November 16, 2018, accessed November 17, 2018, https://www.washingtonpost.com/sports/2018/11/15/babe-ruth-is-finally-awarded-medal-freedom-family-fans-wonder-what-heck-took-so-long/?utm_term=.6151deed0c26.

Epilogue

1. Brother Gilbert, C.F.X., *Young Babe Ruth: His Early Life and Baseball Career, from the Memoirs of a Xaverian Brother*, edited by Harry Rothgerber (Jefferson, NC: McFarland, 1999), 21.

2. "Brother Gilbert Tells About Ruth," *North Adams* (Massachusetts) *Transcript*, April 20, 1929, 3.
3. "Vets Play, Win, Eat and Talk," *Baltimore Sun*, August 9, 1931, 21.
4. Lowell Thomas, "The 'Babe' Grows Up," *Baltimore Sun*, April 14, 1935, 121.
5. "Brother Gilbert Here With Prep Team Today," *Baltimore Sun*, April 9, 1936, 18.
6. "Bro. Gilbert in Fanning Bee," *Baltimore Sun*, April 10, 1936, 14.
7. Source is Brother Tom Puccio, principal of Malden Catholic High School, Malden, Massachusetts, in email to author, April 20, 2017.
8. "Brother Gilbert," in C. M. Gibbs, "Gibberish," *Baltimore Sun*, February 7, 1939, 11.
9. Jesse Linthicum, "Sunlight on Sports. This An' That," *Baltimore Sun*, July 22, 1942, 15.
10. "Brother Gilbert Dies at Lowell; Started Babe Ruth to Fame," *Boston Globe*, October 20, 1947, 1.
11. "Brother Gilbert, Who Found Ruth, Dies in Howell," *Fitchburg* (Massachusetts) *Sentinel*, October 20, 1947, 8.
12. "Youth Subs for Ruth at Funeral," *Berkshire Eagle* (Pittsfield, Massachusetts), October 22, 1948, 10.
13. Jane Leavy, *The Big Fella: Babe Ruth and the World He Created* (New York: HarperCollins, 2018), 471.
14. Email message to author, January 28, 2017, from Brent Stevens, Babe Ruth's great-grandson, owner of the Babe Ruth Central website, sharing responses to questions posed by the author to Julia Ruth Stevens (Babe's daughter), as relayed by her son, Tom Stevens. She died several months later.
15. Email to author from Harry Rothgerber, December 2, 2018.
16. *The Church World*, April 4, 1996, 15.
17. Thomas Shehan, "Brother Matthias Talks of 'George,'" *Boston Evening Transcript*, February 28, 1935, 6.
18. Obituary, *Baltimore Sun*, March 14, 1938, 11.
19. Brother Gilbert, 180.
20. *Xaverian Brothers Auxiliary Bulletin*, October 1942, 16.
21. Brother Gilbert, 181.
22. "George Herman Ruth, Jr.," *Baltimore Sun*, August 18, 1948, 12.

Bibliography

Books

Block, David. *Baseball Before We Knew It: A Search for the Roots of the Game.* Lincoln: University of Nebraska Press, 2005.

Bready, James H. *Baseball in Baltimore: The First 100 Years.* Baltimore: Johns Hopkins University Press, 1998.

Conrad, Margaret R., and James K. Hiller. *Atlantic Canada: A Concise History.* Don Mills, ON: Oxford University Press, 2006.

Creamer, Robert W. *Babe: The Legend Comes to Life.* New York: Simon & Schuster, 1974.

Brother Gilbert, C.F.X. *Young Babe Ruth: His Early Life and Baseball Career, from the Memoirs of a Xaverian Brother*, edited by Harry Rothgerber. Jefferson, NC: McFarland, 1999.

Goldman, Herbert G. *Jolson: The Legend Comes to Life.* New York: Oxford University Press, 1988.

Halloran, Peter C. *Boston's Wayward Children: Social Services for Homeless Children, 1830–1930.* Cranbury, NJ: Associated University Presses, 1989.

Hampton, Wilborn. *Up Close: Babe Ruth.* New York: Viking, 2009.

Hardy, Stephen. *How Boston Played: Sport, Recreation and Community, 1865–1915.* Knoxville: University of Tennessee Press, 2003.

Hensler, Bruce. *Crucible of Fire: Nineteenth-Century Urban Fires and the Making of the Modern Fire Service.* Dulles, VA: Potomac Books, 2011.

Humber, William. *Cheering for the Home Team: The Story of Baseball in Canada.* Erin, ON: Boston Mills Press, 1983.

Brother Julian, C.F.X. *Men and Deeds: The Xaverian Brothers in America.* New York: Macmillan, 1930.

Leavy, Jane. *The Big Fella: Babe Ruth and the World He Created.* New York: HarperCollins, 2018.

Leisman, Lou. *I Was with Babe Ruth at St. Mary's.* Aberdeen, MD: 1956.

Marchi, Dr. Regina. *East Boston, Massachusetts.* Charleston, SC: Legendary Locals, 2015.

Mars, Ken. *Baltimore Baseball: First Pitch to First Pennant.* Parkville, MD: Old Frog Publishing, 2017.

Mencken, H.L. *Happy Days: Mencken's Autobiography, 1880–1892.* Baltimore: Johns Hopkins University Press, 1996.

Montville, Leigh. *The Big Bam: The Life and Times of Babe Ruth.* New York: Anchor Books, 2006.

Moore, James P., Jr. *Prayer in America: A Spiritual History of Our Nation.* New York: Image Books, 2005.

Nemec, David. *The Beer and Whisky League.* New York: Lyons & Burford, 1994.

Pietrusza, David. *Major Leagues: 18 Professional Baseball Organizations, 1871 to Present.* Jefferson, NC: McFarland, 1991.

Ritter, Lawrence S. *The Glory of Their Times.* New York: Macmillan, 1966. Reprint, New York: Perennial, 2002.

Reisler, Jim. *Babe Ruth: Launching the Legend.* New York: McGraw-Hill, 2006.

Ruth, Babe. *Playing the Game: My Early Years in Baseball*, edited by William R. Cobb. Mineola, NY: Dover Publications, 2011.

Ruth, Babe, as told to Bob Considine. *The Babe Ruth Story.* New York: E.P. Dutton, 1948.

Ruth, Mrs. Babe (Claire), with Bill Slocum. *The Babe and I.* Englewood Cliffs, NJ: Prentice-Hall, 1959.

Ruth, George Herman. *Babe Ruth's Own*

Book of Baseball. New York: G. P. Putnam's Sons, 1928. Reprint, Lincoln: University of Nebraska Press, 1992.

Ryczek, William. *Blackguards and Red Stockings: A History of Baseball's National Association, 1871–1875*. Jefferson, NC: McFarland, 2016.

Sarnoff, Gary A. *The First Yankees Dynasty: Babe Ruth, Miller Huggins and the Bronx Bombers of the 1920s*. Jefferson, NC: McFarland, 2014.

Smelser, Marshall. *The Life That Ruth Built: A Biography*. Lincoln: University of Nebraska Press, 1975.

Thorn, John. *Baseball in the Garden of Eden: The Secret History of the Early Game*. New York: Simon & Schuster, 2011.

Voigt, David Quentin. *American Baseball: From the Commissioners to Continental Expansion, Volume Two*. University Park: The Pennsylvania State University Press, 1983.

Wagenheim, Kal. *Babe Ruth: His Life and Legend*. Chicago: Olmstead Press, 2001.

Waring, James H. N. *The Work of the Colored Law and Order League: Baltimore, MD*. Cheyney, PA: Committee of Twelve for the Advancement of the Negro Race, 1908.

White, G. Edward. *Creating the National Pastime: Baseball Transforms Itself, 1903–1953*. Princeton: Princeton University Press, 1996.

Articles

"Astor's 'Babe Ruth Story' Swings Too Wide and Misses," Lew Sheaffer, *Brooklyn Eagle*, July 27, 1948.

"Babe Ruth," Allan Wood, SABR BioProject, https://sabr.org/person/9dcdd01c.

"The Babe Ruth Beginning," Al Kermisch, Society for American Baseball Research Journals Archive, research.sabr.org/journals/babe-ruth-beginning.

"'The Babe Ruth Story,' Starring William Bendix as Baseball Hero Opens at Astor," Bosley Crowther, *New York Times*, July 27, 1948.

"Babe Ruth's Beginnings," Bozeman Bulger, *Saturday Evening Post*, originally published December, 1931, republished April 10, 2017, http://www.saturdayeveningpost.com/2017/04/10/archives/historical-retrospectives/babe-ruths-beginnings.html.

"Baltimore's Civil Rights Heritage: 1885–1929," *Baltimore Heritage*, https://baltimoreheritage.github.io/civil-rights-heritage/overview/1885-1929/.

"Batter Up! Baseball, Baptism, Babe Ruth, and Baltimore," Father Rob Carbonneau, Historian and Director of the Passionist Historical Archives, March 30, 2000, http://cpprovince.org/archives/sesqui/sesqui3.php.

"The Black Sox Scandal," William F. Lamb, Society for American Baseball Research, https://sabr.org/research/black-sox-scandal-bill-lamb.

"Child Welfare: A Brief History," Linda Gordon, Ph.D., New York University, https://socialwelfare.library.vcu.edu/programs/child-welfare-overview/.

"80-Year-Old Ex-Cop Remembers Babe Ruth as a Boy," Rodger H. Pippen, on Ridgely's Delight webpage, http://www.ridgelysdelight.org/PDFs/CopStory.pdf.

"The Foreign Protestants," Nova Scotia Archives, https://archives.novascotia.ca/genealogy/foreign-protestants.

"Hanlan's Point Park," in Closed Canadian Parks, http://cec.chebucto.org/ClosPark/HanPoint.html.

"Harry Hooper," Paul Zingg and E. A. (Betsy) Reed, SABR BioProject, https://sabr.org/bioproj/person/4f4206c6.

"The History of Baltimore," Baltimore City Department of Planning, MD, https://planning.baltimorecity.gov/sites/default/files/History%20of%20Baltimore_1.pdf.

"History of the System," Baltimore City Department of Public Works, https://publicworks.baltimorecity.gov/pw-bureaus/water-wastewater/surface/history.

"Immigrant Ships: Halifax," Glossems on Historical Events, Conditions and Movements, http://www.blupete.com/Hist/Gloss/ImmigrantShips1750-52.htm#Sally.

"Jack Dunn," Jimmy Keenan, SABR BioProject, https://sabr.org/bioproj/person/e1addacb.

"A Jolson Biography: Part 1," Musical101.com: The Cyber Encyclopedia of Musical Theatre, Film and Television, https://www.musicals101.com/jolsonbio.htm.

"The Kids Can't Take It If We Don't Give It!" Babe Ruth, *Guideposts Magazine*, October 1–2 and 23–24, 1948.

"Major and Minor League Baseball in Baltimore," Teaching American History in Maryland, http://teaching.msa.maryland.gov/000001/000000/000176/htm/t176.html.

"The Mines of New Waterford and District," Ted Boutilier, New Waterford Historical Society, https://cbushare.cbu.ca/sites/library/brasdor-collection/Lists/Bras%20dOr%20Collection/Attachments/9332/2544_bdc_0.pdf.

"'My Father Was of German Extraction': Babe Ruth's Ruth/Rudt Ancestors," Druscilla J. Null, *Maryland Genealogical Society* 58 (2017), https://mdgensoc.org/upload/files/allowindex/MGS_Babe_Ruth_Article_2017.pdf.

"Ned Hanlon," Zack Triscuit, SABR BioProject, https://sabr.org/bioproj/person/1e360183.

"Nova Scotia," *The Canadian Encyclopedia*, www.thecanadianencyclopedia.ca/en/article/nova-scotia/.

"Past, Present, and Future Roles of Child Protective Services," Patricia A. Schene, in *Protecting Children from Abuse and Neglect, Volume 8, Number 1* (Spring 1998), http://thesociologycenter.com/GeneralBibliography/vol8no1ART2.pdf.

"Profiles of Brotherhood," Brother Thomas More Page, *Concordia: A Xaverian Sponsored Publication, Volume 10, Number 3* (November 1995).

"Rube Waddell," Dan O'Brien, SABR BioProject, https://sabr.org/bioproj/person/a5b2c2b4.

"St. Louis Cardinals Slugger Pujols gets Babe Ruth Test at Washington University," Gerry Everding, *The Source*, Washington University, https://sourcewustl.edu/2006/08/st-louis-cardinals-slugger-ujols-gets-babe-ruth-test-at-washington-university/.

"St. Mary's Industrial Home: A Grateful Look at the Past," Living the Charism: Exploring the Xaverian Way, http://livingthecharism.com/saint-marys-industrial-home-a-grateful-look-at-the-past/.

"Was Being Left-Handed Ever a Sin?" Fr. Charles Grondin, https://www.catholic.com/qa/was-being-left-handed-ever-a-sin.

"When the Babe Played Second Fiddle," John Thorn, *Our Game*, https://ourgamemlblogs.com/when-the-babe-played-second-fiddle-9f472a4b94c7.

Magazines

Baseball Magazine
Concordia: A Xaverian Sponsored Publication
Guideposts Magazine
New York Clipper
The Sporting News

Newspapers

Baltimore American
Baltimore Sun
Berkshire Eagle
Boston Evening Transcript
Boston Globe
Brooklyn Eagle
Buffalo Commercial
Buffalo Evening News
Canadian Baseball News
Chicago Tribune
Daily News (Newport News, VA)
Fitchburg (MA) *Sentinel*
le Journal de Montréal
New York Daily News
New York Times
North Adams (MA) *Transcript*
Philadelphia Inquirer
Providence (RI) *Journal*
Richmond (VA) *Times Dispatch*
Toronto Daily News
Toronto Globe
Toronto Star
Wilmington (DE) *Morning Star*

Other Publications

Catholic Digest
The Church World
New York Clipper
Our Sunday Visitor
Popular Mechanics
The Sacred Heart Review
Saturday Evening Post
Washington Post
Xaverian Brothers Auxiliary Bulletin

Online Resources

ancestry.com
baseball-reference.com
The Canadian Encyclopedia
newspapers.com
retrosheet.org
Society for American Baseball Research BioProject

Websites

Babe Ruth Central (baberuthcentral.com)

davidstinsonauthor.com
deadballbaseball.com
Ridgely's Delight (ridgelysdelight.org)

Blogs

Babe Ruth 100, by Fred B. Shoken (babe-ruth100.blogspot.com)

Our Game, by John Thorn (ourgame.mlblogs.com)

Other Sources

Babe Ruth Museum
Boston Public Library
Maryland State Archives

Index

Acadia 16
Adams, Babe 102
Adams, Richard 64
Akst, Harry 37
Allen, Mel 12
American Association ("The Beer and Whisky League") 31–32, 108
American League 32, 109, 115
American Legion Baseball junior baseball program 9, 11–12
American Society for the Prevention of Cruelty to Animals 34

The Babe Comes Home (movie) 164
Babe Ruth All Stars 160
Babe Ruth Day 10, 13, 175
Babe Ruth Foundation 11
Babe Ruth: His Life and Legend 4
The Babe Ruth Story (book) 7, 8, 11, 168, 182
The Babe Ruth Story (movie) 8, 14
Babe Ruth's Own Book of Baseball 167
Babe: The Legend Comes to Life 1, 13, 175
Back River Park, Baltimore 106, 117
Baker, Frank (Home Run) 104–106
Baltimore, Maryland 29–30
Baltimore Canaries 31
Baltimore Fire of 1904 61–62
Baltimore Orioles 31–33, 84, 93, 96, 97, 102–109, 112, 114–115, 117, 121, 134, 149
Baltimore Pastimes 30–31
Baltimore Terrapins 32, 93, 105, 108–111, 114, 116–117, 128, 141
Barrow, Edward 109, 116, 144–145, 149, 151, 153, 157, 164
Barry, Jack 143
Bauman, Paddy 131
Beam, George 30
Bedient, Hugh 123
Beebe, Fred 110
Beefelt, Nellie 145
Beefelt, Oliver 145
Bendix, William 8, 11
Bentley, Jack 135
Bergh, Henry 34

Bescher, Bob 107
Bickford, Charles 8, 182
Bielski, Lennie 173
The Big Bam: The Life and Times of Babe Ruth 4, 182
The Big Fella: Babe Ruth and the World He Created 175
Birmingham, Harry C. 51–53
Black Sox Scandal 152–153
Bodie, Ping 125
Book of Sports 19
Borton, Babe 102
Boston baseball history 19–21
Boston Beaneaters 32
Boston Braves 104, 107–108, 127, 130, 134, 177
Boston Red Sox 79, 118, 126–127, 134, 138, 141–142
Boston Red Stockings 20
Boutilier, Alice 18
Boutilier, Eunice Mary 18–19, 26, 181
Boutilier, Francis 18–19, 22, 181
Boutilier, Henry J. 18–19, 22, 26, 181
Boutilier, Jean George 17
Boutilier, Joseph 18–19
Boutilier, Joseph F. 18, 22, 26
Boutilier, Martin Leo 18, 22–26; *see also* Brother Matthias
Boutilier, Mary Ann 18
Boutilier, Mary Margaret 18
Boutilier, Napoleon P. 18–19, 22, 26
Boutilier, Nathaniel 18–19, 22
Boutilier, Sarah 17
Boutilier, Thomas Frederick 18–19, 22–23, 26, 181; *see also* Brother Amandus
Bow, Clara 154
Bowness, Helen 170, 172
Bras d'Or Lake, Cape Breton Island, Nova Scotia 17
Bridges, Tommy 173
Brien, Joanna 122
Brien, Michael 122
Broening, William F. 186
Brother Alban (John T. Bannon) 60, 70, 77, 81, 89–92, 112, 121

209

Index

Brother Amandus (Thomas F. Boutilier) 26–27, 181
Brother Benedict 40
Brother Benjamin 36, 166–167, 181
Brother Bruno 124
Brother Charles 37
Brother Dominic 24, 26, 38
Brother Gilbert (Phillip Cairnes): alerted to young George 89; Babe asks boy to attend his funeral 177–178; as coach at Mount St. Joseph College 84; falling out with Babe 178; introduces young George to Dunn 3, 86, 88, 91, 93; personality 3, 179; sees young George play baseball for first time 89; speaks to baseball writers 177; speeches 176–177; working on memoirs 177–178; writes serialized newspaper story of Babe 89
Brother Godfrey 181
Brother Herman (William Bahr) 40, 41, 60, 70, 81, 89, 92, 112, 121
Brother Matthias (Martin Leo Boutilier): ability with bat and technique 68–69; advice to Jack Dunn 91; advises Babe against divorce 162; ancestry 17–18; appearance 2, 25, 60, 171, 177, 181, 185; birth 18; coaches George Ruth, Jr. 63–68; counsels Babe against becoming a priest 77; counsels Babe in Chicago 161–163; death 181; disciplinarian role 27, 60–61; disciplined for seeing woman 170–172; extra time spent with young George on ballfield 66–67; family's move to Boston 19; father 18; fiftieth anniversary as Xaverian 181; guest of Babe at World Series 160, 166; helps introduce young George Ruth to Jack Dunn 86–87, 90–91; identifies talent in young George 63; joins Xaverians 24–26; makes Babe pitch 78, 186; makes young lefty George write with right hand 64; only press interview 179–181; personality 27–28, 60–61; posted to St. Mary's 26; praised by Babe 2–3, 66–67; praises Babe 1–15, 124, 179–180, 185–186; receives Cadillac as gift from Babe 3, 162–163, 186; receives second Cadillac from Babe 167; retires 181; running technique 68; with St. Mary's band on fundraising tour with Yankees 158–159; siblings 18; teaching in class 65; too big for bedroom 60; welcomes Babe back to St. Mary's 180; words of encouragement for Babe 63; wrecks Cadillac 166
Brother Osmund 172
Brother Pancratius 41
Brother Paul (Peter M. Scanlan) 25–26, 64, 81, 87, 89, 91–92, 95–96, 119, 121, 134, 138, 142, 150–151, 158, 161, 180, 186
Brother Quentin 40
Brother Sebastian 180
Brother Simon 158
Brother Thomas More Page 69
Brothers of Charity 22–23, 34
Brothers of Charity St. Vincent De Paul, Montreal 22
Brown, Joe L. 14
Brundige, Annie 46
Brundige, Milton C. 46
Burns, Leo 145
Bush, George H.W. 11

Cajuns 17
Camden Yards, Baltimore 43, 46–47, 73–74, 139
Canadian Baseball Hall of Fame 129
Candide, Father 23, 26
Cape Breton Colliery League (baseball) 19
Cape Breton Island, Nova Scotia 16
Caporel, Lefty 102–103, 106, 110
Carey, Paul 10, 12–14
Carrigan, Bill 122–126, 135–138, 142
Cashman, Joe 123
Cassin, the Rev. Joseph 24
Cerf, Bennett 11
Chandler, A.B. (Happy) 10, 13
Chapman, Ray 135
Children's Aid Society of New York 33
Cicotte, Eddie 153
Civil War 24, 30, 33, 159
Clark, "Loads" 72
Cobb, Ty 11, 104, 164
Cobb, William 159
Cole, Leonard ("King") 133
Collins, Eddie 104–105, 134
Collins, Ray 123
Comiskey, Charles 42, 153
Congregation of the Brothers of Francis Xavier (Xaverian Brothers) 23
Connor, Roger 159
Conrad, Margaret R. 18
Considine, Bob 10–11, 14, 48, 53, 132, 158, 168, 180, 182
Cottrell, Ensign 97–98, 110, 113–114
Crane, Harriet 144
Creamer, Robert W. 1, 4, 43, 92–93, 101. 106, 114, 134, 161, 175
Cree, Birdie 99, 110, 118–120
Crowther, Bosley 8
Curley, Archbishop Michael J. 170–171

Danforth, Dave 109–110
Daniels, Bert 103
Danzig, Babe 102
Deadball Era 68, 132, 136
Delaney, Frank 12–13
DeLay, Jerry 73
Derrick, Claude 103, 106, 118–120
Digby, Nova Scotia 19
Dolan, the Rev. Thomas 134
Donovan, Bill 129, 132
Dooling, James J. 128
Doty, Babe 102
Dove, Alvin 99

Index

Draper, William H. 134
Dunn, Jack 3, 32, 59, 84, 85, 86, 87–88, 90–93, 95, 97–121, 128, 134, 135, 159, 168, 176, 183
Dunn, Jack, Jr. 102–104
Durant, Myrtle 125
Dyson, Charles 83

East Boston, Massachusetts 19, 21, 24
Eastern League 32, 84
Egan, Ben 96–98, 101, 108, 110, 113, 120–123
Ellison, Babe 102
Engel, Joe 92–93
Excelsior Base Ball Club 30

Federal League 93, 105, 108–109, 111, 115, 117, 140–141
Fell, Lena 75, 80
Felsch, Happy 153
Fewster, Doc 96
Fisher, Cherokee 30
Fitzpatrick, Vincent DeP. 166–167
Flaherty, Dope 72
Ford, Whitey 147
Foreign Protestants of Nova Scotia 17
Fort Louisbourg, Nova Scotia 18
Foster, Rube 123, 134, 137
Fox, Jimmie 169
Frazee, Harry 128, 142, 144, 148–149, 153–154, 156
Frick, Ford 3, 49, 59, 167–168, 173
Fuchs, Emil 174

Gaffney, James 127
Galvin, William L. 170
Gandil, Chick 153
Gate of Heaven Cemetery, Hawthorne, New York 13, 175
Gehrig, Lou 48, 165–166, 169, 174–175
Gerry, Elbridge 34
"Gerry Society" 34
Gibbons, Cardinal James 70
Gilmore, James 108
Gleich, Fred 157–158
Gleichmann, Ed 110, 119
Goldsborough, Phillips Lee 108
Good, Wilbur 133
Graf, Minnie 43
Graney, Jack 122–123

Haggerty, Frank 177–178
Halifax, Nova Scotia 19
Hampton, Wilborn 124
Hanlon, Ned 32, 109, 117
Hardy, Stephen 21
Harris, Paul 80
Hatch, Parker 125
Hemingway, Ernest 11
Hermann, August 116, 129
Hiller, James K. 18
Hodgson, Claire Ruth 167–169

Hofman, Fred 157–158
Holland, Albert 41
Hooper, Harry 124–125, 134, 144
House of the Guardian Angel, Boston 22
Howley, Patrick 18
Hoyt, Waite 165
Huggins, Miller 9, 154, 160–161, 169
Huston, Col. Tillinghast L'Hommedieu 153–154
Hyland, Alexander 172

Igoe, Johnny 148
International Association 108
International Eucharistic Congress, Chicago 161
International League 33, 84–85, 109, 111, 115–116, 118

Jackson, Shoeless Joe 120, 153
James, Bill 137
Janvin, Hal 122
Jarman, Frank 97, 102, 110
Johnson, Ban 32, 116, 129
Johnson, Ellis 131
Johnson, Walter 141
Jolson, Al (Asa Yoelson) 34–37
Jolson, Erle 36

Kaufman, the Rev. Thomas 7–9, 12–13
Keenan, Johnny 156
Kelly, John A. 26
Kerr, Dick 156
Key, Francis Scott 29
Kieran, John 165
Kinder, Edward 168
Kirby, Congo 72, 77
Klingelhoefer, Smoke 103
Koenig, Mark 165

Lander's Coffee Shop, Boston 122, 125, 134
Landis, Judge Kenesaw Mountain 153, 160
Lane, F.C. 79
Lannin, J.J. 118, 126–129, 132, 141–142, 153
Lazzeri, Tony 165
Leavy, Jane 154, 163, 175
Leggett, Joseph B. 30
Leisman, "Fats" Lou 53–54, 61, 63, 66, 69, 72–73, 76–77, 91–92
Leonard, Dutch 123, 126, 134, 148
Lewis, Duffy 158
Lidgate, Gene 97, 103
Lieb, Fred 10, 14, 47
Lingan, Cape Breton Island, Nova Scotia 16–17
Linthicum, Jesse 98–99, 101–104, 106, 109–111, 113, 116
Loden, Daniel J. 74
Lopez, Al 66
Lord Baltimore (George Calvert) 31
Lord Baltimores baseball club 30

Index

Loring, the Rev. Charles Brace 33
Lowenstein, Mel (Mervyn) 10, 14
Lunenburg, Nova Scotia 17, 19

Mack, Connie 12, 84, 99, 103, 116, 118, 122
Mackessy, Monsignor William E. 170
Maisel, Fritz 88, 90, 107, 140
Malden High School, Malden, Massachusetts 177
Malone, Lewis 89
Maple Leaf Park, Hanlan's Point, Toronto 131
Maris, Roger 165
Massachusetts Game (of baseball) 20
Mathews, Bobby 30
Mays, Carl 14, 136, 147, 153
McCall, Skinny 77
McCotter, Harry 82
McGraw, John 32, 107, 149
McMullin, Fred 153
Meadows, Ford 87, 90–91, 176
Melrose Park, Providence, Rhode Island 130
Mencken, H.L. 30
Messina, John 98
Meusel, Bob 158, 160, 165, 180
Midkiff, Ezra 119
Mission Church High School, Boston 168
Moale, Frank V. 75
Montbéliard, France 17
Montreal Royals 32, 109, 113, 130
Montville, Leigh 4, 43, 80, 125, 154, 175
Moore, Wilcy 165
Morgan, J. Pierpont V. 48
Morgan, John 89–91
Morrisette, Bill 80, 85, 91–93, 96, 99, 102–103, 107, 110, 113
Mount St. Joseph College 3, 24, 26, 59, 176–177, 181
Mowrey, Mike 142
Murnane, Tim 123, 133
Murphy, Danny 105
Murray, Red 107
Myers, Hi 141

National Association of Professional Base Ball Players 20–21, 31
National Baseball Hall of Fame and Museum, Cooperstown, New York 141
National Commission (August Hermann, Ban Johnson, John Tener) 115
National High School Band Contest 41
National League 21, 31–32, 107–109
New York game (of baseball) 20
New York Society for Prevention of Cruelty to Children 34
New York Yankees 154–160
Newington Base Ball Park, Baltimore 31
Null, Druscilla J. 44

O'Brien, Father Joseph 45
O'Donnell, the Rev. Hugh Roe 23, 25

O'Leary, Charley 157–158
Onslow, Jack 131
Oppenheimer Shirt Company 57
Oriole Park, Baltimore 93, 102, 105, 107, 110, 115
outbreak of First World War 129
Owens, Brick 143

Peale, Norman Vincent 13
Pegler, Westbrook 49, 58, 65, 159
Pennock, Herb 104, 131
Perrin, Bill 130, 132
Philadelphia Phillies 102–104, 106, 137
Pigtown, Baltimore 43
Pike, Lip 31
Pippen, Rodger 51, 93, 97–98, 100–102
Pittsfield, Massachusetts 20
Players' League 108
pokenins (game) 69
Pratt, Del 158
Presidential Medal of Freedom 175
Preston, James H. 108–109
Pride of the Yankees (movie) 175
Prohibition 154
Providence Grays (Clamdiggers) 115, 126, 128
Pujols, Albert 64

Quinn, Jack 108, 110

Rasin, Carrol 109
Rice, Grantland 141
Ridgely's Delight Neighborhood, Baltimore 43
Risberg, Swede 153
Robinson, John 17
Rogge, Clint 131
Roosevelt, Franklin (U.S. president) 174
Root, Charlie 173
Roth, Dave 84–85
Rothgerber, Harry 178–179
Ruppert, Col. Jacob, Jr. 47, 153–154, 157, 164, 169, 173–174
Russell, Allen 107
Ruth, Babe (George, Jr.): acting 164; auto accidents 112, 129, 137, 143–144, 157–158; "Babe" nickname 100–102; Babe Ruth Day of 1947 10, 175; Baltimore signing 91; baptized 45; bellyache heard 'round the world 160; birth 43; Boston Braves signing 174; Boston Red Sox signing 121; burial 13; buys bar for father 138, 139, 140; "called shot" of 1932 9; catcher with wrong glove 65, 90; childhood years 43–52; coaching by Brother Matthias 63–68; committed to St. Mary's 2, 51–52; counseling by Brother Matthias 161–163; daughter Dorothy 11–12; daughter Julia 11–12, 175, 178; death 13, 175; death of father 145; death of Helen 168; death of Miller Huggins 169; death of mother 79; on deathbed 7–15; decline 173–174; discovery by Dunn 85–88; divorce of parents 75; eating habits 125; fa-

Index

ther (see George Ruth, Sr.); final appearance at Yankee Stadium 12, 175; final major league homer 175; first home run as a professional 98, 132; first home run in a game in Toronto 131; first home run in major leagues 136; funeral mass 13; gives Cadillacs to Brother Matthias 3, 162, 167; grave of 175; handwriting 64; helps St. Mary's fundraising 150–151, 158–159; hits 60th homer in 1927 165; hospitalization 7–15, 160; last rites administered 8, 12; made to pitch 78; made to play all positions 64–65, 144; made to switch to right hand for writing 64; marries Claire Hodgson 168; marries Helen Woodford 134; nickname 54, 157; only no-hitter 143; praises Brother Matthias 2–3, 14–15; retires 174; on St. Mary's ball teams 67, 78; sent to Providence 126; separates from Helen 161; shirt maker training 55–56; signs with Baltimore 87–88, 91–92, 94; sold to New York 135, 154, 155; suspension of 1922 160; suspension of 1925 161; visits St. Mary's with Yankees 180; wants managing job 175; womanizing 144, 160–161; Yankee Stadium 25th anniversary 175
Ruth, Catherine 44
Ruth, Claire 8–13, 66–67, 76–77
Ruth, Dorothy 12, 169
Ruth, Frank 80, 84, 99
Ruth, George Herman, Sr. 1, 43–46, 49–50, 53, 73–75, 82–83, 139, 140
Ruth, Helen see Woodford, Helen
Ruth, Jacob 44
Ruth, John A., Sr. 44–45
Ruth, John, Jr. 44–46, 53
Ruth, Julia (Stevens) 11, 12, 169
Ruth, Katie 2, 43–45, 48–50, 53, 73–75, 79–80
Ruth, Mary 44–46
Ruth, Mary (Mamie, sister) 46, 49–50, 53, 74, 75, 80, 112, 143
Ruth, William 75
Ruth's Café, Baltimore 139, 142, 144–146, 146

St. James House, Baltimore 76
St. John's Preparatory School, Danvers, Massachusetts 168, 172, 176, 179, 185
St. Joseph's Juniorate, Peabody, Massachusetts 181
St. Mary's Industrial Training School 2, 27; Babe committed to 51–52; Babe leaves 95; ball team 67; classroom 65; closes 37; dormitory 39; established 24; fire 41, 149, 150; focus on baseball 40–41; fundraising 150–151, 158–159; role 39; tailoring shop 55, 56
St. Mary's School band 41–42, 70–71, 158–159, 174
St. Xavier High School, Louisville, Kentucky 178
Sally (British ship) 17
Schamberger, Joanna 44–45

Schamberger, Pius 45
Schwarz, Gus 103
Seybold, Socks 68
Shawkey, Bob 152
Sheaffer, Lew 8
Shehan, Tom 179–180, 182, 185, 187
Sherman Act 116
Shocker, Urban 165
Shoken, Fred B. 46, 75, 139, 145, 148
Shore, Ernie 115, 118–123, 125–126, 134, 143, 145, 148
Simmons, Al 169
Sipes, Benjamin 82, 146
Sipes, Ethel 83
Sipes, Martha E. 82–83, 143, 145–146
Sipes, Thelma 83
Sipes, William E. 82
Sisters of Notre Dame 24
Smelser, Marshall 47, 52, 60, 66, 71, 81, 152, 162
Sousa, John Philip 42
Sowers, George 74, 75
Spalding, Bishop Martin J. 23–24
Speaker, Tris 11, 104, 122–124, 134, 141
Spellman, Cardinal Francis 13–14, 175
Steinmann, Scout 96–97, 101
Stenersen, Lawton 54, 72
Stengel, Casey 106
Stevens, Harry 144
Stevens, Julia Ruth 11–12, 169, 175, 178
Stevens, Tom 55, 175
Stoneham, Charles A. 157
Stopford, Emma 145
Strohmann, George 83, 146
Sydney, Nova Scotia 17
Sydney Mines, Nova Scotia 18

Terrapin Park, Baltimore 93, 108, 117
Thomas, Lowell 176
Thorn, John 1, 142
Thorpe, Jim 98
Toronto Maple Leafs 113, 116, 131–132
Tossetti, Linda 55
Truman, Harry (U.S. president) 12
Trump, Donald (U.S. president) 175
Tunstall, Christopher 128
Twombly, George 98, 102–104, 114, 118–120

Union Association 108
Upham, Bill 130

Vaeth, the Rev. Louis C. 166–167
Von der Horst, Henry R. 32

Waddell, Rube 99
Wagenheim, Kal 4, 101, 162
Walker, Tillie 79
Wallace, Charles 170
Wallace, Louise 170
Walsh, Runt 110

Warhop, Jack 136
Weaver, Buck 153
Weeghman, Charles 141
Wickes, Judge Peregrine L. 75
Wicks, Bill 121
Williams, Lefty 153
Williamson, Ned 136, 152
Wilson, Woodrow (U.S. president) 41
Wood, Joe 123–124
Woodford (Ruth), Helen 4, 122, 124, 129, 134, 139–140, 143–144, 157–158, 162
Wright, George 20
Wright, Harry 20

Xaverian Brothers history 23–24

Yankee Stadium 13, 160; 25th anniversary 12, 175
Yerkes, Steve 122–123
Yoelson, Asa *see* Jolson, Al
Young, Nick 31
Young Babe Ruth: His Early Life and Baseball Career, from the Memoirs of a Xaverian Brother 178

Zachary, Tom 165

www.ingramcontent.com/pod-product-compliance
Ingram Content Group UK Ltd.
Pitfield, Milton Keynes, MK11 3LW, UK
UKHW041954140426
5217IPUK00015B/794